NONDISCRIMINATORY MULTIFACTORED ASSESSMENT
A SOURCEBOOK

David W. Barnett, Ph.D.

University of Cincinnati

With a contribution by

Michael C. Forcade, Ed.D.

 **HUMAN SCIENCES PRESS, INC.**
72 Fifth Avenue
NEW YORK, NY 10011

To: Helen and Robert
Carmen, Jeffrey, and Rita

Copyright © 1983 by Human Sciences Press, Inc.
72 Fifth Avenue, New York, New York 10011

Printed in the United States of America
23456789 987654321

Library of Congress Cataloging in Publication Data

Barnett, David W., 1946-
    Nondiscriminatory multifactored assessment.

    Bibliography: p.
    Includes index.
    1. Psychological tests.   2. Educational tests and
measurements.   I. Forcade, Michael C.   II. Title.
BF176.B37   150'.28'7   82-1103
ISBN 0-89885-080-0   AACR2
ISBN 0-89885-082-7 (pbk.)

CONTENTS

PREFACE

The purpose of this *Sourcebook* is to provide a *concise* overview of concepts, techniques and practices in multifactored assessment. Although many excellent references exist, a single source may be helpful for students and others attempting to understand the complexities of current assessment issues. The book is intended for use by psychology students, although established professionals and students in related disciplines, especially special education, may also find the book helpful.

There are several important limitations of the *Sourcebook*. First, the multidisciplinary aspects of evaluation are only alluded to and would warrant further elaboration in a comprehensive text. The potential roles of medical specialists (pediatricians, neurologists, ophthalmologists) and other specialists (physical therapists, occupational therapists, audiologists) are open-ended when discussing assessment and intervention strategies for handicapped children. The roles of regular and special class teachers, resource teachers, and counselors have not been addressed for similar reasons. In practice, there are many ways a multidisciplinary team may function effectively. The specific roles should be decided for each child. There is also, perhaps, a need for a new specialist in the schools; one trained in cultural differences. The study of the many implications of assessment and intervention with culturally different children, nonbiased assessment, is at a very preliminary stage.

Second, the *Sourcebook* is not meant to be a complete discussion of all related assessment issues. Many difficult problems persist. The process of decision making in regard to global assessment strategies requires further development. Psychologists need a wide repertoire of approaches to assessment and require skills in recognizing when to change assessment strategies. Assessment practices must vary according to the nature of the problem, the situation, the resources available, the skills of other team members, and the developmental level of the child. Strategies vary with infants, preschoolers, elementary school children, and adolescents. Especially with infants and preschoolers, family members may become participants in assessment and intervention. Even though tests for infants are available, assessment strategies involving parenting skills may be more efficacious. For example, the almost overnight emergence of severe stuttering in a three year old child may be due to family tension and disorganization. Although a language therapist may serve as a consultant, a closer look at family dynamics is often more important than individual assessment or intervention with the young child.

Also, it appears that an analogue to the concept of incremental validity (Sechrest, 1963) is necessary within education. As one increases the amount of testing, less and less "new" information is generated. Costs increase and the overall benefit to the child is questionable.

There are many ways assessment practices can be "corrupted" (Martin, 1979). For example, several IQ tests may be given to a child before the "right" result is obtained. Children may be tested repeatedly as they proceed through available service "delivery systems." The same test may be given by a resource teacher, school psychologist, private psychologist, special clinic, agency or diagnostic center, etc. Rather than using information to develop an Individual Educational Plan, the information acquired can be used for "case building," e.g., deciding which special education program, already in operation by the school, seems most appropriate. "Overtesting" may result, in part, because testing is an easier, or more clearly defined role for some psychologists. Insufficient or inadequate assessment often results from limited resources or training.

Third, principles of consultation and organizational development are prerequisite to many of the emerging assessment approaches, particularly those stemming from ecological models. Assessment issues are intimately related to "systems" of providing services. In reference to the first two limitations, studies in the organization and development of systems of services are likely to have the most profound overall effect in contrast to other aspects of individual assessment discussed in this book.

Fourth, even though the assessment domain of Cognitive and Intellectual functioning is described in Section II, it is with full cognizance of the lesser role that "cognitive" assessment has actually played in contemporary practices. Various aspects of cognitive assessment are explored throughout the book (Chapters Two and Three, Section II). References to Piagetian and social learning approaches are provided, as are other alternative approaches to intellectual assessment. The most dramatic changes are likely to occur in this area as we begin to know more about neurological functioning, and the interactive processes involved in learning.

Although *not* considered a limitation, problems of definition relating to handicapping conditions are not discussed. Some readers may be confused about the identification of learning disabled, mentally retarded, or emotionally disturbed children. Specific answers are often arbitrary, sometimes resulting from sociopolitical solutions (e.g., numbers of children to be served, who is to provide the services). The children identified may vary simply by changing the test instruments used in evaluation procedures. This is not meant to imply that the problems experienced by children are not real. At the time of writing, there are certain problem definitions, especially those relating to children who are thought to be mentally retarded, learning disabled, or emotionally disturbed. The lack of consensus on (a) theory, (b) assessment procedures, and (c) criteria serve to illustrate the point. The *Sourcebook* is presented, for the most part, in a non-categorical manner. The stress is on identifying the needs of children.

6

Adequate services can be provided in a number of different ways, not necessarily related to the "correctness" of a label.

A complete review of the literature in all related areas was not attempted. However, it is felt that the trends and issues in the areas of intelligence testing, in personality assessment and in recent legal mandates provide a substantial basis for identifying emerging trends in multifactored assessment. Reviews of tests and techniques are troublesome. They soon become outdated, and comprehensiveness is a problem. An attempt was made to select representative, traditional and promising techniques, especially those that are innovative, or demonstrate specific approaches to problem areas. Further, many tests and techniques are described that have not been reviewed in major sources at the time of writing. Global approaches and assessment issues have been stressed in Section II. The author recognizes that language in some earlier quotes would now be considered sexist. However, it does not seem appropriate or necessary to call attention to such errors in each instance.

ACKNOWLEDGMENTS

Many persons have assisted with the preparation of this book, spanning a period of three years. Drs. Joseph Zins and Michael Forcade, both practicing psychologists, as well as adjunct university trainers of school psychologists, read most of the manuscript and suggested extensive revisions. Dr. Sheldon Weintraub (clinical psychology) critiqued parts of the manuscript and provided timely encouragement. Drs. Richard Kretschmer (language), James Stevens (statistics), and Ellen Piel-Cook (vocational assessment) read and commented upon sections relating to their respective fields. Pat Shannon, Steve Byrd, Elizabeth Van Wagener, Luanne Wise, Nancy Hampel (School Psychology students at the University of Cincinnati), Helen Wise, and Dr. George Wolff assisted with proofreading and editing. Special thanks to Fran Floyd for typing seemingly endless rewrites with kindness and understanding. An earlier and briefer manuscript (*A Sourcebook for Nondiscriminatory Multifactored Assessment for Educators*) was made possible through funds awarded by the Dean's Mainstreaming Grant and provided the impetus for the book. I would like to acknowledge Hendrik Gideonse, Dean of the College of Education, University of Cincinnati, for supporting the initial endeavor. Special thanks are also due to Dr. Michael Curtis, Head, Department of Educational Leadership and Coordinator of the School Psychology Program for personal, administrative, and scholarly assistance. The most important sources of help came from an understanding wife, Rita, and a fun loving daughter, Carmen.

The author gratefully acknowledges the use of excerpts from the following sources, reprinted by permission of the authors and/or publishers:

D.N. Bersoff. The ethical practice of school psychology: A rebuttal and suggested model. *Professional Psychology,* 1973, *4,* 305-312. Copyright 1973 by the American Psychological Association. Reprinted by permission.

J.B. Carroll. The nature of the reading process. In H. Singer and R.B. Ruddell (Eds.), *Theoretical models and processes of reading* (2nd ed.). Newark, DE: International Reading Association, 1976. Reprinted by permission.

E.E. Ekwall. *Teacher's handbook on diagnosis & remediation in reading,* Boston: Allyn & Bacon, 1977. Reprinted by permission.

A. Hartman. *The Ecomap: An ecological framework for assessment and intervention.* Paper presented at the meeting of the National Association of School Psychologists, New York, 1978. (The Ecomap is also described in:

Hartman, A. Diagrammatic assessment of family relationships. *Social Casework,* October, 1978, 465-476).

N. Hobbs. Helping disturbed children: Psychological and ecological strategies. *American Psychologist,* 1966, *21,* 1105-1115. Copyright 1966 by the American Psychological Association. Reprinted by permission.

A.S. Kaufman. *Intelligent testing with the WISC-R.* New York: John Wiley & Sons, 1979. Reprinted by permission.

N.M. Lambert. The Adaptive Behavior Scale-Public School Version: An overview. In W.A. Coulter & H.W. Morrow (Eds.), *Adaptive behavior: Concepts and measurement.* New York: Grune & Stratton, 1978. Reprinted by permission.

L.L. Lee. *Developmental Sentence Analysis.* Evanston, IL: Northwestern University Press, 1974. Reprinted by permission.

H.W. Leland. Theoretical considerations of adaptive behavior. In W.A. Coulter & H.W. Morrow (Eds.), *Adaptive behavior: Concepts and measurement.* New York: Grune & Stratton, 1978. Reprinted by permission.

J.R. Newbrough, L.S. Walker, & S. Abril. *Ecological assessment.* Paper presented at the meeting of the National Association of School Psychologists, New York, 1978.

Chapter 1

A SOURCEBOOK FOR MULTIFACTORED ASSESSMENT

The issues relating to multifactored assessment involve decisions about special class placement and the determination of the educational needs of exceptional children. Services are now mandated in federally supported programs to meet the needs of the following children: (a) deaf and hearing impaired; (b) orthopedically and other health impaired; (c) blind and visually impaired; (d) severe and/or multiply handicapped; (e) learning disabled; (f) seriously emotionally disturbed; (g) mentally retarded; (h) speech impaired; and (i) deaf-blind. Multifactored assessment describes part of the solution to what may be considered a "full and fair" evaluation for handicapped children (Martin, 1979). Every area of potential relevance to the suspected disability may become a target for assessment and intervention. An appropriate "multidisciplinary team" may require the services of a physician, optometrist, audiologist, psychologist, school counselor, teacher, speech, hearing and language clinician, physical therapist, or occupational therapist. Multifactored assessment meets the requirement for a broad base of information in order to facilitate educational decisions and, ultimately, to meet individual educational needs.

The following domains of multifactored assessment will help define the needs of most mildly handicapped children. They are treated separately in Section II of this book.

Personal and social functioning
Cognitive and intellectual functioning
Language and communication skills
Adaptive behavior
Visual-motor and gross-motor skills
Academic skills
Vocational assessment

Although most of the techniques subsumed under multifactored assessment are not new, recent legal mandates have required the re-evaluation of all existing practices and have required the formalization of acceptable procedural guidelines. The search for solutions to complex educational problems will be ongoing.

The Legal Context

There are many sources of law regulating services to the handicapped (Martin, 1979). Bersoff (1979) comments that since the middle 1960's there has been an "explosion of litigation and legislation" affecting testing. The major event occurred in 1975, with the passage of the Education for All Handicapped Children Act (Public Law 94-142), incorporating the major legal decisions of the past decade. In effect, PL 94-142 specified the rights of handicapped individuals. Three major points stand out with respect to this book. The law requires that tests and procedures used to identify and place handicapped children in special education programs not be racially or culturally discriminatory and that "no single procedure" be used as the "sole criterion" for making decisions about an appropriate educational placement for a child. In addition, the child's "native language" or "mode of communication" must be used in assessment procedures. However, the three aspects of the law result in practical problems. The guidelines are without specific recommendations. Eliminating bias in testing is complex and controversial, defying simple resolution. Bilingual children, or children using alternative language systems (e.g., signing), can profoundly change existing test practices, especially interpretation. Appropriate multidisciplinary, multifactored assessment and the development of procedural safeguards are the intended solutions to problems associated with test bias and with the identification of the educational needs of handicapped children.

More recently, other court cases have been decided that are likely to have far-reaching implications for the practice of school psychology with respect to nonbiased assessment. The conclusions and legal remedies of the long awaited *Larry P.* case (originally filed in behalf of black students in classes for the mildly retarded in 1971) have been determined. Although initially relating to the testing and placement practices of the San Francisco school system, the preliminary injunction was later expanded to include, in 1974, "black California school children" and those who may be placed through the use of IQ tests. The plaintiffs argued that current IQ tests are biased and their use has resulted in discrimination against black children already in special classes for educable mentally retarded children. "The tests allegedly result in the misplacement of black children in special classes that doom them to stigma, inadequate education, and failure to develop the skills necessary to productive success in our society." (*Larry P.* v. *Riles,* U.S.D.C., N.D., Cal., F. Supp., 1979).

Judge Peckham (Federal District Court for Northern California) summarized the legal conclusions in several ways. Most basic was the decision that:

> In violation of federal statutory law...[the] defendents have: (a) utilized I.Q. tests that are racially and culturally biased, have a discriminatory impact on black children, and have not been validated for the placement of black children into E.M.R. classes; and (b) generally allowed the placement of black children in grossly disproportionate numbers...by procedures that have not been validated. (pp. 100-101)

Peckham also concluded that it was not necessary to determine "intentional discrimination." The legal remedy addresses both testing abuses and the disproportionate number of black children in classes for the mentally retarded. Psychologists are prohibited from using standardized intelligence tests for identifying or placing black EMR children without prior court approval.

At the time of writing, however, the *Larry P.* case has been appealed and another case has been decided that seems diametrically opposed to the outcome of *Larry P.* The U.S. District Court for Northern Illinois refused to bar the use of three major IQ tests in the Chicago School System. Judge Grady, in his decision on *Parents in Action on Special Education (PASE) v. Hannon*, in July 1980, concluded that racial bias in IQ tests (WISC, WISC-R, Stanford-Binet) was "not sufficient," when used with other procedural safeguards and criteria, to prevent their use in placing black children in special classes for the educable mentally retarded. The use of IQ tests, as part of a classification procedure, did not violate the Equal Protection Clause of the Fourteenth Amendment or other federal statutes prohibitive of discrimination.

Of interest was the method Judge Grady used to determine the presence of bias. Empirical findings were not a part of the decision. Judge Grady inspected each item on the three scales (over 400 in all) and found a total of nine biased items, or "at least sufficiently suspect" so that their use would be questionable. He ruled that even so, the few items would not render the use of the tests unfair.

A Need for the Modification of Assessment Practices

Recent conceptual developments in assessment and the social and philosophical context of the legal issues all point toward needed changes. First, the *direct* involvement of parents, teachers, and special educators (and children when appropriate) has considerably modified existing practices and procedures in the schools. Second, with the advent of recent legislation, the types, numbers and complexities of assessments have all increased. Third, multifactored assessment involves more than the individual contributions of special service personnel. The resources of the entire school district are necessarily implicated. School administrators are directly involved, not only from a fiscal-management perspective, but also, more importantly, from a "systems" approach as well. Administrators have responsibilities involving both the establishment of a continuum of services to meet the needs of handicapped children and also the development and maintenance of positive attitudes and professional skills of staff members.

As Martin (1979) points out, assessment practices may be "easily corrupted to serve the convenience of the school system rather than the child" (p. 27). Legal, professional, and ethical guidelines all serve to protect the interests of the child.

The Search for Solutions to Complex Problems

Ready answers are not immediately available for current problems. On the one hand, a process of multifactored assessment has been implicitly mandated by recent legislation. On the other, it has arrived without empirical foundation. Professionals do not always agree upon acceptable assessment procedures for identifying handicapped children, especially learning disabled, mentally retarded, or emotionally disturbed children. The result has been confusion, numerous false starts, and necessarily personal views in looking for viable constructs and assessment techniques. Unfortunately, services cannot be held in abeyance until answers are found. This book represents a personalized view of useful assessment approaches.

Section I of the *Sourcebook* explores three contexts for multifactored assessment. The second chapter discusses issues especially related to the use of intelligence tests. The third chapter presents personality assessment, from a social learning perspective, as a major context for multifactored assessment. The attention given to the area of personality assessment may surprise many readers (and upset others). Traditional personality assessment has, of course, been severely challenged. Along with the criticisms, however, have been significant changes in suggested practices. Many newer developments in personality assessment seem relevant for the highly complex educational problems of children, whereas trends in psychometric theory do not. The focus of traditional psychological assessment for children involving the classification of children as emotionally disturbed is no longer a major emphasis.

Personality assessment, when consistent with a social learning point of view, stresses the study of the child interacting within meaningful environments and emphasizes direct ways of helping. From this perspective, the potential contributions made by parents and teachers and other special services personnel become clearer. For children with severe behavior problems, the possibility of much more powerful treatment alternatives, involving all of the significant factors in the child's environment, can be explored. For children with other handicapping conditions, family and school support systems may be assessed, as well as the child's own personal resources for solving problems. Overall, perfunctory reporting of test scores and diagnostic "impressions" becomes less likely, and the development of assessment strategies designed to facilitate the treatment of children becomes more probable.

The fourth chapter describes, from a conceptual point of view, the legal mandate forming the basis of multifactored assessment and suggested assessment procedures. Section II provides an introduction to many current techniques used in assessing handicapped children. A final chapter is included on low incidence handicapped children because of the very special problems associated with assessing some children.

Section I

CONTEXTS FOR ASSESSMENT

The purpose of this section is to provide several contexts for multifactored assessment. The first context (Chapter Two) alerts the reader to the social consequences of assessment, especially through the use and misuse of intelligence and ability testing. The third chapter presents a context for assessment consistent with emerging trends in personality assessment. The social learning point of view provides an important theoretical framework for assessment techniques and intervention strategies. The fourth chapter includes a conceptual discussion of the aspects of Public Law 94-142 (The Education of All Handicapped Children Act of 1975) that are relevant in considering assessment issues.

Chapter 2

WHY A CAUSE FOR CONCERN?

Concerns about testing are raised by broad personal, social, and political issues. In the public schools, questions have addressed the exclusion of handicapped children from school and the placement of children in special classes, or other potentially restrictive educational programs such as those that "track" or "ability group" students through the use of various intelligence, achievement, or aptitude tests. The complexities inherent in any attempt to quantify human abilities necessarily result in the possibility of error, misinterpretation, and misuse. Unfortunately, all have occurred. Problems still exist, even after several decades of critical awareness. The problems have been compounded by the growth of the testing industry and the corresponding magnitude of the testing movement. Cronbach (1975) reports that "within 30 months of the first publication of a group test, some four million children had been tested" (p. 1). Holmen and Docter (1972), in a study of the testing industry, estimate that more than 200 million standardized achievement tests are used every year in education. Testing has rapidly become a part of American technology for a great many persons and institutions, especially the public schools. In the *Larry P.* trial, the principal focus was on the use of individual IQ tests to classify black children as mentally retarded. The issues, however, are much broader.

The following topics are included for study in this chapter: intelligence testing, the potential social consequences of test usage, and problems associated with reliability, validity, and test bias. The focus of this chapter will generally be on issues relating to minority group children. The problems and dilemmas associated with the assessment of minority and culturally different children have provided much of the impetus that has forced a re-evaluation of assessment practices. However, the basic issues have also set the stage for the consideration of similar topics relating to all exceptional children.

Intelligence Testing

Despite the casual familiarity everyone has with intelligence testing, there are likely to still be a few surprises for the reader who is unaware of historical and recent literature in the area. The diverse theoretical positions associated with the concept of intelligence, the professional practices involving the assessment of intelligence, and the controversies regarding the social outcomes of decisions based on the use of intelligence tests provide the clearest responses to the question "Why a cause for concern?"

The first problem is the lack of a generally agreed upon definition of intelligence. All of us, after a period of reflection, realize that intelligence may be influenced by many aspects of a child's development (e.g., experiential, nutritional, intactness of sensory and sensory motor systems). Furthermore, intelligence has unlimited possibilities for expression in individuals, thus creating unique patterns of abilities. Consequently, when viewed apart from more global personality characteristics, intelligence sometimes tells us relatively little about a person, especially when a single score on a particular scale represents the only source of information. Often, however, the complexity of intelligence as an indication of performance and human potential has been ignored.

Binet is perhaps the most significant historical figure in the assessment of intelligence, as related to modern practices concerned with the identification of exceptional children. A brief look at the origins of the "testing experiment" follow.

Binet believed that a person's intelligence could best be measured by complex abilities: "To judge well, to comprehend well, to reason well, these are the essential activities of intelligence" (Binet and Simon, as reported in Shipley, 1961, p. 886). Binet and Simon also considered intelligence to be related to adaptation involving "good sense" and "adapting one's self to circumstances" (p. 886). In 1904, Binet was appointed to a committee by the Ministry of Public Instruction in Paris, France, with the responsibility for developing an objective method for identifying the mentally retarded. There is evidence to suggest that Binet was highly sensitive to the social issues involving the project. He was also aware of the possibilities of misuse and warned that the procedures used were a sample of a "child's current intellectual behavior" and could not be used as a "rigid, fully developed, finalized test for all time of an individual's (innate) intelligence" (Matarazzo, 1972, p. 41).

Binet and Simon proposed three methods of identifying mentally retarded children, including medical, pedagogical, and psychological examinations (DuBois, 1970). The psychological aspects were to include observations, as well as the measurement of intelligence. Binet and Simon also pointed out important errors that might be made by an "inexperienced" examiner, such as "recording the gross results without making psychological observations...and...without noticing such little facts as permit one to give to the gross results their true value" (in Shipley, 1961, p. 888). At even the earliest stages of the development of tests and procedures for identifying mentally retarded children, a low score on an intelligence test was not necessarily considered synonymous with mental retardation. Intelligence was defined not by a test score, but by global factors stressing judgment. Binet also noted that memory could be "distinct from and independent of judgment" (Shipley, 1961, p. 883). Unfortunately, Binet's name, through the association with the Stanford-Binet Intelligence Scale, has become synonymous with a narrow approach to the assessment of children and the use of a unitary IQ score, concepts Binet would have rejected.

Wolf (1973), in a very readable and interesting biography, describes a brilliant researcher, independently wealthy, with diverse interests in psychology. Wolf points out that Binet was keenly aware of the difficulties inherent in developing intelligence scales and of the need for further research.

Wolf argues:

> Perhaps even more at variance with Binet's conceptions...has been the fact that the scale has not been appreciably or importantly changed by the men who gave it so prominent a place in the United States. Binet's discussions and reflections about the nature and measurement of intelligence seem to be clear indication that he was not satisfied with the scale. At the time of his death he was talking about adaptive, inventive responses, about "attitudes in action" that had not yet emerged in the tests of intelligence. (p. 217)

In reviewing the history of intelligence testing in America, particularly the widespread use of group administered intelligence tests and other aptitude tests used "out of context," it is important to consider Binet's view. He believed that intelligence is an aspect of a person's total personality. It is highly probable that Binet would have also rejected the use of a mathematical interpretation (the IQ was proposed by Stern in 1911) because he recognized the lack of "exactness" in the scale. Wolf further points out that Binet and Piaget did not represent "opposing positions"; Binet was very much interested in the qualitative aspects of intelligence. Binet also stressed the need for naturalistic observations as a method of investigation in addition to laboratory studies (Wolf, 1973), another contemporary position. Binet would also have been at odds with genetic interpretations of intelligence; he was well aware of the impact of the environment.

When Binet's work was "transplanted" to America, his sensitive warnings were ignored. As was brought out in testimony in the *Larry P.* trial, in reviewing the history of IQ testing and special education in California, many early contributors to the development of intelligence tests in this country favored or suggested the genetic interpretation of results. For a brief reassessment of Binet's contributions, see Sarason's (1976) interesting and provocative article. Brody and Brody (1976) point out that by 1905 many of the fundamental contemporary questions about intelligence had been raised, including racial and social class differences, the relative contributions of heredity and environment to the development of intelligence, the modifiability of intelligence, problems associated with the measurement of intelligence, and the definition of intelligence.

Very early, Terman (1916) outlined the possible "uses" of intelligence tests. He recommended testing not only for identifying retarded children, but also for studying delinquent youth and superior children, for considering the appropriate placement of children in school, and for defining individual parameters of vocational fitness, as well as other uses (pp. 1-21). The precise predictive ability and the utility for making important individual decisions or categorizations have not held up very well. For example, while intelligence test scores are closely related to academic skills within public education, the results of IQ tests have less predictive ability and are only moderately related to individual "life adjustment" as indicated by "job success" in later life, occupation, grade point average, or similar indices of success (Matarazzo, 1972). McClelland (1973) reviews evidence concerning the validity of ability measures and similarly suggests difficulties in the prediction of "life outcomes" or "real competence," except for the "advantages credentials convey" when one qualifies for prestigious programs through high test scores (p. 6). Although impressive validity studies exist for intelligence tests in certain areas (e.g., the identification of children likely to experience school failure, Terman's study of gifted individuals and their considerable accomplishments), the most widely accepted intelligence tests (e.g., the Wechsler Scales and the Stanford-Binet) have limitations that may not be generally recognized. They do not test for creative abilities, or factors relating to the processes of cognitive and interpersonal problem solving. Even though ability may be suggested by a particular score, test users have difficulty in estimating the probability that the skills will be applied in everyday situations. Most important, in terms of this chapter, the performance of culturally different children may be penalized. Complex measurement problems may confound individual interpretations. While psychologists are aware of these factors, and can use tests in appropriate ways, intelligence tests lend themselves to a "mystique" and much more is often attributed to test scores than is warranted. In common usage, the definition of intelligence has gone beyond the empirical relationships that have been actually demonstrated. Kaufman (1979) reminds us of other important limitations of intelligence tests: They have not remained current, for the most part, with research in cognition, learning, and neuropsychology.

Definitions of Intelligence

Intelligence is a *hypothetical construct*; that is, we make the assumption that it exists, but in what exact form or manner we cannot say. The adequacy of a hypothetical construct (construct validity) is defined through logical reasoning and through experimentation. There is no one "scientific approach" that can completely legitimize a construct in such a manner that would rule out scientific disputes and varying points of view (e.g., Cronbach and Meehl, 1955). Brody and Brody (1976) further point out the lack of a "simple clear-cut procedure that permits one to determine that tests of intelligence are in fact measures of intelligence" (p. 87).

Many definitions of intelligence have been offered. However, the definitions can be quite distinct from the actual measures of intelligence that have been developed. For example, Wechsler (1958) defines intelligence as "the aggregate or global capacity of the individual to act purposefully, to think rationally, and to deal effectively with the environment" (p. 7). One can see by the description of the test in Chapter Five, the Wechsler Intelligence Scale only approximates the assessment of skills implied by the definition of intelligence.

Piaget views intelligence, or more precisely the development of intelligence, to be a biological adaptation to the environment through the child's gradual attainment of effective cognitive structures (Ginsburg and Opper, 1969). A great number of references exist in this area. DeAvila and Havassy (1975) discuss Piagetian procedures as alternatives to traditional psychometric approaches in assessing the cognitive skills of Mexican-American children. Klein and Safford (1977) and Butterfield (1978) review Piagetian techniques with respect to mentally retarded populations. The work of Uzgiris and Hunt (1975) is likely to have a significant impact with both infants and severely retarded people. Anastasi (1976) reviews a number of Piagetian approaches not included in earlier editions of her book. However, assessment approaches stemming from Piagetian theory have been used informally by most teachers and psychologists and presently serve to complement traditional tests. Social learning approaches to cognition offer further important areas for experimentation (e.g., Rosenthal and Zimmerman, 1978).

Wesman (1968) defined intelligence in a manner that comes close to what may be a consensus position, although not an empirical solution: "Intelligence is an attribute, not an entity" and represents a "summation of the learning experiences of the individual" (p. 267). He believes that intelligence is "*un*structured...[And] differently comprised in every individual—the sum total of all the learning experiences he has uniquely had up to any moment in time" (p. 273). Many other definitions of intelligence have been offered and the reader is referred to other sources for brief, but complete, discussions and additional references (especially Brody and Brody, 1976; Matarazzo, 1972; Sattler, 1974).

Regardless of the definition used, it is relatively easy to lose sight of all of the problems associated with the concept of intelligence. The main point is that the unique qualities of intelligence vary from individual to individual and may have significance only through expression in the complete personality of the individual. Matarazzo (1972) argues that difficulties with the definitions of intelligence and the use of tests themselves seem to transcend the scientific debates: Intelligence becomes less of a psychological or scientific construct and more of a "precious, tenaciously guarded social concept with vast overtones which will profoundly affect the life of every human being who is assessed for this quality of...behavior" (p. 22). Within the field of education, one has only to think of some of the educational categories within special education and the images associated with the following labels: gifted, superior, average, educable mentally retarded, trainable mentally retarded, and severely and profoundly mentally retarded. From the viewpoint of a parent, or child, it is apparent that more meaning is conveyed than the intended simple classification system. From philosophical and social perspectives, strong values on a significant human continuum of desirability are communicated. Socially related values of desirability obscure the functional educational information that otherwise might be conveyed by the terminology.

The Nature-Nurture Controversy

Social and philosophical values provide a context for legal criticisms resulting from the use of intelligence scales in two areas: (a) the consequences of various school placements, especially for minority group children placed in classrooms for the mentally retarded; and (b) aspects of measurement such as reliability, validity, and test bias. Both topics will be dealt with in more detail in the latter two sections of this chapter. A third related factor, however, has contributed greatly to the emotional significance of the social consequences of test usage—the question of the heritability of intelligence. Blacks and other minorities tend to score lower than members of the white middle class. Since the early 1900's when intelligence tests were first used to compare groups of individuals, genetic explanations have been offered to account for group differences. When viewed from the perspective of a minority group member, unfair use and interpretation can have a harmful effect. For example, Gay and Abrahams (1973) suggest that IQ tests have helped "perpetuate negative stereotypes of blacks by demonstrating failures and inabilities" (p. 330). The questions raised regarding the heritability of intelligence have made it a racial issue for some.

Kamin (1974) provides a vivid and alarming account of historical literature, beginning in the early 1900's, hypothesizing racial differences in intelligence. He illustrates the misuse of intelligence tests and attributes the misuse to social and political reasons. In a very persuasive manner, Kamin argues against the heritability of intelligence through an examination of the critical research. He also points out that, throughout the history of intelligence testing in America, the use of the IQ has had a deliberate social impact because of the use of genetic arguments to explain group differences. "The early history of testing in America fixed upon the Binet test an apparently indelible genetic interpretation" (p. 10). Many influential writers were blatantly racist (e.g., Brigham, 1923), as was brought out again in *Larry P.*

Kamin's re-analysis of many sets of data uncovered numerous methodological flaws and errors of scientific judgment that have been perpetuated in the literature. Since the early 1900's various groups, including Indian, Mexican, Southeastern European immigrants, and blacks have all been considered as "inferior." Kamin's analysis is quite disturbing when one considers the profound significance of the use of test results. Kamin (1974, 1975) probably represents, overall, an extreme position: "Since its introduction to America, the intelligence test has been used more or less consciously as an instrument of oppression against the underprivileged, the poor, the foreign-born, and racial minorities" (1975, p. 317). Other, more positive uses can be identified. However extreme the point of view, there is certainly much value in considering the social and political effects of test usage.

Jensen's (1969) widely cited article in the *Harvard Educational Review* was perhaps the most significant publication renewing the heated interest in the heritability debate. Many subsequent reactions to Jensen's position were published (e.g., Cronbach, 1975; Loehlin, Lindzey and Spuhler, 1975; Senna, 1973). Brody and Brody (1976) provide an extensive review of the research involving "black-white differences" in intelligence test scores. Samuda (1975) also has an excellent review of the nature-nurture controversy. Jensen (1980) devotes very little space to the direct question of heritability, although he does not falter from his earlier arguments concerning the relatively high heritability of intelligence. He illustrates the difficulties in estimating heritability and the large amount of uncertainty in estimating the contribution of genotype to test scores. He does state, however, that tests may be "used to estimate an individual's genotype...[But] there is really no point in estimating genotypic values" (p. 245). In a book review entitled "Jensen's Last Stand," Kamin (1980) argues that recent research "is beginning to overturn the simplistic view...[suggestive of the] high heritability of IQ" (p. 117). The bulk of Jensen's book has to do with evidence demonstrating that tests are not, in fact, biased. The major points he presents will be reviewed later in the chapter.

The Effects of Environment

Most social scientists argue that powerful environmental effects can shape cognitive abilities to a significant extent. Brody and Brody (1976) summarize evidence suggesting that "naturally occurring" social environments can produce changes in intelligence scores. The results of direct experimental manipulations are less conclusive, but appear promising. One example will help illustrate the possibilities.

Heber and his associates (1972) have been involved in a longitudinal study (known as the Milwaukee Project) of the prevention of mental retardation in high risk children. The main focus has been on cultural-familial retardation, "almost exclusively found among economically depressed population groups" (p. 1). There have been many interesting results from the study that relate, although indirectly, to the question of racial differences in intelligence. Minority groups, in this case blacks living in Milwaukee, were found to be "disproportionately represented in disadvantaged populations," and yielded a high prevalence of persons characterized as being mentally retarded (p. 1). Another finding was that "the generally acknowledged statement that slum-dwelling children score lower on intelligence tests as they become older held true only for the offspring of mothers whose IQ's were below 80" (p. 5). Also, there was a consistency between maternal and paternal intelligence: "Sixty-two percent of mothers below 70 had husbands who scored below 70 and only 12% of those mothers had husbands who scored about 100" (p. 7). The social environment created by mentally retarded mothers and mothers of normal intelligence was found to be "distinctly different."

The Milwaukee Project is a very comprehensive intervention beginning in infancy (3 months) for high risk children and includes two components: direct cognitive stimulation of the infant and a maternal rehabilitation program. A variety of program evaluation measures are being used. The results, reported when the children had reached the age of 66 months, were very exciting. A thirty point difference in IQ separated the experimental and control groups, with the target children having an average IQ of 124, and the control group having an average IQ of 94. There are concerns about maintaining such gains over long periods of time, particularly since the intervention lasts only until the children go to school. However, Garber (1979) notes that after about ten years, significant differences have been maintained. When compared to the control group, the experimental group (with "rehabilitated families")

> showed normal and above levels of intelligence through the fourth grade, while the controls are a standard deviation below them...Moreover, by fourth grade no children in the specially treated group are below 85 IQ while in the control group 60% of the children are below 85 IQ and more than twice as many are in special class programs (p. 303)

Other social experiments (Feuerstein, 1970, 1979, 1980; Haywood, Filler, Shifman and Chatelant, 1975) have similarly demonstrated the "modifiability" of mental retardation. Feuerstein (1970) discusses various treatment programs and compares the "passive-acceptance" approach to an "active-modification" approach:

> Given the proper social, cultural, and educational policy based on the theoretical framework of the human organism as an open system and further, given an investment in the creation of daring, innovative strategies, retarded performance levels can be raised considerably. (p. 345)

Feuerstein's experiments have different origins and have been directed to older populations (e.g., adolescents). The culturally different or deprived children have been those from Afro-Asian countries referred to Youth Aliyah, the agency concerned with the "ingathering and adjustment" of Jewish children and adolescents to Israel.

Feuerstein (1979) asserts, as have many other researchers, that children categorized as Educable Mentally Retarded are typically socioculturally disadvantaged or culturally deprived. The use of the terms disadvantaged or deprived could be misconstrued. He defines the terms by an individual (or group) "that has become alienated *from its own culture*" (p. 39). The terms have often applied to an external evaluation whereby certain cultures are viewed as "depriving their members" of enriched experiences. By recasting the definition, Feuerstein emphasizes the outcomes of alienation, produced by a variety of causes (e.g., economic, geographic, sociological, etc.), especially affecting "intergenerational transmission" of culture and, most significant for intervention, mediational processes that adults use with children in order to enhance learning of all kinds.

In order to address the problem of low functioning individuals, usually categorized as EMR, Feuerstein has used the term *cognitive modifiability* to define "a transformation in the structure of the intellect that may reflect as well as determine a sharp departure from the individual's expected course of development" (p. xiii). He has also developed the Learning Potential Assessment Device (LPAD) to "Dynamically Assess" retarded performance. *Learning potential* is defined by an individual's capacity to change as a result of a learning experience, and Feuerstein accepts that expectancies concerning modifiability should be much more positive than generally held beliefs would suggest. Dynamic assessment is characterized as an active process. The examiner-examinee interact more like a "teacher and student, as helper and helped" (p. 51). Four changes required by this dynamic approach are reviewed in Section II.

Central to his approach to assessment and intervention is the importance of *mediated learning experiences* which, when limited or impaired, may result in cultural deprivation. A mediated learning experience refers to the manner in which a parent (or sibling, caregiver, etc.) "selects and organizes the world of stimuli for the child" (Feuerstein, 1980, p. 16). In addition to "cultural transmission," the adult role includes the "selection of stimuli," which has the dual importance of attributing meaning to events and focusing the behavior of children on important events.

Other dimensions of mediated learning experiences include "scheduling of stimuli," or the ordering and accentuating of stimuli "along both temporal and spatial dimensions," anticipation, involving expectancies and casual relationships, imitation, the "intentional provision" of specific learning events, and the repetition and variation of experiences. Further, Feuerstein (1980) describes the "transmission" of past and the "representation" of the future as dimensions of mediated learning experiences. Lastly, "comparative behavior," stressing scanning and relational thinking, is presented as an aspect of learning that may be enhanced by active mediational processes (pp. 26-35). Although further research is needed, the changes suggested by his approach have already challenged current thinking about dimensions of assessment and intervention for children with severe learning problems.

In summary, the significance of varying social environments must be considered when discussing differences in intelligence test scores between members of minority groups and middle class persons. When black-white or other culturally related differences are found, they are probably best thought of in terms of "the probability of experiencing environments that are adequate to the fostering of intellectual ability" (Brody and Brody, 1976, p. 189) consistent with skills tapped by current intelligence tests.

Social Consequences of Test Usage

A complete review of all issues related to the social outcomes of test usage would quickly go beyond the scope of this book. The literature is quite extensive and cuts across several disciplines. Other issues relating to decision making and the prediction of significant life outcomes through the use of IQ tests have been briefly mentioned earlier. The primary focus of this section will be on Mercer's (1973, 1979) research leading to the conceptualization of a "System of Multicultural Pluralistic Assessment" (SOMPA). The discussion requires a look at assessment practices, especially those involving decisions about classification, the educational outcomes of classification, and labeling theory from a sociological perspective. The positions of black psychologists and members of various professional groups provide an additional context.

Mental Retardation and Minority Children

Mercer's work is concerned with the exceptionality of mental retardation, especially for culturally different, low SES (socioeconomic status) children. However, it does illustrate the possibility of negative social consequences relating to testing in general. For example, the sociological perspective of labeling theory is extremely relevant for professionals working with all exceptional children. Much of the original thought stemmed from concerns about defining mental illness.

Modern issues surrounding the social consequences of the misuse of tests are perhaps best exemplified by the results of Mercer's (1973) field research in California, especially her data-based description of the over-representation of minority children in classes for the mentally retarded. Highly relevant to the topic of multifactored assessment was the manner by which certain children had become labeled as mentally retarded. Children were identified as being mentally retarded through assessment procedures which emphasized the standardized administration of intelligence scales with children having cultural and/or language barriers. Since the focus of traditional intelligence scales is on the "white middle class range of experiences," test results lend themselves to misinterpretation. The questions and tasks that comprise the scales relate to experiences available only in varying degrees to children of different cultures. Mercer hypothesized that the further the child's family and cultural group from the mainstream of society, the less likely the test scores are predictive of behaviors associated with the construct of intelligence.

Mercer's work heightened the awareness of the professional community to the process of labeling: Mental retardation is a relativistic term, and in the situations that Mercer's research addressed, mental retardation was a label that the children acquired through their contact with the public schools. Many of the children were not retarded in terms of functioning within their own cultural community. The examination of the labeling process has forced a re-evaluation of the measurement issues involved.

The problems associated with the conceptualization and definition of intelligence, as previously discussed, are important to Mercer's concerns. The problems lie not so much with broad definitions of intelligence that emphasize judgment and adaptive behavior, but with the attempt to quantify or measure highly complex abilities, and, even more significantly, to measure these abilities when the child has to function in *two* environments. Cultural values, language, and even judgment as to what constitutes successful adaptive behavior, may be at variance.

Mercer's work, originating in 1963, is quite significant in terms of findings relevant to the concept of multifactored assessment. In the *Technical Manual* for the System of Multicultural Pluralistic Assessment (SOMPA), Mercer (1979) outlines some of the most important outcomes of her earlier research. Only a few global findings are summarized at this point for illustration and discussion purposes.

a. Public schools, in contrast to other community agencies and the lay public, labeled the most persons as mentally retarded.

b. IQ scores were most relied upon in contrast to, for example, medical evaluations.

c. Parents expressed concern about the stigma attached to the label of mental retardation and the possibility that the educational program was a "limiting" one.

d. Minority children (Blacks and Spanish-surnamed) were overlabeled and white children were underlabeled in comparison to the numbers expected in proportion to the general population.

e. Children from lower socioeconomic groups were less likely to be perceived as retarded in their family and social groups. Also, they had fewer physical problems than labeled children from high status families (hence the term "six-hour retardates" relating to failure only in school).

f. Minority children similar in sociocultural aspects to middle class children perform in a similar manner to middle class white children on IQ tests.

g. The number of persons labeled as mentally retarded dropped when a second dimension, that of adaptive behavior, was included in the definition of mental retardation in addition to IQ.

h. For the circumstances whereby persons scored relatively higher on the adaptive behavior measure and lower on the IQ test, it seemed as if the persons were meeting normal social expectations and demands. (pp. 1-4)

Three major recommendations have resulted from the overall conclusions, and they have had a significant impact on the assessment of mentally retarded children. The first reminds us of the global nature of mental retardation. The mentally retarded child should demonstrate difficulties with overall adaptive skills as well as low intellectual functioning (Grossman, 1973). A second recommendation is that people formally labeled as subnormal, or mentally retarded, should fall at or below the performance of 97% of the population or below 70 (approximately) on the major IQ tests. This has been a standard adhered to by many psychologists in clinical and educational practice; however, it has been reinforced by Mercer's work. The major effect of both practices is that it becomes less likely that persons from minority groups or low SES levels will be labeled as mentally retarded. The third recommendation has resulted in the development of "pluralistic norms." Mercer (1979) concluded that it was possible and desirable to develop pluralistic assessment. By doing so, a child's test scores may be compared to those of "similar socio-cultural backgrounds." Mercer assumes that opportunities for learning may be equated in this way, including motivational variables and test-taking experience.

Mercer's work has culminated in the System of Multicultural Pluralistic Assessment (SOMPA). The SOMPA is complex and requires specialized training to administer. Mercer (1979) states that the SOMPA is most useful with children from racial or ethnic backgrounds which vary from the white middle-class experience and/or children from low SES or socially isolated families.

Mercer compares two models stemming from sociological theory. The first stresses conformity to a monocultural society (the Anglo-Conformity Model), the second suggests the possibility of a pluralistic model which would value "non-Anglo cultural heritages" (p. 22). Some of the outcomes of pluralistic assessment, according to Mercer, are: (a) "expanded educational options for all children," (b) "reduced stigmatization of non-Anglo children," (c) "valuing non-Anglo cultural background," and (d) "fostering multilingual, multicultural development" (pp. 24-26).

Three different conceptual assessment strategies contribute to SOMPA: medical, social system, and pluralistic. Information is gained through interviewing parents (or the primary caretaker) and through individually administered assessment procedures with the child. Some of the measures and procedures will be discussed in Chapter Five. The assessment techniques subsumed under Medical Model include a Health History Inventory and Physical Dexterity tasks, a visual-motor test (the Bender-Gestalt), vision and hearing screening, and weight standardized by height. The measures associated with the Social System Model include the Wechsler Intelligence Scale for Children-Revised (WISC-R) or the Wechsler Preschool and Primary Scale of Intelligence (WPPSI), and a measure of adaptive behavior (the Adaptive Behavior Inventory for Children).

The pluralistic model stems from Mercer's interpretation of intelligence tests. Since intelligence tests measure learned behavior, they can be interpreted as achievement tests. Intelligence tests are used as measures of "academic role performance" or "school functioning level."

The pluralistic model is supported, theoretically, by the assumption of "multiple normal distributions." Every child assessed by SOMPA is compared to a distribution of scores appropriate for their sociocultural group. Thus, the IQ scores may be used as an indication of the child's "estimated learning potential" (ELP). The ELP compares the child's performance to that of children "from similar sociocultural backgrounds."

The primary result of using SOMPA is to prevent both the misclassification and misplacement of children differing significantly in their racial or ethnic backgrounds or children from economically disadvantaged or socially isolated backgrounds. From this perspective, Mercer (1979) discusses the concept of "adaptive trajectory": "An *enabling trajectory* facilitates the individual's movement into ever-broadening circles of social systems...A *disabling trajectory* takes the child into social systems that are dead ends" (pp. 88-89). The concept of adaptive trajectory seems very useful in considering special programs for children, assigning labels that may be stigmatizing, and considering long range outcomes of educational decisions. Mercer believes that placement in special classes for the educable mentally retarded children may result in disabling trajectories for culturally different children.

At least one study (Fisher, 1978) has considered the classification-declassification issue by systematically varying the criteria for inclusion in programs for the mentally retarded. Fisher compared four approaches to the classification of children as educable mentally retarded, trainable mentally retarded, and not retarded. The first approach used the traditional cut-off of two standard deviations below the mean with an individually administered IQ test (Wechsler Full Scale IQ of 70). The second approach, termed "psychometric," required the child to meet each of five criteria: (a) a full scale IQ of less than 70, (b) Verbal and Performance scales below 75 (The WISC-R, described in Chapter Five, is made up of these two scales, each having five subtests and a supplementary test), (c) no more than two individual subtests within the normal range, (d) achievement test scaled scores below 80, and (e) performance on a visual-motor test two standard deviations below the mean.

The third approach to classification used Mercer's "Pluralistic" norms approach (the Estimated Learning Potential) by statistically "adjusting" the WISC-R scores relative to the degree of proximity to the cultural mainstream. The fourth was termed the "Adaptive Approach" and made use of the traditional "psychometric" tests, in addition to an adaptive behavior measure (the Adaptive Behavior Inventory for Children, described in Chapter Five).

The results relating to the category of "educable mentally retarded" (EMR) are described as follows. The first approach (Full Scale IQ below 70) classified the greatest number of children as EMR (77%). The second approach (psychometric), with five separate criteria, reduced the number of children that would be categorized as EMR to 63%. The Pluralistic Approach reduced the number even further, to 42%. The Psychometric and Adaptive Behavior approach reduced the number of classified students to 23% (pp. 5-6). The findings relating to the declassification of children are similar, as were the trends for Trainable Mentally Retarded (TMR) children. The Adaptive Behavior Approach seemed to be the "most conservative" with respect to minorities. Fisher states: "The Adaptive Behavior approach appears to have the greatest impact on Mexican-American and Black students. Approximately 70% to 85% of the minority students were declassified" (p. 10).

Although Fisher's research included a relatively small sample (110 children), in a circumscribed geographic region, the results are likely to be replicated in other public school systems. The impact of using pluralistic norms and a measure of adaptive behavior will most certainly result in far fewer children from minority groups being placed in classes for mentally retarded children. However, as Fisher (1978) points out in his discussion, questions at the instructional level are unanswered. The children referred for psychological and educational evaluation are likely to have serious problems, noticeable to teachers and perhaps parents, that are impeding their progress in school. The child, referred to as the "six-hour retardate," does have serious academic problems independent of what might be considered adequate adaptive behavior outside of the school situation. Fisher (1978) notes that

> in some instances, not providing a student with a special program appears to be contrary to the current educational trends and legal guidelines which require that the student receive the "most appropriate instructional arrangement." (p. 12)

The issues surrounding nondiscriminatory testing and social outcomes relating to minority group children have not been clearly resolved. Goodman (1977) has challenged Mercer's orientation to nondiscriminatory testing, saying it: "while seemingly progressive, refined, and fair-minded, is actually unsound, unhelpful, and even dangerous for educational policy" (p. 204). The arguments she presents are complex, but can be considered from two major perspectives. The first questions Mercer's diagnostic approach to mental retardation and the second raises pragmatic concerns with the utility of Mercer's system.

Goodman (1977, 1979) views the "diagnostic fallacy" of Mercer's conceptual approach to mental retardation as inconsistent with other research and logic.

> It assumes that since a child's learning failure must be due either to lack of opportunity...or to biological defect, controlling for the former will automatically yield pure cases of the latter. But this is not the case. (Goodman, 1977, p.200)

Goodman argues that the two categories involving environmental versus biological reasons for retardation are not independent and can overlap. A more serious problem with Mercer's approach to mental retardation is the assumption that etiology and prognosis are highly related. Given the state of current research, it may be untenable to assume that a more successful outcome may result from interventions with children having a low IQ due to "cultural . . . or economic deprivation" than when the low IQ is related to "brain damage or other organic sources" (p. 201). Goodman continues by stating: "The fact is that biological integrity, IQ, and prognosis are relatively independent factors" (p. 201).

Besides the problems with Mercer's conceptualization of mental retardation, Goodman (1977) expresses concern as to the "educational utility" of the assessment system. One possible outcome of using SOMPA, which Goodman points out, is that children may be denied services unless they are "comprehensively" retarded. Children needing services other than full-time special class placement, or other special services, for a limited time period may not meet established criteria. Goodman views mental retardation as a "statistical designation" that reflects community values regarding education. If a white middle-class cultural system is actually encouraged by the local community and school, pluralistic standards would be inappropriate. She advocates a "descriptive" approach to assessment. Mental retardation would be defined by a relative failure on a cluster of socially determined behaviors, "and would be likely to both vary across cultures and change over time" (p. 204). The *School Psychology Digest* (*8* (1,2), 1979) presents special issues relating primarily to the SOMPA and the ensuing debate.

Many of the subscales are of interest to practicing psychologists (e.g., the Adaptive Behavior Inventory for Children (ABIC) and the Sociocultural Scales). The Sociocultural Scales of the SOMPA (including Family Size, Family Structure, Socioeconomic Status, Urban Acculturation) provide an important tool for assisting with the interpretation of normative tests. Spanish and English translations are available. Approximately 3600 psychologists have been formally trained to use the SOMPA thus far (*The SOMPA Scene,* 1, 1979). At the same time, as brought out in the symposium on the SOMPA in the special issues of the *School Psychology Digest*, a number of criticisms have been raised. Of special concern is the absence of validity information on the Estimated Learning Potential (ELP), and the lack of attention given to how to address the difference between a child's School Functioning Level (SFL) and ELP. The school is relatively ignored by SOMPA. Oakland (1979) concludes that the SOMPA is only one approach to nondiscriminatory assessment. It is incomplete in terms of meeting the needs of children and teachers. However, Oakland agrees that the SOMPA does provide "some potentially useful strategies" (p. 213).

To briefly summarize the points covered thus far, one of the major controversial issues relating to the social consequences of test usage has been the placement of minority group, or culturally different, children in special classes for the mentally retarded, based largely on low scores on IQ tests. Mercer noted the overrepresentation of these children, found it indefensible, and designed a system of assessment stressing cultural pluralism and adaptive behavior (to one's social milieu outside of school). This approach tends to "declassify" children as mentally retarded, even when they have problems with school functioning, if their "estimated learning potential" and "adaptive behavior" suggest a higher level of ability, or more adequate performance, outside of school. One study (Fisher, 1978), cited in some detail, examined the number of children classified or declassified as a result of varying the criteria for mental retardation. Mental retardation is a relativistic concept, and the number of children so labeled can be easily manipulated by changing the placement criteria. The result of using pluralistic norms and measures of adaptive behavior is to "declassify" a relatively large number of children previously described as mentally retarded, or to preclude such a classification when culturally different children are referred because of academic problems.

Goodman (1977, 1979) argues that the diagnostic assumptions may be misleading and that the utility of the procedures has not been demonstrated. The SOMPA "fails in the attempt to establish intellectual potential" (1979, p. 48). A clear solution is not apparent and there may not be sufficient information to allow one at this time. Longitudinal studies of educational outcomes, perhaps best depicted by Mercer's use of the terms describing "enabling" versus "disabling trajectories," are needed. There is much uncertainty about the long range effects of educational decision making relating to the questions raised. Dunn's (1968) widely cited article, as well as Cronbach and Snow's (1977) analysis of a wide variety of educational experiments, serve to warn us about the possibility that narrowly conceived, short term "good" may result in negligible, or unintended, negative long term effects. Dunn (1968) provided an early criticism of placement practices for "socioculturally deprived children":

> Regular teachers and administrators have sincerely felt they were doing these pupils a favor by removing them from the pressures of an unrealistic and inappropriate program of studies. Special educators have also fully believed that the children involved would make greater progress in special schools and classes. However, the overwhelming evidence is that our present and past practices have their major justification in removing pressures on regular teachers and pupils at the expense of the socioculturally deprived slow learning pupils themselves. (p. 6)

Cronbach and Snow (1977) suggest that Binet's original work was an experiment as to whether or not special education would benefit selected children. However, only the selection issues appear to be systematically raised. One must question not only the accuracy of the assessment, but, more importantly, the educational benefit to the child. In addition to the concerns relating to the efficacy of special class instruction for certain groups of children, the sociological perspective warns us against possible harm that may accrue by assigning labels, even when it appears that the best interests of the child have been considered. Cronbach and Snow (1977) remark that "Investigators have been asking, since 1920, whether assignment to the slow-paced section is advantageous for the child with low scores and whether assignment to the fast section benefits the able child," and they conclude that "systematic research has been surprisingly sparse" (p. 334). This general problem is compounded with minority and culturally different children.

Reactions From Black Psychologists and Professional Groups

Despite the lack of answers concerning assessment issues and adequate programming to meet the individual needs of children, progress has been made. The warnings concerning the use of standardized intelligence tests with culturally different children have been expressed in a very clear manner, sometimes rather vehemently. For example, Williams (1971) pointed out that

> the single. most salient conclusion is that traditional ability tests do systematically and consistently lead to the assigning of improper and false labels on black children, and consequently to dehumanization and black intellectual genocide. (p. 62)

In 1969, the Association of Black Psychologists' statement concerning abuses in testing "called for an immediate moratorium on the administration of ability tests to black children" (Williams, 1971, p. 67). Very clearly, Williams views testing and subsequent special class placement as a "disabling trajectory":

> Tests do not permit the masses of black children to develop their full intellectual potential. Tests are used to sort and consequently to misplace black children in Special Education classes. (p. 67)

Jones (1980) provides a comprehensive view of issues related not only to assessment but also to broader concerns of many black psychologists. Jackson (1975), writing as chairman of the Association of Black Psychologists, presented a reaction to proposed definitions of test bias.

Other events, such as the Congressional hearings that occurred during the 1960's (Brim, 1965), demonstrated an "antitesting sentiment" from both lay and professional groups. The groundwork for recent federal legislation is evident in the major concerns: inaccessibility of test data, invasion of privacy, rigidity in the use of test scores, types of talent selected by tests, and the question of fairness to minority groups (Brim, 1965). Individual psychologists and professional groups, such as the American Psychological Association and the National Association of School Psychologists, have been deeply concerned about such issues for a number of years. This is evident in the number of articles in the major journals relating to minority children, measurement issues, and professional aspects of psychology, as well as numerous presentations at national conferences.

Similarly, the 1972 National Education Association Annual Conference explored the topic "Violations of Human and Civil Rights: Tests and the Use of Tests," and recommended a moratorium on testing (Bosma, 1973). The criticisms and expressed concerns from major professional groups help to guard against continuation of the misuse of tests with minority children. Even so, Gay and Abrahams (1973) note that although

> "cultural pluralism" has become the vogue of American education in the 1970's, the melting pot model still is operating, and much to the detriment of those children who come from culturally different backgrounds. (p. 330)

The *Journal of School Psychology* (Guest Editor: Oakland, *11*(4), 1973) is an excellent source for further reading, as is Oakland's (1977) more recent book on the assessment of minority group children. Sattler (1974) also provides a valuable chapter on the topic.

Other Issues: Labeling and Exceptional Children

Most recently, theory regarding the social consequences of test usage has dealt with problems associated with minority or culturally different children. Yet, the sociological perspective of deviance and "labeling theory" are potentially relevant to all exceptional children. Much contemporary theory regarding labeling arose from reactions to psychiatric diagnosis. The topics are introduced here because of the sociological emphasis of Mercer's work and also because the problems of labeling and classification have broad applicability.

Becker (1963) reviews several approaches to deviance. One is a statistical view: "Deviance includes anything varying too widely from the average" (p. 4). Another definition analyzed by Becker describes "deviance...as something essentially pathological, revealing the presence of a 'disease'" (p. 5). One can see how statistical data are automatically translated into social, followed by disease interpretations: a low score on an IQ test becomes a diagnosis of mental retardation—"a disease."

Another sociological view defines deviance "as the failure to obey group rules" (Becker, 1963, p. 8). However, this definition is also limited in that it "fails to give sufficient weight to the ambiguities that arise in deciding which rules are to be taken as the yardstick against which behavior is measured and judged deviant" (p. 8). Becker suggests that

> deviance is not a simple quality, present in some kinds of behavior and absent in others. Rather, it is the product of a process which involves responses of other people to the behavior. (p. 14)

Scheff (1966) points out that "labeled deviants" may actually be encouraged or rewarded for continuing "stereotyped" deviant behavior and that "labeled deviants" can be punished when they attempt to return to a normal position in life. Bandura (1969) provided convincing arguments against traditional psychiatric "disease interpretations" and the subsequent labels of deviant behavior. Such labels can impede the search for effective methods of helping, they have "led to heavy reliance upon physical and chemical interventions...as quick remedies for interpersonal problems, and long-term neglect of social variables as influential determinants of deviant response patterns" (p. 16). Bandura's contributions will be explored in greater depth in Chapter Three. The expansive two-volume treatise, *Issues in the Classification of Children,* edited by Hobbs (1975), explores these issues in depth. It should be noted that labeling may serve useful purposes. Labels, or "classification systems," may open doors for services by demonstrating needs (e.g., studying the prevalence or rate of a particular problem). Classification systems may assist with the organization of services to children and with the professional exchange of information (e.g., research in autism, schizophrenia, drug abuse). Also, systems are needed for accountability and fiscal management. Classification systems, if related to treatment and predictive of future behavior, may be important for remedial and preventative programs. From a legal viewpoint, Bersoff (1979) notes that

> The equal protection clause [of the Fourteenth Amendment] is not an absolute barrier to classification and not all classifications resulting in disparity are unconstitutional. If the classification is reasonably related to the purposes of governmental activity and is performed fairly, the fact that persons are treated differently does not necessarily create a constitutional violation. (pp. 3-4)

Measurement Problems

In order to more fully comprehend the potential hazards involved in the assessment of human abilities and characteristics, it is necessary to consider measurement problems in testing. Even with the best and most widely accepted test instruments (e.g., the Wechsler Scales and the Stanford-Binet), measurement problems persist and the interpretation of individual test scores requires prior background in the understanding of measurement concepts. Traditionally, these have included the topics of reliability and validity. Newer developments in measurement theory will also be introduced. Generalizability theory has helped reconceptualize approaches to measurement and error. A brief consideration of test bias is also highly relevant.

Reliability

There are three common methods of estimating a test's reliability, most often interpreted through the use of correlation coefficients representing the relationship between two sets of scores. One way is to retest the person later with the same test. *Test-retest reliability* provides an estimate of the stability of measurement. The question may be asked, "If a person is tested on one day, would the score be similar on the following day, or soon after?" The scores resulting from test-retest reliability may be influenced by memory, changing conditions in test administration, or any other possible factors that may vary over time. Scores resulting from retesting with an *alternative or equivalent form* may be influenced by the same factors that occur over time. Since, however, the exact test is not used twice over a brief span of time, the effects of memory and practice are reduced.

The reliability of a test can also be estimated from a single administration of a test indicating the degree of "internal consistency" of responses to test items. The *internal consistency* can be determined by the average correlations among test items. Coefficient alpha is the basic statistical approach for determining this type of reliability and establishes the "upper limit" for the test's reliability (Nunnally, 1978). *Split-half* reliability provides two sets of scores for each person by dividing the test into equivalent sections. Similarly, split-half reliability yields an estimate of test "consistency" rather than stability over time.

In practice, the determination of the reliability of any test is a complex matter. The classical approach to measurement defines each score by two components, the obtained score and test error. Test error can take a multitude of forms, often not readily recognizable or identifiable. The reliability of a test allows for the estimation of test error and is generally accurate for large groups of children. Thus, sources of error are thought to be *randomly distributed*, having an equal chance of affecting every individual. Different types of reliability provide estimates of different sources of error (*Standards*, 1974).

Estimates of traits obtained by different methods, or during different time periods, are not often identical. For example, a child does not really have *an* IQ. If the same test were given over and over again to the same child, theoretically, a normal distribution of scores scattered around a mean would result. In practice, a child may gain about seven IQ points on retesting after a brief time interval. If a child is given different tests, the results are rarely identical. Different IQ tests yield different estimates and often emphasize different skills.

The amount of error in a test score for an individual can be estimated, and is called the *standard error of measurement*. Comparisons between tests which attempt to measure the same attribute are not as straightforward. The *true score,* or actual IQ in the case of intelligence tests, is always unknown and it does not exist as such. Classical measurement theory suggests that any "observed" score is simply an estimate of a hypothetical true score. The standard error, derived from the standard deviation and reliability of the test, allows for the interpretation of a score around a *confidence interval*. While, for example, test-retest reliability compares the consistency of two different performances of a group of persons on separate occasions, the confidence interval suggests, for an individual, the probability of including the hypothetical true score within a range of scores. The standard error of measurement is important in order to estimate the possible range of scores for an individual due to "irrelevant" or "chance factors" (Anastasi, 1976). Since the reliability of a test may vary by age and ability level, by the type of skill measured, and by the way it is estimated, test manuals should provide detailed information in order to enable appropriate interpretations. The standard error of the Binet ranges from 2.4 to 6.8 depending on age and ability level (from Sattler, 1974). An example with the Binet (for a bright six year old child) yields a confidence interval of about 10 points (plus/minus one standard error of measurement of about 5). If the child achieved an IQ score of 120, we can estimate that about 68% of the time, the score will be in the range of 115 to 125, if the "true" IQ is 120. Confidence intervals can be constructed in terms of any probability level based on the properties of the normal curve. For the example given, if we wanted to be 95% certain of including the true score, the confidence interval would be from 110 to 130. An IQ score, as well as other standard scores, should always be interpreted by using the confidence interval, thereby taking into account the reliability of the test.

Salvia and Ysseldyke (1978) suggest a more conservative procedure for establishing confidence intervals with relevance for special class placement. From an equation by Nunnally (1978), an *estimated true score* can be determined. Nunnally comments that estimated true scores are most important for obtaining the center of the confidence interval. Estimated true scores are computed in the following way. The difference between the child's test score and the group mean of the test (e.g., 100, with an IQ test) is found. This difference is multiplied by the reliability coefficient of the test. The product is then added to the group mean. Using estimated true scores can have important consequences for intelligence testing because, as Nunnally (1978) points out, "obtained scores are biased estimates of true scores. Scores above the mean are biased upward, and scores below the mean are biased downward" (p. 217). The more extreme the scores, the more biased they are. In the above example, with a child who had an obtained score of 120 on an IQ test, the estimated true score would be approximately 118 and the confidence interval (68% level) would range from 113 to 123 (mean = 100; standard deviation = 16; reliability = .91). If a child scored 70 on an IQ test, the estimated true score would be approximately 73.

For a long time, measurement experts have discussed concerns about the classical approach to test theory stemming from Spearman's early work (1904). This approach assumes that an obtained score is comprised of two components: a true score and error. Logically questions can be raised about both components. First, the assumption of a hypothetical true score may be called into question. The realities are that if a person is tested on different occasions, or under different conditions, variation in scores is the rule. The second component, error, likewise has conceptual difficulties. Test error may not be randomly distributed, but may be biased or systematic in its influence on test scores. More importantly when considering classical test theory, a careful analysis of the variation in scores usually attributed to test error can be carried out. Error is assumed to be attributable "to multiple sources," and experiments "can estimate how much variation arises from each controllable source" (Cronbach, Gleser, Nanda, Rajaratnam, 1972, p. 1). In other words, when circumstances surrounding testing vary, the amount of influence of the changing conditions may be estimated.

The problems associated with the classical approach to test error can be best viewed by illustrating the problems of defining the reliability of a test. Test constructors have had many options in studying reliability, previously discussed. They are not interchangeable, however. Different approaches to reliability account for different sources of error. Cronbach and his associates (1972) have considerably advanced conceptual approaches to measurement through the development of *generalizability theory,* replacing classical reliability theory for both traditional tests and also observational approaches to assessment. The question of the *reliability* of a measurement procedure is recast *"into a question of accuracy of generalization, or generalizability"* (Cronbach, *et al.,* 1972, p. 15). A careful analysis is made of how scores yielded by a particular measure generalize to other subjects and to the "universe" of possible "conditions" that enable behavioral scientists to observe the performance of subjects. The conditions which might be studied could include the "tasks or stimulus," the time of observation, the setting, and the performance of different raters.

Many sources can be found for further reading. Wiggins (1973), Cone (1977) and Mitchell (1979) discuss generalizability theory within the framework of observational studies. Campbell (1976) applies it within the context of industrial and organizational psychology.

In educational and psychological testing, the assumption of random distribution or error may be unwarranted for a particular child or group of children. Even though test error is assumed to be randomly distributed, having an "equal chance" at affecting all persons, it may have a systematic, nonrandom effect on a child or subgroup of children. This consideration is important for individual test interpretation. Sources of test error, whether systematic or random, become sources of information, when considered from an experimental viewpoint.

Validity

Validity is concerned with the determination of what the test measures and to what degree. Test names (e.g., intelligence, aptitude, and achievement) are not always very meaningful or accurate descriptions for tests. Construct validity was discussed earlier in the chapter within the context of defining intelligence. *Construct validity* is important from a theoretical or scientific viewpoint in furthering an understanding of what a test measures. Another type of validity, content validity, is more appropriate to a discussion of achievement tests. *Content validity* addresses the question of the adequacy of the items and "involves essentially the systematic examination of the test content to determine whether it covers a representative sample of the behavior domain to be measured" (Anastasi, 1976, pp. 134-135).

Especially important in educational and psychological decision making is the *criterion-related validity* of a test, indicating "the effectiveness of a test in predicting an individual's behavior in specified situations" (Anastasi, 1976, p. 140). APA's *Standards* (1974) make the distinction between concurrent and predictive validity. *Concurrent validity* provides information about the child's status at the time of testing, as in making a "diagnosis." *Predictive validity* concerns future performance on test-related dimensions.

Tests do not have high or low validity in a general sense. A statement concerning validity must always be qualified in terms of the specific population the test was standardized on and the experimental procedures used in developing the test. Furthermore, as Messick (1980) points out, the social consequences of assessment are not distinct from measurement issues. In addition to determining the adequacy of a test, the "potential social consequences" must be appraised.

What are some of the most serious problems relative to intelligence testing and validity? First, IQs can and do change. Intelligence test scores of infants are not very predictive of adult intelligence. Measured intelligence in school-aged children becomes more predictive of adult intelligence. However, relatively large changes in intelligence can be observed through the repeated testing of groups of children. In one classic study (Honzik, Macfarlane and Allen, 1948), changes of a magnitude of 15 IQ points were observed in more than half of the children in the study, a change in IQ of 20 points was not that unusual, and a change as great as 50 points was reported (for further discussion see Brody and Brody, 1976; Mussen, Conger and Kagan, 1974; Sattler, 1974).

Second, IQs are only moderately correlated to our most important "life goals," such as academic success, as reflected in grade point average, or a person's job success. A higher correlation exists between IQ and the number of years spent in school. There is also a rather large range of abilities, as measured by intelligence tests, within separate occupational groups, such as accountants, truckdrivers, lawyers, and teachers. Brody and Brody (1976) and Matarazzo (1972) have both summarized validity studies in terms of occupational status. One impressive example of validity is that provided by the classic study of gifted persons by Terman. The lives of a group of about 1,500 gifted individuals (the top one percent of the population) have been followed since 1921. On the whole, the group has had a list of remarkable achievements providing substantial evidence for the long-range predictive validity of IQ tests. At middle age, many individual members of the group had made major contributions and had won widespread recognition, including impressive numbers elected to Phi Beta Kappa, the National Academy of Science, and *Who's Who,* etc. Terman and Oden (1959) concluded that "the capacity to achieve far beyond the average can be detected early in life through tests of general intelligence" (p. 144). Even so, a small percentage of this extremely bright group of individuals either dropped out of high school or did not complete college, and, similarly, some were underemployed at mid-life, working in clerical, or semi-skilled positions. Terman and Oden (1959) suggest that in terms of personal and emotional adjustment, the group did not appear to differ appreciably from the norm.

In summary, intelligence should best be viewed as one facet of personality. In order to make predictions about the future of an individual, it is best to view results of intelligence tests within this perspective. Intelligence is not a static characteristic of the person. A single IQ score does not approximate the complexities of the skills and other attributes of a person, including creative thinking, interpersonal problem solving, motivation, value systems, and other qualitative factors. Although impressive validity studies can be found for groups of people, extreme caution is in order when tests are used for individual decisions, especially with young children, or with children and adults of divergent cultural backgrounds. The construct of intelligence and the tests designed to measure intelligence may serve useful purposes if interpreted properly.

Test Bias

The problems and attempted solutions associated with *test bias* are exceedingly complex and without clear resolution. Test bias relates both to problems of measurement as well as to social and political issues. Mercer's work has been important in this regard. Mercer, as previously illustrated, has emphasized significant sources of bias that may result from sociocultural differences. In the sense that placement decisions based on biased testing may bar certain groups of children from educational opportunities or may stigmatize them, the use of tests may result in discriminatory practices. Thus a closer look at *test bias* is in order.

There are many ways that a test may be biased. Flaugher (1978) notes that "an important complicating aspect is the widespread failure to interpret test scores appropriately" (p. 67). For example, a specific test can be used as a measure of past instruction and might be considered as an *achievement test*. If it is used in a broader sense and does not reflect specific content relating to an instructional program, a test with similar questions may be viewed as an *intelligence test*. In this case, the test is reflective of all past learning opportunites as well as biological development. If the test is used to predict future performance, the test is usually regarded as an *aptitude test*.

Differences in interpretation can have great social significance. If a test is interpreted as an achievement test, and scores are low, better instruction, or an alternative method of instruction is indicated. If interpreted as an aptitude test, social and political factors may become involved in making a case for the *"withdrawal* of educational resources":

> Low achievement scores reported for groups of minority students have led to demands not for the improvement of the educational system but for the abandonment of those "lying" tests, which are seen as indicating that the capacity to achieve does not exist. (p. 672)

In cross-cultural testing, there may be other sources of bias that would possibly affect the test scores of a minority subgroup. Anastasi (1976) lists several possibilities as follows: language or dialect difference; speed, or the value of a rapid performance; test content; cultural conditions affecting the child's interests; and motivation and attitudes in approaching the testing situation (p. 287). The sex, age, and personal characteristics of the examiner and other, possibly unknown, variables relative to the situation may affect the test performance of an individual (Anastasi, 1976, pp. 39-41), although specific studies have been less conclusive.

Historically, there have been many attempts to resolve the problems associated with test bias, particularly as it relates to cultural differences. Anastasi (1976), Samuda (1975), and Sattler (1974) outline experiments with "culture-free" and "culture-fair" tests. They have not been very successful because of the overall importance of culture: "intelligence tests cannot be created so that differential exposure to learning has no influence on test scores" (Sattler, 1974, p. 32). The most important aspects of learning take place in a social-cultural environment. Other approaches to testing minority children have included translating the tests into different languages (see Sattler, 1974, for a concise discussion). However, the experiments have not been very successful. The difficulty level of items can easily and unintentionally be changed and the significance of the items (or test content) may turn out to be relative only to a specific culture. The answers are not straightforward. For example, when a test is translated from English into Spanish, it can become a "hybrid belonging to neither culture" (Sattler, 1974, p. 39). Culture specific tests yield interpretations relative to a specific culture, but not in relationship to the "American core culture" (Mercer, 1979, p. 24). For example, Williams (1975) has developed the Black Intelligence Test of Cultural Homogeneity (BITCH-100) and reported a correlation of .39 with the California Achievement Test for 28 black high school dropouts. For whites, a test like this may measure "awareness and familiarity" with "black experience."

A number of statistical approaches to minimizing test bias have also been attempted. Most have been in the context of industrial (e.g., job selection) or educational applications not directly related to problems associated with the identification of exceptional children (e.g., decision making for entry into graduate or professional schools like medicine, law, etc.). Mercer's SOMPA, as previously discussed, is an example of one statistical approach to minimizing test bias directly relevant to exceptional children. A brief overview of statistical approaches follows.

Test bias can be defined as differences in average scores obtained by distinct cultural groups. Intelligence tests have been said to be biased in this manner because blacks and other minority groups score lower than whites. Flaugher (1978) argues that

> Knowing what we do about the relative status, socioeconomic and otherwise, of ethnic minorities in the United States, it would be surprising if most kinds of tests didn't show mean differences in favor of the majority group. (p. 673)

An alternative approach may view the mean score differences between groups as less important and defend the use of a test if the test appears to predict, in a fair manner, the performances of both groups. A third definition may ignore both mean differences and predictions and note the end effect: whether or not the persons selected are representative of the overall population (a quota system). Other solutions and combinations of solutions have been offered. Schmidt and Hunter (1974) and Hunter and Schmidt (1976) review the statistical approaches to test bias and conclude "that any purely statistical approach to the problem of test bias is doomed to rather immediate failure" (Hunter and Schmidt, 1976, p. 1069). McNemar (1975) warns that if one chooses a particular definition of test bias with the intent of being "fair," one may still be charged with the "unfair" use of the test through a conflicting definition. Hunter and Schmidt (1976) see the various statistical approaches as actually supporting different ethical positions, representing sometimes "irreconcilable values" (p. 1069). Each approach may have advantages or disadvantages, depending on one's point of view. Cleary, Humphreys, Kendrick, and Wesman (1975) also provide an important review of the statistical issues relating to test bias. A special issue of the *Journal of Educational Measurement* (*13*(1), 1976) explores "bias in selection."

Jensen (1980) has brought the emotionally charged issue of test bias again into the forefront of public attention (Kamin, 1980). For this reason alone, the major points of his recent book warrant review. That many researchers, however, have been examining the theoretical and practical implications of test bias can be ascertained by the number of publications relating to the topic. Assumptions relating to test fairness with minorities have to do with predictive validity, the significance of situational influences in test scores, and test content. Many sources suggest that tests may be useful under certain circumstances with minorities, contradicting some of the important early recommendations (e.g., Fishman, et al., 1964). Research relevant to the use of the WISC-R is cited in Chapter Five.

One potential source of bias is a test's predictive validity. An absence of bias would be indicated by the lack of systematic under or over prediction of a criterion performance for persons in either the minority or majority groups. A finding of *differential validity* implies a statistically significant difference between validity coefficients for members of distinct groups. Jensen (1980) reports: "Differential validity for the two racial groups is a virtual nonexistent phenomena" (p. 515). However, one point raised by the *Larry P.* decision is the relative absence of information on the predictive validity of IQ tests with minority children scoring between two and three standard deviations below the mean. The important question was *not* whether standardized IQ tests *generally* predict the academic performance of black children. The tests require validation for the placement of black students into classes for the educable mentally retarded.

Another important method of examining test bias is through studying the internal characteristics of the test (e.g., reliability, item discriminability, the factorial structure of the test). Again, Jensen concludes that the results of many studies "fail to support...the expectation that...most current standardized tests of mental ability are culturally biased" (p. 587). A "rational" approach to determining bias may lead to inaccurate results. For example, Sandoval and Miille (1980) found that judges, college students representing black, Mexican-American, and whites, were unable to identify, by inspection, items on the Wechsler Intelligence Scale for Children-Revised that were empirically demonstrated to be more difficult for minority in contrast to white children.

Furthermore, situational influences (factors relating to the testing procedure such as examiner characteristics, testing atmosphere, test sophistication) often seem to have negligible effects. For example, Jensen's interpretation of thirty studies exploring the influence of examiner race failed to support the hypothesis that "subjects...perform better when tested by a person of the same race" (p. 618).

Jensen does *not* advocate giving IQ tests routinely to school children in his book. Even though concluding that tests are not biased, he does find many faults with current test usage. He remarks that tests are not "good *in principle.*"

They are good only to the extent that they can serve useful and beneficial purposes and can do so more objectively, reliably, and efficiently than other available means. (p. 736)

Several points stand out from the brief review of intelligence testing and bias. First, when interpreted in a positive way, it appears that intelligence tests may be beneficial in assessing the problems of children relatively independent of cultural influences. Second, as with Heber's research (the Milwaukee Project), IQ tests may serve as important outcome measures for socially significant interventions. Third, many potential sources of bias may influence test scores in individual cases. Procedural safeguards, discussed in Chapter Four, become paramount. Reschly (1979) notes that the evidence for item bias and atmosphere bias (relating to situational influences on test scores) is inconclusive. Furthermore, research evidence does not suggest differential validity for different groups of children. Reschly reminds us that the sources of bias have to be studied with respect to social consequences.

The ultimate criteria that should guide our evaluations of test bias are the implications and outcomes of test use for individuals... [T]est use is fair if the results are more effective interventions leading to improved competencies and expanded opportunities for individuals. Test use is unfair if opportunities are diminished or if individuals are exposed to ineffective interventions as a result of tests. (p. 235)

Summary

The second chapter has stressed the difficulties associated with one aspect of psychological testing, the assessment of intelligence. After considering problems in defining intelligence, social issues that arise out of test usage, as well as measurement problems, one may be somewhat puzzled and pessimistic about the value of assessment for helping children. Indeed, the problems are substantial when viewed within the traditional context. As was emphasized in the discussion of test bias, many questions thought to be technical might be better considered to actually reflect different ethical positions encompassing personal values not reconcilable through the use of statistical techniques. The examples cited stressed the measurement of intelligence, especially with minority group children, in order to help illustrate serious contemporary concerns. Similar assessment issues may arise in testing exceptional children. The third and fourth chapters (and Section II) will provide a more adequate context for multifactored assessment.

Chapter 3

PERSONALITY ASSESSMENT

Recently, the topic of personality assessment has been either ignored in major texts relating to educational assessment, or has suffered severe criticism. Even in traditional references, the topic has often been treated by offering examples of tests commonly used to identify the emotional problems of children who may then be placed in special classes, residential settings, or referred to outside agencies for therapeutic help. This type of discussion oversimplifies personality assessment and is difficult to justify. Personality assessment has not been a popular topic in recent years for many psychologists, teachers, and well-informed parents. Some school psychologists avoid the term "personality assessment" because they anticipate negative reactions from parents, teachers, and principals, due to ties with psychodiagnosis, emphasizing pathological, abnormal behavior, or because of the many problems surrounding personality tests from a measurement point of view. Although it is easy to understand this practice from a historical perspective, it may not always be necessary. While the widespread criticisms and negative attitudes are understandable in light of past practices and potential abuses, personality assessment has much to contribute to the concept of multifactored assessment.

Why Does Personality Assessment Represent a Major Context?

In many respects, the negative influences of personality assessment parallel the concerns attributed to intelligence testing as presented in Chapter Two. Personality tests have been criticized because of pervasive measurement problems and also because of legal, ethical, and social issues that have stemmed from test usage. The use of tests to classify children as emotionally disturbed has been widely challenged for all of the above reasons. Also, the ambiguities and potential dangers of classification systems themselves are of great concern to many social scientists, as well as to parents and society in general. Finally, the classification of children, per se, has not been necessarily equated with effective treatment approaches.

44

Even after five years of planning, the development of the third edition of the *Diagnostic and Statistical Manual of Mental Disorders* (American Psychiatric Association, 1980) is not without similar criticism (McReynolds, 1979). Often, the traditional outcomes of personality assessment tended merely to confirm observations of parents and teachers. Insights may have been offered with respect to a child's personality characteristics, but did not necessarily lead to specific programs for intervention.

Despite actual abuses and meaningful criticisms, personality assessment, as characterized by traditional as well as innovative approaches, has undoubtedly made contributions to the understanding and helping of children with emotional problems by skilled psychologists. Most significantly, since the middle 1960's there have been many conceptual advances in psychological assessment. The broadened scope of personality assessment has allowed for the reconsideration of many of the criticisms resulting from a search for acceptable practices. The newer, emerging models of personality assessment provide a context for measurement problems encountered, and focus on empirically verified methods of helping children. The recent trends in personality assessment have been very much influenced by the concerns involving classification, legal and ethical issues, accountability, as well as the measurement problems typical of traditional personality assessment.

One trend can be characterized by a "problem-solving" approach to assessment whereby the psychologist enlists the aid of parents, teachers, and child (if at all possible) to help identify barriers to adjustment and, more important, to generate possible solutions to the problem. A second trend has been a reconceptualization of trait approaches in personality. Rather than viewing personality dimensions as traits, implying immutable characteristics of the person, they are perhaps better considered as "organizing factors in behavior" (Stern, Stein and Bloom, 1956), for example, as in how children view themselves (self-concept) and others (others-concept).

Personality dimensions may be explored through the traditional or non-traditional use of tests. The child's repertoire of personal and social skills may be assessed, and new skills or coping strategies may be taught where lacking (as in taking turns, making friends, living under stressful life circumstances, etc.). When the child has the necessary skills, but they are not practiced in certain circumstances, "self-control" procedures may be taught. Suggestions may be made to assist those working with the child in a particular setting to help maintain the desired behavior. Another significant trend is the focus on the child's environment. The social systems of the child (family, school, community) are all considered, together or in part, as potential targets for assessment and intervention. In addition to the usual concerns involving efficiency, the emerging models also stress accountability through a careful consideration of the impact of the intervention.

One can see that the procedures may be helpful, not only for children traditionally characterized as emotionally disturbed, but for other children as well. As special education teachers will attest, many children have highly complex learning problems that cut across the arbitrary "boundaries" of exceptionalities. Any child, whether considered learning disabled, mentally retarded, blind, or hearing impaired, may have emotional or adjustment problems. One approach has been to try to distinguish the "primary" from the "secondary" symptoms. For example, the child may be learning disabled but have an "emotional overlay." Newer models of personality assessment are less concerned with the problems associated with the classification of individuals. They permit one to fully consider the complex problems of children and to identify a wide range of potential resources for helping both within the child and within the child's social environment.

This chapter will have the following plan. Following a few definitions, a brief discussion of the "decline" of personality assessment will be presented, summarizing criticisms and concerns of the use of traditional techniques and approaches. Recent trends will then be explored.

A Few Basic Definitions and Parameters

Psychological Assessment is conventionally used as a broad term, encompassing traditional ability and personality measurement. Personality tests refer much more narrowly to "measures of such characteristics as emotional adjustment, interpersonal relations, motivation, interests, and attitudes" (Anastasi, 1976, p. 18). Behavioral assessment, rather than using indirect measures, such as tests, stresses "direct measurement of the individual's response to various life situations" (Goldfried and Kent, 1976, p. 34). Behavioral assessment is usually contrasted to traditional approaches to personality assessment. Modern writers stress that personality assessment includes other practices in addition to testing. Sundberg (1977) conceptualized personality assessment as

> the set of processes used by a person or persons for developing impressions and images, making decisions and checking hypotheses about another person's pattern of characteristics which determine his or her behavior in interaction with the environment. (pp. 21-22)

A very common mistake within the educational perspective is to equate the use of personality tests with personality assessment. Sloves, Docherty, and Schneider (1979) describe the difference in the following way: "Psychological assessment is systems and problem oriented, dynamic, and conceptual; whereas psychological testing is methods and measurement oriented, descriptive, and technical" (p. 28). McReynolds (1975) notes that both in theory and in current practice, psychological assessment must go beyond the giving of psychological tests:

> Properly conceived, the field of assessment encompasses the development and utilization of the full range of techniques—tests, interviews, experimental manipulations, and naturalistic observa-tions—for gathering systematic information about persons, groups, and human institutions. (p. X)

The actual use of the terms is somewhat confusing. Writers in the area of personality assessment frequently refer to cognitive aspects of functioning, including problem solving and creativity, as well as more traditional personality dimensions. Behaviorists have encouraged the use of a set of assessment procedures that seem, at least on the surface, to have little relationship to traditional approaches. Nelson and Hayes (1979) offer the following comparisons. While sharing some techniques (e.g., interviews, observations, questionnaires) "the two approaches differ radically...in their assumptions and levels of inference" (p. 491). Behaviorists have minimized inferences about underlying causes of behavior. The "functional utility" of behavioral assessment is stressed; the adequacy of behavioral asessment is judged not only by its ability to enhance the understanding of behavior, but also by its ability to alter behavior. They characterize traditional personality assessment by the assumption that "behavior is a function of relatively stable intra organismic (e.g., intrapsychic) variables" (p. 491). The assessment of the situation "is thought to be of little relevance" because "the causes of behavior lie within the person" (p. 491). Recent developments in behaviorism emphasizing a "multimodal approach" (e.g., Keat, 1979; Lazarus, 1976, 1977; Nay, 1979) stress the importance of observable behavior as well as the cognitive and phenomenological aspect of functioning. Also, behaviorists have gone beyond the analysis of "current environmental variables" and stress person or "organismic" variables ("individual differences produced by physiology and past learning") (Nelson and Hayes, 1979, p. 495). Furthermore, Hartmann, Roper, and Bradford (1979) make the following comment:

> The potential value of norms (and norm-referenced tests) should not be quickly dismissed by behavioral assessors. Norm referenced tests have served a number of useful purposes for applied behaviorists, and can continue to do so in the future. (p. 9)

They list a number of possible uses of normative tests including (1) screening, (2) assessing target behaviors, (3) noting the "degree of convergence between alternative measurement procedures," (4) evaluating intervention strategies, and (5) in establishing the "clinical significance or social validity" of interventions (pp. 9-10). Although clear differences in approaches are sometimes suggested in the literature, in practice the usefulness of such distinctions becomes less apparent.

Personality tests are popularly categorized as being either projective or objective, although the distinction may not be an important one (Lanyon and Goodstein, 1971). Projective Techniques are characterized as "unstructured." The child may be asked to respond to an ambiguous stimuli (e.g., a picture to be interpreted, a sentence stem to be finished such as "I like..." or "I am sad when...") or to make a drawing of a person, a house, or of their family. Traditionally, the major assumption has been that persons presented with the ambiguous task will structure the task in such a manner as to provide insights into their own needs or conflicts. Psychological interpretations have considered sources of anxiety, defense mechanisms (e.g., repression, denial and regression), and the types of controls that a child exhibits. Projective techniques have been historically associated with a psychodynamic orientation reflecting inner needs and private processes. They have also been characterized by considerable difficulty in applying suitable research methods.

Objective tests are characterized by more structure. Rather than eliciting open ended responses, children taking objective tests are commonly asked to choose from alternative responses presented in a multiple choice or true-false format. In contrast to projective techniques, the development of objective tests has not been tied to a particular theoretical approach and has given rise to large-scale attempts at empirical validation of many measures. Statistical tests of research hypotheses derived from particular personality theories lend themselves to the use of objective measures. Most objective techniques attempt to describe the person in terms of a number of traits. The resulting tests vary widely depending on the author's theoretical orientation. Historically, many approaches to assessment involved aspects of psychiatric classification (e.g., hypochondriasis, schizophrenia, paranoia), a description of temperament or psychosocial functioning (e.g., withdrawal, depression, dominance, conscientiousness), or comparisons involving interests, values, and attitudes.

Personality assessment techniques should help in understanding a person experiencing a psychological problem. Kanfer and Goldstein (1975) define psychological problems

> by a person's feelings of anxiety or tension, dissatisfaction with his own behavior, excessive attention to the problem area, inefficiency in reaching desired goals, or inability to function effectively in psychological areas. (p. 6)

With children and especially young children, as Nelson and Evans (1977) point out, the "referral may bear little relationship to the child's own subjective feelings of stress" (p. 603). Psychological problems are likely to be identified by persons in the child's social environment. The child may not be experiencing difficulty, it may be that:

> Others in his social environment are adversely affected by his behavior or judge him to be ineffective, destructive, unhappy, disruptive, or in some other way acting contrary to his best self-interest or the best interest of the social community in which he lives. (Kanfer and Goldstein, 1975, pp. 6-7)

In other words, "abnormal child behavior can be defined by what bothers adults" (Nelson and Evans, 1977, p. 604). For these reasons, especially with young children under the strong social control of adults, assessment strategies should include the significant social environments of the child.

Historical Influences

Although related in general to the origins of research in measurement and the study of individual differences, another significant influence in personality assessment resulted from early efforts in individual clinical assessment of abnormal behavior or psychopathology (see DuBois, 1970; Lanyon and Goodstein, 1971; or McReynolds, 1975, for a brief history of personality assessment). The influence of psychoanalytic theory with its corresponding emphasis on "deeper," "hidden," and "private" facets of personality led to the growth of projective tests such as the Rorschach (1921), Human Figure Drawing (Machover, 1949), and the Thematic Apperception Test (Murray, 1938) as techniques to explore unconscious mechanisms. Even though research interest in projectives seems to have waned in recent years, the instruments are still used widely. Sundberg (1977) comments: "In the popular mind the ten inkblots came to symbolize much of what a psychologist does, and implied a mysterious and magical image of the profession" (p. 206).

Surprisingly, the Rorschach has received some recent positive reviews (e.g., Buros, 1972) and there has been innovative research with alternative approaches to projective tests. For example, Fulkerson (1965) explored cognitive interpretations of projective tests with the Rorschach. Winter, Ferreira, and Olson (1965) adapted Arnold's (1962) method of story sequence analysis involving the Thematic Apperception Test for the study of family problem solving processes. Although the innovations are unlikely to result in new standardized procedures, experimental approaches may offer valuable information under unique circumstances. Klopfer and Taulbee (1976) present what might be considered as a consensus view of persons using various projectives in describing the TAT:

> We seem to be approaching the conclusion that the TAT is not a psychometric instrument at all, but rather a multidimensional method for studying complex personality and for evaluating needs, values, motivations, and attitudes. (p. 554)

The influence of the study of individual differences from a measurement perspective has led to tests characterized as objective. Objective tests cover a broad range of applications, including the identification and classification of persons with psychiatric disorders, and the description of interests and values of normal persons for the purpose of, for example, helping with career choices, or job screening. Personality research, using tests having a paper and pencil format, has proliferated in part because the tests lend themselves to statistical procedures. Tests such as the Minnesota Multiphasic Personality Inventory (1940), and the California Psychological Inventory (1957), have been studied with very large samples of persons and are still very widely used. Sundberg (1977) notes that "objective techniques have been the most powerful long-run force in personality assessment" (p. 196). Most of the research, however, has been done with adults, making the transition to children's problems difficult. Also, much of the research has concentrated on the theoretical study of personality of either normal or disturbed persons and has not been associated directly with practical considerations in planning treatment or intervention programs. Even modern, well-researched, and standardized tests for children (e.g., The Children's Personality Questionnaire, Porter and Cattell, 1975) can be criticized with respect to utility. Personality measures may, however, be helpful in terms of ''conceptual validity''; that is, they may assist the psychologist in understanding certain children and thus may be helpful in certain circumstances.

Another strong influence in the study of abnormal behavior was the early tie to the field of medicine and consequent attempts to provide diagnostic classification systems for those considered mentally ill. The assumption was that the discovery of specific treatments would follow. The term ''psychodiagnosis'' reflects this particular historical trend. Weiner (1972) comments: ''Psychodiagnosis, defined as the clinical use of psychological tests to facilitate personality classification, is currently in a state of seige'' (p. 534). A great many writers (e.g., Bersoff, 1973a; Mischel, 1968, 1973, 1977; Peterson, 1968) have been extremely critical of traditional approaches to personality assessment characterized by the ''psychodiagnostic model'' and the use of tests for classification and prediction.

Is Personality Assessment Declining?

There are a great number of references documenting the concerns related to testing and changing patterns of test usage among psychologists. Cleveland's (1976) article entitled ''Reflections on the Rise and Fall of Psychological Assessment'' is a good example. Cleveland comments on the ''Period of Triumph'' of testing, occurring directly after World War II and lasting for about ten years. Following the brief period of very rapid growth, there has been skepticism about testing from both lay and professional groups, perhaps culminating in the 1960's with the severe criticisms and anti-testing sentiment expressed in congressional hearings (Brim, 1965) and in the influential writing of Mischel (1968) and Peterson (1968). Cleveland (1976) stresses factors such as ''changing social values'' and research describing ''a steady flow of failures'' as contributing to the demise of traditional assessment practices using tests.

The Major Criticisms of Personality Assessment

Numerous research studies have shown that tests in the area of personality, commonly used to identify or diagnose emotionally disturbed persons, have low reliability and validity. Expert clinical judges have had difficulty agreeing in matters of interpretation. Tests do not adequately predict behavior for many potential groups of persons belonging to different diagnostic groups. Another factor that Cleveland (1976) cites is that: ''test reports tend to emphasize pathology and to ignore assets,

constructive characteristics, and healthy mechanisms used by the clients"
(p. 314). Others have expressed concern about the possibility that
widespread use of personality assessment might constitute an invasion of
privacy.

The problems are equally severe within a public school context. Salvia
and Ysseldyke (1978), in an important book relating to the assessment of
exceptional children, are highly critical of traditional personality
assessment. In addition to the above problems, they cite concerns
regarding accountability, especially with the "educational relevance" of
traditional personality assessment.

A great number of other references exist criticizing the use of
personality tests. However, the same points relating to measurement
problems, usefulness, and social consequences of classification are most
often mentioned. Wiggins (1973) presents an excellent review of the
measurement and prediction problems in personality assessment.

Writers advocating the use of traditional approaches to psychosocial
assessment and personality measurement in research have attempted to
outline the circumstances for which testing may be useful (see, for example,
Hogan, DeSoto, and Solano, 1977, and Weiner, 1972). In response to the
criticisms have come suggestions for acceptable practice. Included are
broadening horizons and methods applicable to the problems of a wide
range of exceptional children, not just those labeled emotionally disturbed.
The objectives of recent models of personality assessment have transcended
the traditional interest in personality classification by stressing specific ways
of helping people. Therefore, since most people react to personality testing
on the basis of traditional conceptions, it is important to consider the major
criticisms in more detail. When appropriate, lines of debate will also be
briefly outlined.

The first criticism is that personality tests do not predict behavior very well.
Mischel (1968) and Peterson (1968) have severely criticized traditional test
usage, especially for the study of clinically relevant behavior. Mischel
points out that personality tests have correlations with criterion behaviors
of no more than .30. He views this as a ceiling or limit for how well
personality tests can predict behavior. Peterson (1968) similarly decries the
use of tests in the clinical assessment of significant social behaviors:

> Personality test validities have not approached the level required for
> individual decisions, and it is becoming more and more apparent that
> the fault lies not merely in the instruments but in the basic rationale on
> which they are founded. (p. 138)

Both Mischel and Peterson point to the necessity of studying the person in
context. However, Hogan, Desoto, and Solano (1977) comment that
studying the "situation" or context may not lead to greater predictive
ability than that evidenced through the use of tests. They cite more
optimistic evidence of successful predictions made in certain experiments
with personality tests and socially significant behaviors. Weiner (1972) feels
that writers like Mischel and Peterson have "misconceptualized" the

purpose of psychodiagnosis. He argues that psychodiagnostic testing is not used to predict behavior, but to further the understanding of "personality processes."

Secondly, trait approaches have not fared well in personality research. Peterson (1968) comments that psychological tests have often been developed as an "economical way" to determine the important "general characteristics" of a person (p. 140). Similarly, Mischel (1973) notes that various traits, or personality dispositions, have been proposed as "basic units of personality study" that would demonstrate "widely generalized causal effects on behavior" (p. 253). The attempts have included the development of hundreds of tests designed to measure either specific factors or very broad dimensions, thought to have explanatory or predictive significance. Mischel (1968, 1973) questions the usefulness of trait-like approaches. He notes that evidence for consistency can be found in several areas, such as cognitive or intellectual aspects of personality, behavior relating to cognitive styles and problem solving skills, and for specific samples of behavior across similar situations. Socially significant behaviors related to the "traits" measured by personality tests have not been easily predicted. There is evidence, however, to suggest a more significant link when, from an individual viewpoint, persons rate the relevancy of the trait and estimate their own consistency in various situations for the behavior in question (e.g., Bem and Allen, 1974).

Weiner (1972) acknowledges that "inferences" about test performance increase the chances for measurement error. He balances the critical view with the observation that behavioral assessment, in contrast, is "theoretically impoverished." It may enable "a prediction of what someone will do but not any understanding of why he will do it" (p. 536). Zubin, Eron, and Schumer, (1965) similarly comment: "Personality structure cannot always be the basis for a correct prediction of future behavior, but it can form the basis for explaining or interpreting observed behavior" (p. 13). Hogan, *et al.* (1977) review the arguments concerning the use of tests as measures of traits and suggest that many modern writers and researchers share a common view: "Trait terms refer to stylistic consistencies in interpersonal behavior" (p. 256). They comment that reliable and valid measures of personality are predictive of important behaviors and that "most personality researchers do not believe traits are enduring psychic structures or that personality tests are designed to measure such traits; nor are most test users trait theorists" (p. 257).

A third criticism has been that traditional personality assessment with origins in psychiatric diagnosis has not demonstrated a usefulness for newer approaches to treatment. Phillips, Draguns, and Bartlett (1975) characterize the traditional view as being based on medical concepts of illness: "The individual...is sick...suffering from an illness that prevents his normal adjustment in society....The underlying pathological process needs to be elucidated" (p. 27). The person's symptoms are important for diagnosis but may be considered "trivial" in determining treatment.

The same authors note, in raising the question of how well the medical model has fared, that: "Seven or more decades of biological, biomedical, and genetic research have isolated remarkably few physical bases for recognized forms of psychopathology" (p. 29). Phillips, *et al.* (1975) view the modern trends in classification as being "flexible," "open to change" and most important, responsive to unintended negative outcomes (p. 45). Classification systems should reflect modern research, and, for children, they should be tied to the unique problems of childhood and stages of development. They should stress the "classification of behaviors," not children. The systems should be "multidimensional," and should emphasize a social and situational context. The authors also point out the importance of public understanding of classification systems in recognition of the fact that they can be easily misunderstood. Especially with children characterized as, for example, "behavior disordered," the public may regard the problems associated with the diagnostic labels as "immutable," or "difficult to change" (p. 47). It is partially for this reason that Coleman, Butcher, and Carson (1980) prefer the term "maladaptive" rather than "abnormal." The term has the advantage of shifting the focus of the concern from the person to the behavior. Consequently, there is an implication of more possibility for change. Phillips, *et al.* note that, despite the criticisms and concerns cited, "classification" or the need to classify, has not been eliminated. Instead, greater caution is required in the use of classification systems.

> For . . . practical and theoretical reasons, the task of assessing and classifying individuals faced with problems of adaptation is here to stay. (pp. 43-44)

Weiner (1972) offers a somewhat similar opinion. In reference to traditional diagnostic categories, he notes that the terms are widely used, thus serving to facilitate communication, and the behaviors are real. Weiner suggests psychodiagnosis may be helpful for treatment planning as, for example, in providing for an estimate of "personality resources" (p. 539).

Goldfried and Kent (1976) compare the traditional approach to personality assessment with the behavioral approach. The traditional approach, with its focus on the understanding of deeper personality traits and processes, has placed little emphasis on the "utility" of assessment in determining therapeutic approaches (p. 34). However, Davidson and Neale (1978) suggest that traditional assessment instruments "cannot predict the usefulness of psychotherapy because we know so little about therapy" (p. 77). It is therefore unrealistic to expect assessment tools to be able to predict future outcomes that are not well understood. Personality assessment procedures have been expected to predict many ill-defined outcomes and, as a result, their weak predictive validity should be expected in many instances (e.g., Mischel, 1968). In contrast, the specific intent of behavioral assessment has been to generate information that would have a direct relationship to treatment, characteristically, "the selection and implementation of appropriate behavior-modification procedures" (Goldfried and Kent, 1976, p. 34). Bersoff (1973a), in a widely cited article, also questioned the usefulness of psychological tests in the development of intervention strategies and offered possible solutions, discussed later in this chapter. Wiggins (1973) notes that "social behaviorists" (e.g., Peterson, Mischel) have ignored traditional personality assessment problems stressing classification and decision making and have concentrated "on the development of assessment procedure for the single case" (p. 364).

The nature of the classification problem is changing and is being influenced by developments in many fields. Theoretical issues associated with labeling were introduced in Chapter Two. Overall, an important trend is that classification systems are more likely to be descriptive of the types of services needed by the child, thus requiring assessment of the resources of the system attempting to provide services. The change in emphasis may be highly significant in the field of education.

A fourth area involves humanistic concerns. Many humanistic principles result from problems associated with the classification of persons leading to discriminatory treatment, and stigmatizing, dehumanizing labels and conditions, as previously discussed. Weiner (1972) agrees that "humanistic principles are expressed in such a way that it is almost impossible to take exception to them" (p. 537). However, he continues by stressing that the humanistic concerns result from "abuses of psychodiagnostic assessment," but not with its objectives (p. 538). Sugarman (1978) reviewed humanistic concerns of psychodiagnostic assessment (finding 31 in all) and warns that the "criticisms could be valid" if procedural safeguards are not followed.

A View of Current Practice

In light of the many criticisms of psychological assessment, especially personality assessment, one might wonder if such procedures have actually declined in popularity. For example, Garfield and Kurtz (1976) reported that the diagnostic activities of clinical psychologists had "diminished in relative importance . . . continuing a trend noted in the late 1950s" (p. 3). It seems, however, that the "decline" in assessment reflects only a narrow, traditional approach, as suggested by both the critical literature and the emergence of newer approaches to assessment. McReynolds (1977) stresses that "the overall role of assessment in applied psychology has been increasing in recent years" (p. 3). He notes, further, that both humanists and behaviorists have developed approaches consistent with their theoretical positions, and that "rapprochement" has subsequently enriched the whole field of assessment (p. 2).

What are practicing psychologists actually doing in their approaches to personality assessment? This seemingly straightforward question is difficult to answer. Surveys of psychologists are often used, but they are inconclusive and are, in themselves, objects of criticism and controversy because of methodological problems. Bias introduced by sampling, return rate, question format, etc., make clear interpretations difficult. The following study provides one estimate of current usage.

Wade and Baker (1977), in a survey of clinical psychologists, provide some rather surprising findings following earlier reviews predicting the declining importance of testing. The major findings *do not* replicate earlier surveys or confirm predictions concerning the demise of testing. Many types of tests (e.g., projective and objective) are used by psychologists, even those with sharply varying therapeutic orientations: "Clinicians have definitely not abandoned testing" (p. 879). For example, Swan and MacDonald (1978) found, in a survey of members of the Association for the Advancement of Behavior Therapy, that 20% used personality inventories and 10% used projective tests. The interview with the client was the most commonly used technique (89%).

One of the most interesting commentaries relates to the evident differences in opinions between clinicians (practicing psychologists) and researchers. Researchers have been generally interested in the accuracy of tests or test batteries (combinations of tests) in diagnosing specific problems or conditions and in predicting specific behaviors. As suggested previously, the results have often been less than encouraging. Somewhat surprisingly, clinicians appear to be indifferent to the low reliability and validity of the tests and feel that the "negative research findings lack credibility" (Wade and Baker, 1977, p. 879). As evident in this one survey, clinicians apparently do not use tests consistent with the goals of researchers. They are less interested in using tests for diagnosis or prediction. Clinicians appear to view testing as an "insightful" process rather than an objective skill. Many clinicians apparently use tests in order to better understand the "personality structure" of the individual. Many clinicians would not automatically accept test results that differed from their own hypotheses. In summary, clinicians seem to doubt negative research; personality dynamics may be too subtle for experimental study. When confronted with an experimental literature critical of testing, it seems as if many clinicians have embraced their tests and spurned the literature. Personal experience with the tests were viewed as more significant than negative research findings.

Intuitive approaches are not without criticism (see Chapman and Chapman, 1969; Garfield, 1978; Meehl, 1954; and Wiggins, 1973, for distinct views on various facets of the problem). The study by Wade and Baker (1977), however, serves well to highlight the many problems associated with personality assessment. It is, in actuality, a very idiosyncratic process, hard to define or research. In a rejoinder to a criticism of the survey, the authors reply that "clinicians of today may be like 18th century physicians—looking for effective, successful assessment techniques where few currently exist" (Wade and Baker, 1978, p. 850).

Recent Trends in Personality Assessment

Personality assessment has been influenced by advances in humanistic, behavioral, and cognitive-learning areas. Recent trends in assessment include (a) the extension of assessment into significant social groups of the individual, (b) a reconsideration of the importance of naturalistic observations, (c) a formalization of problem-solving approaches to assessment, (d) an emphasis on the client's direct role in assessment, and (e) stress on the utility of assessment for treatment purposes.

The recent trends and influences reflect awareness of the complexity of behavior and the corresponding need for "multiple goals for measurement" (Mischel, 1977). Mischel summarizes this point: "If...behavior is determined by many interacting [personal and environmental] variables...then a focus on any one of them is likely to lead to limited predictions and generalizations" (p. 246). The multiple goals include the relevant characteristics of people as well as situations or environments. Following an overview of major trends, three perspectives of assessment will be explored: environmental and ecological; psychosocial and psychosituational; and cognitive-behavioral.

An Overview of Recent Trends

The *humanistic* perspective, especially in regard to the handicapped, re-emphasizes the value of all people, the potential for personal growth, and attention to improving the quality of life for individuals. Humanistic values have had a pervasive influence on recent legislation and assessment practices, as will be noted in Chapter Four. In the area of personality assessment and intervention, several principles bear mention at this point. Ellett and Bersoff (1976) stress that techniques should generate "information directly related to the problem and questions posed by the referral agent and the client" (p. 486). Further, they emphasize that any information should be considered in light of its usefulness to the individual desiring assistance: "A concerted effort is made throughout the assessment to avoid seeking and interpreting information not related to assessment questions and expressed goals" (p. 486). Obviously, exploitation and deception are to be avoided; explanations should be clear and appropriate for the client's level of understanding. A related principle is that of "least intervention," whereby one intervenes "in the client's everyday life only to the extent that the client desires a change" (Kanfer and Goldstein, 1975, p. 12). A goal should be to "establish mutually agreed upon behavior change" (Ellett and Bersoff, 1976, p. 485).

The *behavioristic* position stresses the importance of the environment in understanding a person's adjustment. Direct observation, the application of learning principles, and empirical demonstration of the effect of the intervention are all characteristics of this approach. Numerous successful cases have been reported in the literature involving a wide variety of problems (e.g., O'Leary and O'Leary, 1977). The behavioral approach can be considered as an experiment with one subject and is highly appropriate for school or other applied settings (Kratochwill, 1977). Assessment procedures are evaluated by their usefulness in designing and implementing intervention techniques.

Another significant influence on assessment has been a renewed interest in the *cognitive* activities that mediate behavior. The importance of cognitive mechanisms are stressed by social learning theorists: The emphasis is on "the prominent role played by vicarious, symbolic, and self-regulatory processes in psychological functioning" (Bandura, 1977, p. vii).

> Social learning theory approaches the explanation of human behavior in terms of a continuous reciprocal interaction between cognitive, behavioral, and environmental determinants.

There has been a burgeoning of research and application relating cognitive processes to the adjustment problems of children (e.g., Meichenbaum, 1979).

Maloney and Ward (1976) raise the question "How can the process of assessment be valid when there are so many problems with the tools of that process?" (p. 73). This problem is at the crux of the need to consider psychological assessment from a *problem-solving* perspective. They propose the process of arriving at "conceptual validity" as a solution to pervasive measurement problems. Conceptual validity stresses the uniqueness of the individual and reduces the possible influence of preconceptions that psychologists may have regarding the significant traits or attributes in question. Conceptual validity refers to the process of accurate description of a person through personality assessment techniques. "To the extent that hypotheses are confirmed and consistent observations follow from the constructed model, the process is validated" (Maloney and Ward, 1976, p. 74). They suggest that the "validity of the model" is established by noting its "logicalness and internal consistency."

Sloves, Docherty, and Schneider (1979) characterize the complexity of the assessment process from a problem-solving perspective. The person conducting the assessment must consider:

> (a) the object of the referral, (b) the referral process within the social system, (c) the referral agent, (d) the precipitating factors that led to the referral, (e) possible sources and causes of the problem(s), (f) constraints operating against problem definition and resolution, (g) availability of resources to conduct an assessment and plan an intervention strategy, and (h) the social, political, organizational, and the structural context in which the problem is embedded. (p. 30)

The issues dealt with go beyond individual personality assessment and necessarily address the relationship between assessment and intervention.

What about the *client's role* in assessment? With adults, and perhaps adolescents and some children, direct participation of the person referred is becoming more commonly accepted. The client is requested to actively participate "in a self-corrective enterprise" (Mahoney, 1974, p. 275). Peterson (1968) and Mischel (1977) have similarly described the importance of "the subject as expert and colleague." Mischel (1977) states:

> The moral, for me, is that it would be wise to allow our 'subjects' to slip out of their [passive] roles...and to enroll them, at least

sometimes, as active colleagues who are the best experts on themselves and are eminently qualified to participate in the development of descriptions and predictions—not to mention decisions—about themselves. (p. 249)

The utility of having young children reflect upon their own behaviors is more variable, but valuable insights may be gained. For example, Murdock (1979) found, consistent with earlier research, that the children's perception of family environments were significantly related to classroom adjustment, while the parents' perceptions were not. Nelson and Evans (1977) discuss the major aspects of assessing children's behavior. With regard to interviewing children, two types of information may be gained. The first involves children's perceptions of their relationship to the problem and includes levels of self-understanding and analyses of the problem. This information may be unique and unobtainable through other sources. The second kind of information is indicative of "how well the child can handle himself. . . in a social situation with an adult" (Nelson and Evans, 1977, p. 616). Yarrow (1960) provides worthwhile parameters for interviewing children. Interviewing, role-playing, and traditional, as well as the experimental, use of tests (e.g., Ellett and Bersoff, 1976; Meichenbaum, 1977), may provide an understanding of the potential for the child's role in assessment and intervention.

Environmental and Ecological Approaches to Assessment

Stokols (1977a) comments that "during the late 1960's and early 1970's, the study of human behavior in relationship to the physical-social environment emerged as one of the fastest growing areas of psychological research" (p. 1). Although the terms are often used interchangeably, the origins of ecological and environmental approaches are different. *Ecological psychology* may be defined as the study of the relationships between organisms and environment with an emphasis on "collective processes" of groups of persons and their "adaptation" to the environment (Stokols, 1977a, p. 7). *Environmental psychology* has taken a different focus by including the study of individual psychological processes such as perception, cognition, and learning (Stokols, 1977b, p. 6). Stokols (1977b) characterizes research in environmental psychology: "Direct emphasis has been placed on the manner in which psychological and social processes interact with features of the physical environment to yield varying patterns of behavior" (p. 12).

The influences of environmental psychology are very broad, and recent comprehensive reviews are available (see Altman, 1978; Stokols, 1977a, 1978). From the viewpoint of multifactored assessment, several areas of significance can be identified.

The first is the necessity of studying personality as an *interaction* between the person and environment. The interactionist position has had a long history, but, at times, the practical influence has been marginal, especially in the schools. Very early, Murray (1938) stressed the importance (and difficulty) of identifying or characterizing the environment or situation before predictions about actual behavior could be made. Mischel (1968, 1973, 1977) has also been influential in stressing the interactionist position. Even though attention to person/situation interactions in personality assessment cannot be considered a recent idea, further development is required before practical approaches will be widely accepted (Magnussen and Endler, 1977).

The assessment of environments is of equal interest. Insel and Moos (1974) state: "Like people, environments have unique personalities" (p. 179). They point out that, in actuality, the assessment of environments is not usually carried out in a very practical manner. Few techniques exist that can be used across the wide range of problems associated with children, schools, and families. It may be unlikely that environmental assessment will ever develop as a "test-oriented" science. The quality, complexity, and idiosyncratic nature of person-situation interactions will probably prevent the development of many test-like assessment techniques for environments. Interviews and direct observation may remain the standard techniques, especially when the objectives of assessment change for each person-environment situation.

Despite serious difficulties related to the complexity of characterizing environments, Moos and his co-workers have found three broad dimensions that seem to be relevant for many environments. The first is a *relationship dimension,* assessing "the nature and intensity of personal relationships within the environment"; the second is a *personal development dimension,* estimating "the potential or opportunity in the environment for personal growth and the development of self-esteem"; the third is a *system maintenance and system change dimension,* assessing "the extent to which the environment is orderly and clear in its expectations" (Insel and Moos, 1974, p. 181). Several experimental assessment techniques have resulted from the research of Moos and his colleagues (e.g., The Family Environment Scale discussed in Chapter Four, and The Classroom Environmental Scale).

Parke (1978) reviews the effects of the child's home environment on social and cognitive functioning. Many powerful influences, particularly in the early developmental years, can be identified. For example, language stimulation, parental styles of discipline and punishment, provision of play materials, maternal warmth and quality of interaction, are among the significant variables. The caregiver's role in *mediating* (interpreting, explaining, guiding) the environment plays an important role in cognitive development. Heber's (1972, 1978) longitudinal study with high risk children (discussed in the second chapter) is a good demonstration of the influential possibilities of the home environment for cognitive development. Parke (1978) has also analyzed aspects of the physical environment (e.g., the effects of television or noise) and the impact of the social organization of the home (e.g., privacy and crowding).

Gump (1978) provides a recent review of school environments. Consideration of both the "objective" and "subjective" environments is necessary. School environments may be organized in a global way around values characterized as "traditional," "progressive," or "laissez-faire." Classroom environments vary in physical as well as in subjective ways, and the same environment may have unique effects on individual children because of the way the environment is perceived. Gump recommends research into the objective settings of schools as they relate to effects on the subjective environments. School environments are especially important in the development of alternative educational programs necessary for meeting individual educational needs of exceptional children as mandated by law. The legal requirements, referring to "an appropriate educational program" for each handicapped child, are discussed in Chapter Four.

A third important contribution of the environmental and ecological perspective has been the influence of a *systems* approach. Hobbs (1966, 1979) applied a systems approach in working with emotionally disturbed children. In doing so, one major assumption was "that the child is an inseparable part of a small system of an ecological unit made up of the child, his family, his school, his neighborhood and community" (1966, p. 1108). Project Re-Ed (re-education of emotionally disturbed children) was established as a reaction against psychiatric hospitalization based entirely on traditional psychotherapy. Hobbs (1966) noted that hospitals may "make children sick"; the "expectancy of illness may confirm a child's worst fears about himself" (p. 1105). "Cure" is abandoned as a goal in treatment; the problem from a systems perspective is defined as "doing what we can to make a small social system work in a reasonably satisfactory manner" (p. 1108). Hobbs (1966) recognizes that children "have learned to perceive themselves in limiting or destructive" ways and may perceive the world as "an uncertain, rejecting, and hurtful place" (p. 1108). Also, one must recognize that for some children, sources of "affection" and "support" are not always available. In developing concepts for the process of re-education with emotionally disturbed children, Hobbs (1966, 1979) proposed twelve considerations (although going beyond a systems approach) consistent with contemporary thought. Some are applicable for children with a wide variety of handicapping conditions. From the perspective of personality assessment, the twelve points serve as significant dimensions for assessment.

1. *Life is to be lived now.* No one waits for a special hour [for treatment].... [The] task is to contrive each day so that the probability of success...outweighs the probability of failure.
2. *Time is an ally.* Children are kept too long in most traditional treatment programs.... [The] expectation of a prolonged stay in a treatment center becomes a self-validating hypothesis.
3. *Trust is essential.* The disturbed child is conspicuously impaired in his ability to learn from adults.... He faces each adult with a predominant anticipation of punishment, rejection, derision, or withdrawal of love.

4. *Competence makes a difference.* The ability to do something well gives a child confidence and self-respect and gains for him acceptance by other children, by teachers, and, unnecessary as it might seem, even by his parents.

5. *Self-control can be taught.* Children and adolescents [can be] helped to manage their own behavior without the development of psychodynamic insight; and...symptoms can and should be controlled by direct address ...not by an uncovering therapy (from Hobbs, 1979).

6. *Cognitive competence of children and adolescents can be considerably enhanced...* They can be taught generic skills in the management of their lives as well as strategies for coping with the complex array of demands placed upon them by family, school, community, or job (From Hobbs, 1979).

7. *Feelings should be nurtured.* We are very interested in the nurturance and expression of feeling, to help a child own all of himself without guilt.... Anger, resentment, hostility are commonplace...and their expression is used in various ways.

8. *The group is important to the child.* When a group is functioning well, it is extremely difficult for an individual child to behave in a disturbed way.

9. *Ceremony and ritual give order, stability and confidence.* [Many disturbed children live chaotic lives, a predictable environment may be helpful.]

10. *The body is the armature of the self.* Clearer experiencing of the potential and boundaries of the body should lead to a clearer definition of the self, and thus to greater psychological fitness and more effective functioning.

11. *Communities are important.* Many children...come from families that are alienated or detached from community life or that are not sufficiently well organized or purposeful to help the child develop a sense of identity with his neighborhood, his town or city.

12. *A child should know joy.* There is an extensive literature on anxiety, guilt and dread, but little that is well developed on joy. (1966, pp. 1109-1113)

Newbrough, Walker, and Abril (1978) outline the steps of an ecological approach in the following way. (a) A "broad perspective" of the situation is needed. (b) The professional tries to understand the "network" of relationships between all of the significant individuals and the environment. (c) All persons involved should realize that the "problems belong to a system," not only the individual being referred. (d) The professional involved with the intervention should evaluate the normative behavior in the systems and the "expectancies" for normal behavior of the significant persons in the settings. (e) The identification of the strengths of the system representing resources for problem solving and for carrying out varying aspects of the intervention should be stressed. (f) One should evaluate the possibility of indirect or unintended effects. The last point bears elaboration. The necessity of evaluating the possibility of unintended, undesirable side effects that may result from the intervention is a very important consideration of the ecological approach. Willems (1977) provides warnings to this effect in the context of behavioral treatments: "Behavior-environment systems have important properties that change, unfold, and become clear only after long periods of time" (p. 42). An ecological approach includes the careful consideration of ways in which "simple intrusions can produce unintended effects," "indirect harm may follow from narrowly defined good," and "long-term harm may follow from short-term good" (p. 42).

Another ecological perspective is that there is often "no best solution." Problems can be usually resolved in a variety of ways through any combination of modifying the problem behavior, changing the expectations of persons encountering the problem behavior, and altering the situation. The identification of the strength of the system is important because, as Newbrough et al. (1978) point out, the intervention itself is a temporary "artificial" situation, and a final goal is that the system will rely on its own resources for solving problems. Several techniques will be described in Chapter Five that provide an environmental or ecological perspective. Ecological and systems approaches are gaining increasing recognition with respect to the development of comprehensive treatment programs for significant child syndromes such as hyperactivity (e.g., Whalen and Henker, 1980), and for psychotic behavior and neurological impairments (e.g., Brubakken, Derouin and Morrison, 1980).

Psychosocial and Psychosituational Approaches

The emerging trends in personality assessment differ mostly with respect to varying points of emphases. A high degree of overlap and continuity are characteristic of newer assessment approaches. In many respects, psychosocial and psychosituational assessments are continuous with the ecological and environmental approaches. However, both psychosocial and psychosituational assessment stress more specific units of analysis, rather than the broad networks described in the previous section, and also emphasize the detailed specification of intervention strategies. A framework involving psychosocial assessment has been suggested for classifying emotionally disturbed children (Prugh, Engel, and Morse, 1975), but the actual procedures may have relevance for a broad range of handicapping conditions.

The origins of the psychosocial and psychosituational models relate to a high degree to earlier writing in clinical assessment by Peterson (1968) and Mischel (1968). In an attempt to provide a translation from clinical applications to more useful assessment strategies within the schools, Bersoff (1971, 1973a) has stressed the principle that the traditional assessment environment, whereby the child is removed from the classroom and tested under optimal circumstances, may not be comparable to the child's functioning in the actual school situation. Assessment of "optimal functioning" may be important, but it is unlikely to have as much direct relevance for developing intervention techniques as assessment that is carried out in a manner consistent with the circumstances of the child's actual behavior.

Greiger and Abidin (1972) describe psychosocial assessment as appropriate for the "School Community Psychologist." The principal techniques are interviewing and observation, thus enabling the study of an individual's behavior and situation. The interview stresses (a) the definition of target behavior, (b) the identification of contingencies that maintain the behavior, and (c) "the detection of irrational ideas" that persons may have about the child's behavior (pp. 113-114). The last point refers to unreasonable, negative, illogical, and self-defeating thoughts a person might bring into a situation, preventing more objective communication (Ellis, 1970). Observations focus on "the social behaviors displayed by all members of the situation," the "attitudes and affective states of those individuals who constitute the system" and the "physical situation" (Greiger and Abidin, 1972, p. 116).

Psychosituational assessment has been similarly described (Bersoff, 1971; Bersoff and Greiger, 1971; Ellett and Bersoff, 1976). Bersoff and Greiger (1971) suggest that the analysis of the problem within a behavioral framework is important for developing plans for remediation. It also reduces the tendency to blame "someone" for the child's problem behavior. Responsibility is shared. Along with the identification of maladaptive or target behaviors is a parallel need to be able to describe "expected behaviors." Being aware of expected behaviors enables a check on the "appropriateness" of the intervention and helps establish objectives. Ellett and Bersoff (1976) state: "Any data, whether obtained through systematic observation, interviewing, or the more traditionally administered psychometric and projective instruments can be used within the psychosituational assessment framework" (p. 486). The use of tests is advocated only when they "can facilitate a more complete understanding of the client's behavior, provide information not forthcoming from other assessment procedures, and further delineate strategies for attaining referral goals" (p. 490). The use of nonstandard techniques and the modification of existing tests may also be used.

Cognitive-Behavior Approaches

There has been a very definite resurgence of interest in the cognitive aspects of the study of behavior as they relate to both assessment and intervention techniques. Mahoney (1977) describes the cognitive-learning approach as "diversified," appearing to avoid "formalization," but also as one of the clearest trends in psychology. The cognitive approach, consistent with a social learning viewpoint, has had a pervasive effect in three areas of potential importance to exceptional children: Cognition and language (e.g., Rosenthal and Zimmerman, 1978), personality assessment (e.g., Mischel, 1968, 1973, 1977) and behavior modification (e.g., Bandura, 1969; Mahoney, 1974; and Meichenbaum; 1977). Perhaps even more important are the interrelationships of the three areas and their overall significance to the multifactored assessment of exceptional children. As Nelson and Evans (1977) point out with respect to the behavior problems of children, behavior assessment should be "linked" to cognitive as well as other aspects of a child's development. Similar to previously described approaches, another salient characteristic of cognitive-behavioral methods is the direct correspondence between assessment and intervention. The assessment techniques lead directly to the specification of interventions. Assessment is seen as a continuous process and intervention is viewed as an experimental method, revised on the basis of behavioral data.

Mischel (1973) outlines "person variables" consistent with the interactionist position of social learning theory that might serve as possible targets for assessment in personality measurement. Rather than "broad dimensions," "basic factors," "pervasive motives," or "characteristic life-styles," the stress should be on variables that allow the study of the unique organization of behavior within the individual (p. 253). Mischel (1973) suggests five "person" variables, allowing the study of interactions between specific situations, thought or cognition, and actual behavior, as follows:

1. The individual's *competencies* to construct (generate) diverse behaviors under appropriate conditions
2. The individual's *encoding* and *categorization* of events
3. The subject's *expectancies* about outcomes
4. The *subjective values* of such outcomes
5. [And the individual's] *self-regulatory systems and plans.* (p.265)

Mischel (1973) summarizes the social learning approach to personality by emphasizing the following:

> The interdependence of behavior and conditions, mediated by the constructions and cognitive activities of the person who generates them, and . . . the human tendency to invent constructs and to adhere to them as well as to generate subtly discriminative behaviors across settings and time. (p. 279)

Bandura (1969, 1977a) has been a central figure in describing and developing the social learning point of view. The theoretical perspectives and applications of social learning are diverse. In personality assessment, two areas are of critical importance. The first is the central role of cognitive processes in learning and in mediating the environment as previously mentioned. The second is the concept of social learning as a "reciprocal-influence process" and "reciprocal-determinism" as a basic principle for the study of behavior. Reciprocal determinism is an important reconceptualization of the interactionist position and addresses the long standing debate whether person variables or situation variables exert greater influence on behavior. Bandura (1978) stresses that "behavior, internal personal factors, and environmental influences all operate as interlocking determinants of each other" (p. 346). For example, an angry child (an internal personal factor) may behave in an angry way (hit or yell), thus evoking angry reactions from friends (social environment). The angry reactions of people in the environment may reinforce the angry child's internal hypotheses about people and events. Behavior may affect the environment, environment may affect behavior, and both may affect internal or personal predispositions. Bandura further points out: "The relative influence exerted by these three sets of interlocking factors will vary in different individuals and under different circumstances" (p. 346).

Patterson's work with the socially aggressive behaviors of children helps to illustrate the reciprocal influence process. Patterson, Reid, Jones, and Conger (1975) found that children referred for the treatment of socially aggressive behaviors exhibited high rates of disapproval, negativism, noncompliance, teasing, yelling, whining, destructiveness, and crying, among other behaviors. Also, they found that aggressive boys were likely to come from families "in which all members demonstrate high rates of aggressive behaviors" (p. 4). Patterson and his co-workers hypothesized that the children studied might lack the social skills necessary for normal socialization and are subsequently rejected by families and peers. They found that "such children tend to receive three times as much punishment from their social environment as do non-problem children" (p. 4). Another related finding was that aggressive children are punished more often than children without problems, even when their behavior is acceptable, "Thus an aggressive child teaches his siblings and his parents to accelerate their rates of coercive behaviors" (p. 6). Aggressive children can have an extremely negative view of themselves that results in unacceptable behavior and in the maintenance of negative reactions from the environment. The treatment Patterson and his associates designed consisted basically of stopping the cycle of coercive behaviors. The parents, peers, and teachers were trained to use "non-violent" consequences for the child's aggressive and deviant behaviors. The social learning point of view stresses not only the characteristics of the person, behavior, and environment, but, more importantly, the reciprocal relationship between all significant variables.

Mahoney (1974) comments, in describing the rationale for a cognitive-behavioral approach, that "only a small percentage of a person's behaviors are publicly observable.... Our lives are predominantly composed of private responses to private environments" (p. 1). Mahoney reviews a wide range of theoretical and practical problems in providing a foundation for a cognitive approach to behavior modification. His analysis, from a cognitive learning perspective, of possible factors relating to maladaptive behavior is helpful for assessing children. Problems in attention, relational processes, "response repertoire features," and "experiential feedback" all may contribute to "performance variance" (p. 167).

Attentional problems can be related to diverse processes. For example, *selective inattention* involves "ignoring" relevant or important stimuli; *misperception* stems from the "inaccurate labeling" of events; *maladaptive focusing* results from attending to stimuli which have a negative effect on performance; and, *maladaptive self-arousal* occurs when the person creates "private," but "irrelevant," stimuli that may have a negative effect on performance (pp. 151-153).

Mahoney (1974) describes relational processes in terms of four possible problems in mediating events that may prevent adaptive behavior. The first involves *classification error,* whereby events can be simply misinterpreted. The second is referred to as a *comparator process,* involving standard setting and evaluation: "Private evaluations are made relative to past, vicarious, and ideal standards" (p. 155). The third area implicates *retentional deficiencies:* "If prior mistakes and intervening successes [can be recalled]. . .chances of adaptation are enhanced" (p. 156). The last type of "mediational dysfunction" includes the possibility of *inferential errors,* as when "we. . .infer conclusions poorly supported by our personal data" (p. 157).

Response repertoire features refer to whether or not an individual is capable of making an appropriate response in a particular situation. Mahoney lists the areas that may limit a person's response potential: "physiological limitations, insufficient learning, poor retention, or inappropriate response utilization" (p. 165). Experiential feedback relates to motivational factors, including environmental contingencies or "consequences" of behavior, and "self-generated" rewards (p. 166).

Mahoney sees a trend toward emphasizing "general strategies of adjustment" requiring "broad and effective coping skills" (pp. 272-273). Coping skills training, self-instructional training, and problem solving are all possible approaches for working with exceptional children.

Meichenbaum (1977) describes a "cognitive-behavioral" approach to assessment, arising from a "need to develop more explicit ways of assessing our client's affects, cognitions, and volitions" (p. 229). The approach attempts to analyze "sequential psychological processes" necessary for a specific task in order to determine "what can affect a change from incompetence to competence" (p. 232). The client's "thinking processes" are analyzed, and an "inventory" of "cognitive strategies" is noted, both in terms of their correspondence to adequate performance (p. 236). In order to gain insight into the psychological processes required in a task, one may modify the requirements of the task (as with speed, with modality, or by noting attempts at training subsets of skills). The environmental variables surrounding the task may be explored, and "supports" may also be contributed, such as "direct task aids" (e.g., memory prompts), or other instructional aids (e.g., helping the client to analyze the task, or to pay attention) (pp. 241-242). Specific techniques may include interviews, behavioral assessment, videotapes, and the modified use of projective tests (e.g., the employment of TAT-like pictures related to the target behavior). Meichenbaum's work with hyperactive-nonreflective children illustrates the use of self-instructional training.

The research and practical applications consistent with the cognitive-behavior approach are becoming exceedingly diverse. Two areas will be briefly presented as possible targets for assessment and intervention. The first is self-control. As Kazdin (1975) points out, self-control procedures are important because: (1) much behavior of practical significance would be "missed" by the direct observation procedures of behavioral assessment; (2) problems associated with maintaining desirable behaviors and transferring the behaviors to new situations have presented difficulties for traditional behavioral techniques; and (3) performance may be enhanced by having the person contribute to the intervention technique. Workman and Hector (1978) review the literature relating to self-control in classroom settings and note, despite a lack of follow-up studies for most research reported, that self-control procedures may be promising in such areas as increasing on-task behavior and improving academic behavior. Fagan, Long, and Stevens (1975) describe curricular intervention in the area of self-control. Karoly (1977) and Meichenbaum (1979) also provide important reviews of the literature involving self-control in children.

Another topic of broad significance for multifactored assessment is individual problem solving skills. D'Zurilla and Goldfried (1971) define problem solving as:

> a behavioral process, whether overt or cognitive in nature, which (a) makes available a variety of potentially effective response alternatives for dealing with a problematic situation and (b) increases the probability of selecting the most effective response from among these various alternatives. (p. 108)

They point out that "general effectiveness" may be facilitated by training in independent coping skills with critical, everyday problems (p. 109). The stages are generally as follows: (a) identification of the problem; (b) problem definition; (c) generation of alternative solutions to the problem; (d) evaluation of the possible consequences of the alternatives; and (e) verification (pp. 111-119). D'Zurilla and Goldfried (1971) suggest that problem solving approaches may be appropriate "whenever it appears that the client's difficulties are resulting from the ineffectiveness with which he handles a broad range of problematic situations" (p. 120).

Spivack and Shure (1974) and Spivack, Platt, and Shure (1976) have distinguished between "impersonal" problem solving skills (as with intelligence tests) and "interpersonal" cognitive problem solving skills. They have introduced assessment procedures and curricular strategies in the area of interpersonal problem solving for children. Although the significant factors may vary with the age of the child, they have stressed the study of the following skills and processes in their research: (a) a sensitivity to human problems; (b) the skills needed to "generate alternative solutions to problems"; (c) the ability to generate the steps necessary to carry out potential solutions; (d) the understanding of the "social consequences" of one's acts; and (e) "an awareness of social and personal motivation in oneself and others and awareness that current interpersonal events have a continuity with past events" (1976, pp. 5-7). In early childhood, the most significant skill related to behavioral adjustment is the ability to "conceptualize alternative solutions to interpersonal problems" (1976, p. 50). With children between the ages of nine and twelve, "alternative problem solution" and "means-end thinking" both seem to be related to good adjustment.

Summary

Personality assessment provides a major context for multifactored assessment for both negative and positive reasons. On the negative side, the concerns parallel those of intelligence testing. Issues relate to measurement problems, as well as personal, social, legal, and ethical concerns. All point to the most serious consideration of possible abuses with regard to test usage. However, despite the serious concerns, the field of personality assessment can be thought of as expanding. Conceptual advances, consistent with a social learning point of view, include: (a) a reconsideration of the role of the client; (b) an emphasis on assessing the social systems of the client; (c) a formalization of problem solving approaches to assessment and intervention; and (d) an imaginative search for psychological constructs and assessment techniques that will directly help people rather than refine classification schemes. The point was also made that specific areas of personality assessment may have relevance for a wide range of adjustment problems of exceptional children, not only those thought of as emotionally disturbed.

Chapter 4

THE LEGAL, ETHICAL, AND
PROFESSIONAL CONTEXT

The third major context for multifactored assessment has resulted from the passage of Public Law 94-142, The Education for All Handicapped Children Act of 1975. Federal law requires that all children, regardless of the handicapping condition, receive a "free and appropriate" public education. Also, safeguards arising out of concerns about parents' and children's rights are addressed. The law is complex and based upon many years of development, marked by numerous significant court cases and prior legislation. Only the most basic concepts relating to multifactored assessment will be discussed and references that include earlier milestones will be noted. Procedures and professional and ethical guidelines for nondiscriminatory multifactored assessment will be suggested.

The Education for All Handicapped Children Act of 1975 (P.L. 94-142)

There are four major purposes of P.L. 94-142. The first is to guarantee that special education will be available to all children from ages 3 to 21. Exclusion from school or postponement of educational opportunities are no longer valid options or excuses for not providing services to handicapped children. Services need not be made available to children in the 3 to 5 or the 18 to 21 age ranges when such provisions are "inconsistent with state law or practice or any court decree" (Abeson and Zettel, 1977, p. 122).

The second major purpose of P.L. 94-142 is to ensure "fairness and appropriateness in decision making with regard to providing special education to handicapped children and youth" (Ballard and Zettel, 1977, p. 177). This area clearly has had the greatest impact on assessment practices in education and will be elaborated upon in this chapter. Problems associated with decision making for handicapped children are extremely complex and relate to a wide variety of factors associated with

69

multifactored assessment. Historical concerns with test usage and labeling were noted in previous chapters. In this chapter, the focus is on legal safeguards, individual rights, and professional practices. Legal and ethical concepts take on added importance because many questions about assessment practices and educational decision making are simply unanswerable from a scientific standpoint. Everyone involved should agree, if possible, that an educational decision is best for a particular child. Parents' and children's rights to involvement in the decision-making process, the concept of least restrictive alternative (and related concepts of normalization and mainstreaming), and the concept of an Individual Educational Plan (IEP) are all aspects of the law directly relevant to problems and procedures in multifactored assessment.

The third and fourth purposes of P.L. 94-142 are mentioned for reference purposes and will not be discussed further in this chapter. P.L. 94-142 addresses "management and auditing requirements and procedures regarding special education at all levels of government" and establishes procedures and mechanisms to "financially assist the efforts of state and local government through the use of federal funds" (Ballard and Zettel, 1977, p. 178).

Background References

Many excellent references exist for the reader desiring more information about various topics relating to P.L. 94-142. Abeson, Burgdorf, Casey, Kunz, and McNeil (1975) provide a background discussion of the problems and potential solutions associated with providing services to special children, especially the early conceptual development of the Individual Educational Plan (IEP). The major innovation stemming from past legislation is the use of a contractual system (the IEP) to reach agreement between parents, children and school officials concerning educational services.

Theimer and Rupiper (1975) review thirty-two lawsuits filed on behalf of handicapped children. The major areas relate to children's rights to appropriate education, problems with test bias, and tracking systems. Abeson and Zettel (1977) provide an excellent review of the history of the passage of P.L. 94-142. Ballard and Zettel (1977), in a question-and-answer format, cover the major points of the law. Kabler (1977) and Prasse (1978) review the implications of P.L. 94-142 from the viewpoint of school psychologists. Lambert and Cole (1977) also discuss equal protection and due process and stress areas that may cause legal problems for psychologists. Martin (1979) provides a complete discussion of the legal requirements in public education regarding handicapped children. A special issue of the *Journal of Education*, (*161*, 3, 1979) analyzes the initial impact of P.L. 94-142 following its implementation.

Problems with Implementation

As one might expect, the implementation of such a complex law has resulted in some major problems for professional groups despite an "impressive" national commitment (*Progress toward a Free Appropriate Public*

Education, 1979). Many school districts are now struggling with the practical aspects of P.L. 94-142, such as due process, nondiscriminatory testing, and the development of a continuum of special services. Many psychologists are concerned that the "intent" of P.L. 94-142 may not be followed (e.g., *The School Psychologist, 33*(5), 1979). For example, Hoff, Fenton, Yoshida and Kaufman (1978) found that parents had considerable difficulty understanding placement team decisions. Their findings cast "serious doubt on the degree to which it can be said that parents were actively involved in decision making" (p. 270). Four problem areas were identified: (a) informing the parents of the placement team decisions, (b) providing adequate notice to "encourage parental participation," (c) "informing parents of relevant due process safeguards," and (d) "documenting crucial communications in writing" (p. 271). Although the study was small, involving only four elementary schools, the results could probably be replicated in other schools as well. Similarly, Goldstein, Strickland, Turnbull, and Curry (1980) observed conferences related to the development of Individual Educational Programs (IEPs) and found critical problems with full representation and participation of professional team members and parents. They found a need for systematic training for parents and professionals in implementing IEP conferences. There is also the potential for major problems in coordinating services, even with good intentions (e.g., times and locations for conferences, communications between parents, teachers, other school personnel, and professionals representing agencies outside the school).

Another serious problem with the implementation of P.L. 94-142 relates to the persistence of either negative attitudes or low expectancies from both lay and professional people. Voeltz (1980) and Horne (1979) provide important discussion of attitudes and expectancies, as they relate to mainstreaming. Professional, parental, sibling, and peer attitudes all provide an extremely important context for intervention strategies. Negative attitudes and lower expectancies may affect "social, psychological, and emotional growth" of "special needs students" (Horne, 1979, p. 64).

A third problem area relates to the expansion of services. Cohen, Semmes, and Guralnick (1979) discuss the implications of the public laws with a special emphasis on developing programs for preschoolers. Other problem areas remain with older teenagers and young adults, and handicapped children in the regular classrooms. The problems and potential solutions for expanded services will be discussed further under the topic of "least restrictive alternative" in this chapter. Martin (1979) reviews the legal mandates involving educational alternatives and handicapped children. He warns that "schools must clearly move away from the old habit of placing a child in whatever services are already available; they must create the full range of services needed" (p. 91).

In the first semiannual update on the implementation of P.L. 94-142, it was apparent that much had been accomplished. Still, problems were evident in many areas, some already cited. Other difficult areas included:

1. Problems, especially in rural areas, with implementing the least restrictive environment philosophy and the concomitant continuum of

services. Relatedly, deaf, blind, and orthopedically handicapped children may, more frequently, have limited contact with non-handicapped children;

2. The number of evaluations needed;
3. Confusion between agencies requiring interagency agreements;
4. In-service training to meet the needs of teachers working with handicapped children, particularly with low incidence conditions;
5. Problems with Individual Educational Plans (e.g., services listed based on services *available*; participation of parents and teachers);
6. Problems with communications with non-English speaking families;
7. Procedural and paper "overkill."

P.L. 94-142 and Assessment Issues

The remainder of this section will discuss parents' and children's rights, the concept of least restrictive alternative, the requirement of an Individual Educational Program, and procedures in nondiscriminatory multifactored assessment.

Parents' and Children's Rights and Due Process

The "right to due process of law" is the mandated "solution" to problems that exist in the assessment and placement of handicapped children (Abeson and Zettel, 1977, p. 125). Abeson & Zettel (1977) describe the purpose of due process as follows: "The presence of due process is designed to allow for equal consideration of the interests of all who are involved in the education of a handicapped child—the child, the family, the schools" (p. 125). Due process involves five major areas: notice, access rights, consent, hearing rights, and appeal rights.

Notice involves several different, but related, aspects. The local school system must notify the parent, and consent must be received "prior to an evaluation for a child who is hypothesized to be handicapped and in need of some sort of special education or related services" (Pryzwansky and Bersoff, 1978, p. 176). Due process procedures exist for both school representatives and the parents. If the parents refuse consent, the school administration may decide, in the best interest of the child, to proceed with the evaluation. Legal recourse is available for school officials as well as parents in case of disagreement (see Turnbull, Turnbull and Strickland, 1979). The local educational agency also must notify the parents about the information that will be needed, the sources of the information and the manner in which the information will be used. For example, the schools cannot disseminate the obtained information to other "interested parties" outside of the schools without written parental permission.

The psychologist must not only list the psychological tests that will be given, but must also describe, in a comprehensible way, the evaluation techniques. Thus, the parents give *informed consent* to the evaluation.

Parents should also be notified when any changes are made in the educational placement of the child, such as when the child may no longer require special services. The parents should also have a clear grasp of all of the due process rights. Included are the right to *access*, or the right to examine, and to have a copy made, of the information and data related to the identification and evaluation of the handicapping condition and the placement decision; the right to *challenge* the content of a record of the evaluation, if they feel it contains inaccurate or misleading information; and the *right to obtain an independent evaluation* of their child's needs, at the school's expense, if the school's evaluation is found inappropriate.

The child should be *reevaluated* every three years, or more frequently if requested by a parent or teacher. (Instructional objectives are evaluated annually.) Consent must be granted by the parent not only for the evaluation, but also before any change is made in the school program requiring special classes or special services. Parents have the right to a *hearing* if they disagree with the evaluation, or with the final placement decision. Parents may also *withdraw consent* at any time and, in effect, stop the process. Either the school or the parents may *appeal* the decision reached in a hearing and ultimately if agreement cannot be reached, appeal may be made to the courts. Most important, in terms of minority issues, notification efforts must be made in a manner understandable by the parents. The primary language of the parents, or other mode of communication, must be used. The child has a right to a surrogate parent if parents or a legal guardian cannot be identified.

As outlined in the first chapter, most would consider fairness in educational evaluation and placement to be directly tied to testing. Prasse (1978), however, makes the following point: "Referral systems, staffings, case conferences, multidisciplinary teams, and final decision-making responsibilities for placement are potentially racially and culturally discriminatory" (p. 595). One major assumption about the notice requirement is that direct parental involvement will reduce the possibility of such discrimination. Pryzwansky and Bersoff (1978) make excellent suggestions that are consistent with the intent of the law regarding parents' and children's rights (some have been edited, expanded, or modified to a slight degree). (a) The parents should be given correct information, including "disadvantages and risks" in evaluation (this is also true regarding placement decisions, e.g. in explaining problems associated with special classes, programs, or labeling). (b) Parents should be given adequate time for consent. Some psychologists and school administrators may try to cover *all* information in a single one hour session. The advantages of more frequent contacts are that parents have time to evaluate the situation, visit with the special class teacher, and to participate in decision-making meetings. (c) Parents may be referred to other knowledgeable parents or people representing advocacy groups for special children for "advice and information." (d) Parents should know that they can bring other people to assist them at the various conferences (especially helpful for persons from differing socio-cultural backgrounds). (e) Parents should not perceive any "threats concerning loss of rights" if they fail to give consent (e.g., the parents should not feel that if they refuse to give consent, school officials may be "angry" and "take things out on their child"). (f) Finally, parents may need to be reminded that their permission is not permanent; they have the right to "revoke consent" (p. 279).

There are other reasons, distinct from the legal mandates, for involving parents in educational decision making. Parents can be contributing members of a multidisciplinary team, since they have the most knowledge and insight about their child in all but the most extraordinary circumstances. They have the potential to make definitive contributions in the area of assessment that cannot be overlooked. For example, parental observation and involvement is crucial in areas of adaptive behavior for children suspected of being mentally retarded, or in the behavioral assessment of hyperactive or emotionally disturbed children. Particularly within areas of the low incidence handicapping conditions (e.g., blind, deaf, multiply handicapped) and with preschool handicapped, parental involvement in assessment through interviewing and the use of rating scales or checklists may be one of the most practical and appropriate procedures yet developed, as will be discussed in the last chapters.

In addition to contributing evaluation input and fulfilling an advocacy role, parents need information upon which to base decisions, since they usually have sole responsibility for long-term planning for their child. Parents, even of young handicapped children, will have many questions involving the vocational, community, social, and personal adjustment of their children and many will need to understand how to develop a continuity for the care of the child that is not usually met in the public school situation. Baker (1976) presents an excellent review of the potential for parental involvement with developmentally disabled children. He stresses that "parents cannot simply wait for this service continuum to emerge for their child because they themselves are in fact an integral part of that continuum, especially in the early years" (p. 694).

One final point should be mentioned in discussing parental participation and legal safeguards. Although due process is a legal concept, adherence to due process does not necessarily establish an adversary relationship between the parents, the child and the schools. Abeson and Zettel (1977) stress: "Many school systems operating under well established and understood due process systems have found that they can provide an effective means of guiding communications with the families of children with handicaps" (p. 126). Losen and Diament (1978) provide a helpful resource for professionals desiring to improve relationships with parents. Many techniques and useful guidelines for working with parents as "partners or coequals" are outlined. They discuss problems with both "parent defensiveness" as well as "staff defensiveness." Marion (1980) reviews principles useful for communicating with parents of culturally diverse exceptional children.

The Least Restrictive Environment

Providing educational services in the least restrictive environment raises philosophical and moral issues, as well as being an instructional imperative. Abeson, Burgdorf, Casey, Kunz, and McNeil (1975) present the following perspective. Services for handicapped persons should be "provided in the most normal setting in which the individual can function effectively" (p. 275). Ideally, there should be "one system of public education for all children" (p. 275).

Several concepts are central to a discussion of the least restrictive environment: normalization, mainstreaming, and the provision of education and related services through a continuum of instructional choices. *Normalization* was first described by Nirje (1969) within the context of institutional settings for the retarded. Wolfensberger (1972) has broadened and restated the definition as follows: Normalization refers to the "utilization of means which are as culturally normative as possible, in order to establish and/or maintain personal behaviors and characteristics which are as culturally normative as possible" (p. 28). Normalization is both a "process" and a "goal"; it does not imply a guarantee that the goal will be reached and that persons will "become normal" (p. 28).

> It does imply that in as many aspects of a person's functioning as possible, the human manager will aspire to elicit and maintain behaviors and appearances that come as close to being normative as circumstances and the person's behavioral potential permit; and that great stress is placed upon the fact that some human management means will be preferable to others. (p. 28)

Normalization as a principle sounds deceptively simple. However, the implications and changes required are complex and vast. Wolfensberger (1972) makes the distinction between physical and social integration. Physical integration relates to such things as the location, physical context, size, or access to a building or facility. Social integration refers to "role perceptions" and "stereotypes" and the various interactions between the handicapped person and social systems. Zipperlen (1975) provides an excellent discussion of the principles of normalization. She views it as the move away from "the large, hierarchical, isolated institutions" (p. 287). Zipperlen also notes potential dangers involved "when adopted as official policy": It may lead to "standardization rather than to the necessary diversity of options" that are required by such a principle (p. 287). From a sociological perspective, Gelman (1978) gives the following view: "Normalization is a rational attempt to deal with those conditions which have tended to deepen and reinforce prejudice and set the mentally retarded apart from the rest of society" (p. 86). The principle can be applied to all handicapped persons, not only the retarded. Baker (1976) sees the principle of normalization in terms of the acceptance of developmentally disabled persons; they should be considered "as an integral part of society" instead of being separated from society, however "well intentioned" (p. 693). Two implications that follow from the principle need to be emphasized. The first is that "individuals and social institutions" need to adapt to handicapped persons. The second is that handicapped persons also need to reach their highest potential in interacting with other persons and institutions (Baker, 1976).

The concept of least restrictive (or alternative) environment is sometimes confused with the similar concept of mainstreaming. They are not precisely equivalent terms. Mainstreaming is not addressed or mentioned in P.L. 94-142, but the two terms have often been used interchangeably. Neisworth and Smith (1978) define *mainstreaming* as "developmental integration; integration of handicapped individuals with nonhandicapped persons as a means toward normalization" (p. 544). The potential difficulty with the term "mainstreaming" is that it has been understood by some to mean that all handicapped persons should be placed into present educational settings as a means for deinstitutionalization without provisions for support services or a range of educational alternatives. Birch (1974) discusses mainstreaming and suggests the following:

> Central to the mainstreaming movement is the theme that given the desire, facilities, and reasonable professional preparation, the average teacher can learn to educate exceptional youngsters in the regular class with the support and consultative services of special education personnel. (p. 1)

Birch (1974) further notes that mainstreaming is not for every child or teacher: both have to be carefully selected. He lists a number of reasons for mainstreaming, many of which have been addressed elsewhere in this book (e.g., labeling and parental concern, the question of effectiveness of special education for some children, court actions, and alternative models for special services). Interestingly, another reason Birch sees for the mainstreaming movement is that "nonhandicapped children are deprived if they are not allowed to associate with handicapped children" (p. 6). He further states:

> Understanding, helpfulness, satisfaction of curiosity, overcoming of handicaps, acceptance of differences—these are a few of the concepts and feelings which can be developed among normal children through constructively managed interactions in school with the exceptional children who are their classmates. (p 6)

Thus, the terms can be clarified by the principle that mentally retarded children (as well as other handicapped children) "must be mainstreamed in the least restrictive environment possible" (Smith, Forsberg, Herb, and Neisworth, 1978, p. 353). Meisgeier (1976) and Sarason and Doris (1978) also provide excellent discussions of mainstreaming issues. Johnson (1980) explores the significance of the mainstreaming movement for the black child.

Parallel and necessary to the concept of least restrictive environment is a *continuum of instructional choices* for children and handicapped adults. All of the prior discussion stressing normalization as a major principle underscores the importance of additional flexibility in the provision of education and support services to handicapped individuals. Models presented by Deno (1970) and Reynolds (1962) are widely cited and frequently used as frameworks for describing the issues and practical problems involved in implementing the concept of education within the least restrictive environment. Reynolds (1962) stresses that "special placement should be no more 'special' than necessary" (p. 368). A continuum of instructional choices implies that the classification of children for the purpose of instruction is always "tentative and subject to revision" and that assessment should be continual, so children can be returned to "more ordinary environments as soon as feasible" (p. 370). Reynolds (1962) describes a hierarchy of special education program alternatives. Children with the most severe handicapping conditions may be served within hospitals or other treatment centers, residential schools, or special day schools. The fewest number of children would be served in such settings. Children with less severe handicaps may receive instruction in special classes, either part or full time, depending on each child's needs. Most exceptional children may be served in the regular classrooms by providing ancillary services through resource rooms, supplementary teaching, modification of regular class instruction, or through consultation with specialists knowledgeable in the handicapping area. The key points are that the child should be moved "only as far as necessary" from the mainstream of education, and should "return as soon as possible" (Reynolds, 1962, p. 368.) Although Reynolds' earlier work is widely used as a model for services, Reynolds and Birch (1977) have updated the earlier "cascade" system of instructional choices. They acknowledge several criticisms of the approach, the major one being that it is "too place oriented." They stress that: "regular schools and classes should have diversified staffing and should offer many forms of individualized instructional programs so that a great variety of students could be accommodated there with good results" (p. 35). Their text reviews mainstreaming issues, delivery systems, and major handicapping conditions. The book by Gearheart and Weishahn (1976) is a useful reference on mainstreaming, and includes an overview of handicapping conditions and practical suggestions for classroom teachers. Turnbull and Schulz (1979) have written a good introduction to mainstreaming and also include recommendations for specific areas of instruction. Paul, Turnbull, and Cruickshank (1977) examine a different and complementary view of mainstreaming issues through a "systems" and organizational analysis.

The Individual Education Program

Each child identified and placed in special education by the multidisciplinary team requires an *Individual Education Program* (IEP). Abeson and Zettel (1977) consider the IEP to be the "central building block" of P.L. 94-142. The IEP requires a written statement of the unique needs of the child, consistent with the findings of a multidisciplinary assessment, and includes information about the child's present performance, short term objectives, annual goals, specific supportive services required, a time line for providing services and meeting objectives, and criteria for evaluating progress towards the objectives. The IEP must also address participation of the handicapped child in the regular school program and the total program plan must be evaluated at least annually. In addition, various teaching methods (such as those necessary in overcoming sensory modality problems, motivational problems, etc.), and special materials may be suggested. Torres (1977) considers the IEP to be:

> A management tool designed to assure that, when a child requires special education, the special education designed for that child is appropriate to his or her special learning needs, and that the special education designed is actually delivered and monitored. (p. 1)

The chapter by Abeson and Weintraub (in Torres, 1977) summarizes the major points in developing and understanding the IEP. Other chapters in Torres (1977) develop and elaborate upon the key concepts relating to the IEP. Also, a sample IEP is illustrated in the Appendix and may serve as a useful guide for school districts. Turnbull, Strickland and Brantley (1978) have developed a comprehensive guideline for the development of IEP procedures.

Multifactored assessment has direct relevance for the development of the IEP. The discussion of specific techniques for determining the child's needs will be treated more fully in Section II. The procedures for establishing a child's needs are outlined next.

Procedures for Nondiscriminatory Multifactored Assessment

A child's need for a special education program should be documented by a comprehensive multidisciplinary assessment. The exact procedures will vary widely with children having different handicapping conditions. Some children will require a great deal of flexibility and ingenuity on the part of the persons doing the assessment, particularly with unusual or "low incidence" handicapping conditions. For minority children, the legal issues are not clearly resolved at the time of writing. Furthermore, the issues have been addressed by the courts and not by empirical methods. As pointed out in Chapter One, the outcomes of *Larry P.* and *PASE* resulted in different opinions about bias inherent in tests, although each had a different emphasis. Both cases have important limitations from a professional standpoint. Neither banning the use of IQ tests for placement purposes, nor minimizing the amount of potential bias for a child, may necessarily result in sound practice.

Background References

A great many recent references exist concerning specific assessment procedures. Assessment procedures generally applicable for mentally retarded, learning disabled, and behavior disordered children will be outlined in Chapter Five, and procedures for low incidence assessment will be discussed in Chapter Six. The legal mandate, however, requires that assessment procedures be "appropriate," and, for certain children, acceptable procedures are difficult to find. A few references are offered that may be helpful in establishing special procedures for more unusual circumstances relating to assessment. Often the solutions are not straightforward and are not easily predicted. For example, Swanson and Deblassie (1979) found that, for Mexican-American children with Spanish as the dominant language, the English version of the verbal part of an individual intelligence test (Wechsler Intelligence Scale for Children) yielded higher mean scores than the Spanish version.

Mowder (1979) also reviews the special concerns in assessing bilingual students. Chinn (1979) discusses the general parameters in assessing, for example, black gifted children, Mexican-American children who may have learning disabilities, and visually impaired Asian-American children. Hynd and Garcia (1979) describe the problems associated with assessing Native Americans.

Procedures for Multifactored Assessment

The procedures that follow can be applied only in a general sense. The necessary steps are summarized at this point in outline form and specific techniques related to the procedures will be discussed in Section II.

1. A psychoeducational evaluation should cover as many of the following areas (or domains) as are appropriate for a particular child, based on the state program standards for the handicapping condition: (a) emotional and social areas; (b) language and communication skills; (c) academic achievement; (d) cognitive and intellectual skills; (e) adaptive behavior; (f) gross motor, fine motor, and perceptual skills; and (g) vocational and occupational assessment.

2. An individual psychological and educational evaluation (psychoeducational) should include *norm*, as well as *criterion referenced tests*. Norm referenced tests, like traditional IQ and achievement tests, compare an individual's score to others of the same age or grade by using percentiles or standard scores. This type of evaluation may be helpful for the designation of a global program for a child by being predictive of success in the mainstream of education, thus estimating the degree of support that may be necessary. Criterion referenced tests are made up of questions sampling sets of skills or knowledge in particular content areas, without regard to the performance of other children. For example, the tests might focus upon math facts, sight words, phonics skills, and basic language concepts. They can be constructed by a teacher or obtained from a publisher. Criterion referenced tests are most helpful for the designation of short term and long term instructional objectives. Both norm referenced tests and criterion referenced tests should be used for the determination of program effectiveness and accountability.

3. *Direct observation* of the child in a variety of natural settings (e.g., school classroom, playground, home) should be used in combination with traditional assessment techniques. Classroom teachers and parents can make perhaps the greatest contribution in this area, as will be discussed in Section II. Observational procedures are particularly important in defining personal and social objectives of the IEP. Observa-

tional skills may help clarify short term objectives and methods (e.g., reinforcers, contingencies) and help translate the somewhat vague, but descriptive, terms, such as poor self-concept, misbehavior, etc., into suggestions for specific intervention strategies. Consultations with the professionals on the multidisciplinary team regarding the child's behavior in a variety of testing and instructional settings is usually helpful in understanding the child's functioning in the natural environment. Direct observation should be used to corroborate test measures when possible. Formal observation and recording strategies may be very helpful in assessment and intervention in specific problem areas, such as hyperactivity or aggressiveness.

4. Psychoeducational assessment should include *interviews* with a significant person in the child's life outside the school setting (usually a parent). In this manner, adaptive behavior can be assessed and information can be gathered regarding the child's educational and developmental history (medical problems, medication, developmental milestones). The SOMPA, introduced in the second chapter, formalizes this approach. The Sociocultural Scales of the SOMPA may be highly useful in determining the suitability of assessment procedures.

5. The child's *native language*, or most usual mode of communication (e.g., signing), should be used for assessment purposes. If an examiner proficient in the child's native language, or skilled in a particular mode, is not available, an interpreter can be used while testing, although this is often not the best practice. Verbal portions of a test with bilingual children, even with a relatively high degree of proficiency in both languages, will usually underestimate abilities (Gerken, 1978). When testing a child with severe problems in such areas as speech, hearing, vision, and, most especially, a combination of areas, it is often difficult to differentiate between the estimate of the child's ability and the communication or sensory deficit. Therefore, a consultation or assessment by specialists in the appropriate area is usually necessary, as well as the adaptive use of test measures (e.g., making necessary changes in the administration of a test item to compensate for a specific sensory problem). With children having unique problems, the traditional norms may not apply, except in defining the most general parameters of functioning, and the scores should be considered a *minimal estimate*, and should be clearly labeled as such. The scores may be useful for educational and vocational planning, but stigmatizing labels should be avoided under these circumstances, if possible.

6. Tests should be validated for the specific purpose or evaluation area in question and should be administered by trained personnel (see APA's *Standards for Educational and Psychological Tests*, 1974).

7. A medical evaluation may be required by the appropriate state program standard for the particular handicapping condition or deemed necessary or pertinent to educational programming.

Professional and Ethical Guidelines for Psychoeducational Assessment

There is not now a "best" set of procedures to follow, or a set of tests or assessment techniques that do not have limitations or have not been criticized by a segment of the lay or professional community. For example, Coles (1978) reviews the most frequently used assessment techniques in evaluating learning disabilities and raises very serious doubts about common assessment practices. However, following the above procedures and adhering to established safeguards for psychological and educational assessment should minimize problems related to sources of bias and should provide helpful information for educational decision making and instructional programming.

Matarazzo (1972) notes three "crucial elements in assessment" as follows: (a) Each instance for assessment should have a clearly identifiable "purpose or end"; (b) A "set" battery should not be used—there should be "deliberate selection" of appropriate assessment techniques to help in decision making for each "individual case"; and (c) "Socioprofessional guidelines and safeguards" should be "acknowledged in order that the rights and prerogatives" of individuals and society are upheld (p. 13).

There are other critical issues to be aware of before proceeding to the details of testing. The following list provides an appropriate context (adapted from Anastasi, 1976):

1. Rapport is essential. It is the responsibility of the examiner to attempt to elicit the child's interest and cooperation.
2. The examiner must attempt to reduce test anxiety and must help to remove the "surprise and strangeness" of the test situation, if it is affecting the performance of the child.
3. The test user must be qualified: the examiner must choose the appropriate test and must know the technical merits of the instrument.
4. Protection of privacy must be insured. A child must not be tested under false pretenses, and matters not relevant to the referral problem should not be "explored."
5. Confidentiality must be upheld and is an obligation of all members of the multidisciplinary team (teachers, school psychologist, special educator, speech and hearing clinician, principal, etc.).
6. The explanation of the test results to the parent or child should be by a trained professional with qualifications appropriate to the specific techniques employed (pp. 34-57).

Bersoff (1973b) summarizes the writing of Fischer (1970) from the viewpoint of school psychology and recommends the following steps that seem highly consistent with the intent of P.L. 94-142. Although all the steps could not be followed in every possible circumstance faced by school psychologists, even an approximation of the procedures may avoid professional "malpractice." The first is that of *coadvisement*, an elaboration of informed consent.

The psychologist tells the child and his parents how he functions; informs them of the identity of the referral agent and the purpose for referral; and describes the nature of the assessment devices he will use, the merits and limitations of those devices, what kind of information will be put into a report, and who might eventually read the report. The psychologist then asks the child to tell how he perceives the purposes of testing and what he feels the consequences of such an evaluation might be. The psychologist secures agreement from the child and his parents to proceed with the assessment subsequent to full and mutual disclosure concerning the purposes of the evaluation.

A second procedure is that of *sharing impressions*:

Immediately after the administration of the psychometric instruments the psychologist, the child, and his parents engage in a dialogue in which the psychologist gives his interpretation of the child's test behavior as he has just experienced it. By conferring with the child he attempts to extrapolate from the testing situation to other situations similar to the one represented by the test stimuli. Such a dialogue provides immediate feedback to the child about how others perceive his behavior and enables the assessor to check out hypotheses about how equivalent the test behavior observed is to actual classroom behavior and to develop possible strategies he may use to intervene in the instructional environment. . . . It also gives the child a chance to disagree with the psychologist's initial interpretations and to offer his perceptions about his own behavior.

The third procedure is a joint *critique of the written evaluation*:

After the evaluation is complete and the psychologist has prepared his report, he shows the child and his parents a copy of the written evaluation. This insures that the report will be recorded so that it is understandable to all concerned. . . . Then, the child and his parents are given the opportunity to clarify the points made, to add further material, and, if there is disagreement between the psychologist and the clients, to provide a dissenting view (in writing if warranted). Finally, the psychologist receives permission to disseminate the report to those whom the child and his parents agree to. (p. 310)

Summary

Aspects of P.L. 94-142 relating to nonbiased, multifactored assessment were explored. The major areas considered were parents' and children's rights, due process, and the concepts of least restrictive environment and the individual educational plan. Procedures for multifactored assessment that follow from the intent of the law were outlined. Although acceptable procedures are often difficult to find, adherence to suggested strategies will minimize bias in testing and in the provision of services, while the likelihood of an appropriate educational program for a child will be increased. The important points include: (a) adherence to procedural safeguards; (b) use of appropriate test instruments and assessment techniques; (c) awareness of critical elements of assessment; and (d) actualizing the potential for parental and child contributions.

Section II

THE PRAGMATICS OF ASSESSMENT

The purpose of this section is to discuss specific approaches to assessment. Chapter Five presents seven domains of multifactored assessment. Chapter Six stresses the special problems associated with the assessment of low incidence handicapped children.

Chapter 5

MULTIFACTORED ASSESSMENT

Multifactored assessment, along with the procedural safeguards described in Chapter Four, are, taken together, the emerging "answers" in meeting the requirements of nonbiased, comprehensive evaluations required by Public Law 94-142. Reschly (1979) notes the basic assumption is that bias may be reduced "if a broad variety of information is collected and considered systematically in making classification decisions" (p. 237). Tucker (1977) provides the following analysis:

> A state of art in nonbiased assessment clearly exists in the form of broad professional resources, sound principles and practices, legislative and legal guidelines and intervention techniques which, if applied, can alter and improve children's behaviors. (p. 91)

The information obtained from the specific techniques may be used for any or all of the following purposes: (a) the identification of children with handicapping conditions; (b) the determination of a global program with sufficient resources to meet children's needs; (c) the individualization of instructional planning including short and long term goals and objectives; and (d) the evaluation of both the progress of individual children and the effectiveness of the total program.

Even though the chapter is outlined by separate assessment domains (Personal and Social Functioning, Cognitive and Intellectual Functioning, Language and Communication Skills, Academic Skills, Adaptive Behavior, Vocational Assessment, Visual-Motor and Gross-Motor Skills), several points detract from the overall convenience of this type of organization. The overlap between many areas is striking. For example, with young children, problems in cognition, language, and behavior are often closely linked together. For adolescents, the same may be true of the areas relating to Personal and Social Adjustment, Adaptive Behavior, and Vocational Assessment. The significance of Language and Communication Skills may be of potential importance to all areas (e.g., assessing a deaf child with motor problems). A second problem, not often discussed, relates to the vagaries sometimes associated with specialization or "expertise." A high degree of specialization is required and multidisciplinary assessment is implied throughout the chapter. One may, however, be easily misled by the role of the "expert," if information is not jointly shared or analyzed by members of the multidisciplinary team. For example, even though psychologists may have formal coursework in personality assessment, they would be remiss to assume that a teacher or parent could not make valid observations or could not contribute to the problem solving process. The role of "expert" in assessing reading may vary from situation to situation. Some teachers (or psychologists) may have excellent backgrounds in reading diagnosis, while others do not. Some speech, hearing, and language clinicians may have less familiarity in analyzing the utterances of severely emotionally disturbed children than special education teachers or psychologists with training, interests, and experience with such children. The examples are not meant to malign any speciality. The point is that flexible and open communication and decision-making systems are needed for multifactored assessment. It is unrealistic to assume that individual professionals can be trained to competently assess infants, preschoolers, school-aged children, adolescents, and adults across all handicapping conditions, for any specialty. At the same time, however, an in-depth awareness of each assessment domain facilitates communication and consultation between the primary members of the multidisciplinary teams and allows for appropriate referrals to other specialists. Collaboration in consultation is a learned skill.

The ordering of the assessment domains is at odds with other recent lists of categorical assessment. Despite the many problems associated with the assessment of personal and social functioning, it is felt that this area comes closest to the priorities that should be established when intervening in the lives of children. The stress should be on the most significant sources of life satisfaction (e.g., Hobbs, 1966) and the most complete view of the child. The placement of the other domains was a difficult matter. The cognitive and intellectual section follows for historical reasons, contemporary interest, and also because of the possible future impact of studies of children's cognitive development. Except in unusual circumstances, the assessment of academic skills will probably be more curricular in nature in the future (e.g., Wallace and Larsen, 1978; Faas, 1980). Many teachers will have had specific training in the diagnosis and remediation of reading, arithmetic, handwriting, and spelling. The remaining areas can be grouped in a number of ways. For example, the significant dimensions of adaptive behavior may relate to personal-social skills for one child and communication and language behavior for another.

Assessment of Personal and Social Functioning

Contemporary trends in personality assessment were presented in Chapter Three. In brief review, the major points included: (1) the assessment of relevant and often unique person variables; (2) the assessment of environmental or situational variables; and (3) the analysis of ongoing interactions between persons and situations.

Because of the serious nature of school referrals in the area of personal-social functioning, several guidelines are necessary for adequate asessment. First, there is not a single best approach to assessment. Often the many required resources necessitate a close working relationship between the members of the multidisciplinary team, especially parents, referring teacher, school counselor, and psychologist. The school principal may also be actively involved because of the potential effects on other children and teachers. Second, assessment should lead directly to interventions and the results of the interventions should be evaluated. Third, if not successful, the ethical requirement is to refer the child and parent to other resources (e.g., Mental Health Centers, available university facilities, clinical psychologists in private practice) and to establish a cooperative relationship between the school personnel and the treatment agent.

One of the first steps for a psychologist working with a child experiencing a severe emotional problem is to identify the potential resources for helping and to define the specific roles that may be assumed by various persons. Teachers have important roles in both assessment and intervention, and a wide variety of references exist describing approaches from a "classroom ecology viewpoint" (e.g., Brown, 1978; Moos and Trickett, 1974; Simon and Boyer, 1974; Wallace and Larsen, 1978; and Weinberg and Wood, 1975). In addition to classroom interventions, a number of behavioral programs include the parents or siblings as direct participants (e.g., Atkeson and Forehand, 1979; Mash, Hamerlynck and Handy, 1976; O'Dell, 1974; Patterson, 1975; and Weinrott, 1974).

As with the other sections, a comprehensive treatment of the topic is not possible within the scope of this book. Omissions include: (1) psychiatric diagnosis; (2) psychophysiological and neuropsychological assessment (e.g., Epstein, 1976; Filskov and Boll, 1981; Nay, 1979; and Reitan, 1976); (3) observation techniques for the analysis of classroom interactions (ecologies) as referred to above; (4) a review of the many traditional as well as emerging constructs in personality theory and assessment (e.g., basic needs, defense mechanisms, moral development, attribution theory, cognitive style, etc.); and (5) a further elaboration of behavioral and cognitive-behavioral assessment techniques as reviewed in Chapter Three. Special note should be made of Buros' *Personality Tests and Reviews* (1970) and the eight Mental Measurements Yearbooks which provide extensive reviews of major personality assessment techniques.

The following topics will be discussed: problems associated with the assessment of minorities; behavioral diagnosis; psychosocial and cognitive constructs; and specific assessment techniques.

The Assessment of Minorities

The assessment of personal and social functioning of minority people has not received widescale discussion (Pettigrew, 1964). With blacks and other minorities, personal and sociocultural variables (e.g., language, cognitive style, limiting opportunities, adaptive and coping mechanisms, prejudice) may confound the search for assessment and intervention techniques. Many controversies exist with respect to problem identification. One, especially, is the attribution of the problem to either social, political, or individual factors. For example, some believe that individual intervention may result in a disservice when problems stem from more profound economic, social, or political concerns. The edited book by Jones (1980) presents important minority views. The procedures and steps outlined in Chapters Three and Four apply directly to the problems encountered. Barriers to interracial assessment have been addressed by: (1) establishing a position of advocacy; (2) exploring cultural differences; (3) furthering attempts at rapport; (4) enlisting the aid of a professional (e.g., psychologist, teacher, social worker) of the same ethnic background; and (5) using behavioral assessment approaches (e.g., those of Kanfer and Saslow, described in the following pages). Savage and Adair (1980) suggest a team approach to help establish the *ethnic validity* of the assessment process. The team, comprised of such persons as parents, administrators, teachers or community members, are at the center of the assessment process and advise an "expert" in assessment with regard to procedures. The team directly participates in decision making. Most significantly, "the team serves as an anchor to the assessment" by making the process and procedures relevant to the community and overall cultural context of the problem (p. 199).

The difficulties inherent in assessing minorities should not be neglected, despite confusing research. Anderson, Bass, Munford, and Wyatt (1977) warn, with respect to psychiatric assessment and treatment of blacks, that "important sociocultural factors in assessment and treatment of black patients are often overlooked and when acknowledged are misinterpreted" (p. 340). On the other hand, at least one empirical study has suggested that bias in diagnostic labeling towards blacks and lower-class populations may be less prevalent than generally believed (Bamgbose, Edwards, Johnson, 1980). The subjects in the study were 21 black and 40 white clinical psychologists. The race and socioeconomic status of the cases presented to the psychologists did not seem to influence the diagnosis.

Many standardized (objective) tests in personality assessment do not report information on ethnic differences. Those that do (e.g., Barnett and Zucker, 1980a; McDaniel, 1973; and Wirt, Lachar, Klinedinst, and Seat, 1977) suggest that ethnic differences may be apparent across important personality dimensions. When empirically studied, striking differences have sometimes been found (e.g., Jones 1978). However, Yando, Seitz, and Zigler (1979) reported a relative absence of ethnic differences in six personality and motivational factors in two carefully controlled studies with 304 eight year old children. They used a wide variety of behavioral tasks distributed over six construct areas (creativity, self-confidence, dependency, curiosity, frustration threshold, and autonomy) and found that Socioeconomic Status was much more predictive of behavior than ethnic group membership. Significant SES differences were found in the first four constructs. The most important finding was that when differences were found, the superior performances did not always belong to the children of a particular group (i.e., advantaged).

Specific interpretations of subtests may require item-by-item analysis of tests like the Personality Inventory for Children (Wirt, et al., 1977). The Thematic Apperception Test (Murray, 1943) has been used extensively in studies across many cultures. Significant differences have been found relating to social class and ethnic variables (Harrison, 1965). A Thematic Apperception Test in which blacks are depicted (Thompson, 1949) was used for research purposes, but interest has been limited. Custom made pictures structured for a particular purpose show promise for personality assessment with members of ethnic groups (Bailey and Green, 1977; Harrison, 1965). The Paired Hands Test (Zucker and Barnett, 1977) may be a valuable aid because it presents biracial stimuli in the form of a series of black and white hands interacting in various poses. Abel (1973) presents a comprehensive treatment of cross-cultural assessment with projective techniques.

Behavioral Diagnosis

Kanfer and Saslow (as reported in Mash and Terdal, 1976) suggest the major dimensions of behavioral diagnosis that serve as guidelines in considering various therapeutic interventions.

1. Initial Analysis of the Problem Situation (including behavioral excesses, deficits, and assets)
2. Clarification of Problem Situation
3. Motivational Analysis
4. Developmental Analysis (including biological limitations or self-limiting expectations; sociological and behavioral aspects)
5. Analysis of Self-Control
6. Analysis of Social Relationships
7. Analysis of the Social-Cultural-Physical Environment

Assessment in each dimension of significance to the individual should generate information about areas for intervention, targets for intervention, possible treatment alternatives, and sequences of treatment goals. Lazarus (1976) has suggested the mnemonic BASIC ID which represents the following assessment domains: Behavior, Affect, Sensation, Imagery, Cognition, Interpersonal, and Drugs (including organic and physiological processes).

Nay (1979) reviews sources of clinical assessment errors and further emphasizes the need for broad based assessment approaches. His orientation to assessment closely follows that of Kanfer and Saslow, and Lazarus. He summarizes the process of assessment in three major steps, each a potential source of clinical assessment error. The first involves the "detection" of the important problem areas. Interventions may ultimately fail because information was not obtained, or was inaccurate, or biased. Problems of detection may be due to the "inadequate choice of modality" (e.g., the modalities of Lazarus' BASIC ID, or the domains suggested by Kanfer and Saslow), thus significantly restricting, at the outset, the range of information central to a complete understanding of the client's circumstances.

Problems in detection may also be the result of the choice of methods used by the psychologist. For example, relying on either direct observation or self-report techniques alone would necessarily narrow the perspective of the psychologist. Each method is associated with unique sources of error (involving reliability and validity). Also, error can be a result of "sources of bias" in either the client or psychologist's perception of the problem.

The second major source of clinical assessment errors results from the integration and interpretation of the obtained information. Nay describes key sources of error involved in clinical decision-making:

> Error of congruence has to do with a bias in favor of perceiving congruence in information...independent of the actual consistency or inconsistency of the findings.
> Overgeneralization...[involves reaching a conclusion]...based on limited information.
> Another source of error occurs when the interpretation...results either from inadequate conceptualizations or theoretical biases. (pp. 280-282)

The final major source of error involves the selection of goals for treatment:

> If important aspects of the client's life situation have not been detected or if clinical findings are inadequately integrated or incorrectly interpreted,...[the psychologist or behavior change agent]...cannot be in a position to select goals for intervention that best meet the client's needs. (p. 283)

Psychosocial and Cognitive Constructs

The search for important personal and social variables and constructs for assessment has been presented in some detail and is necessarily open-ended. Peterson (1968) described relevant theory about clinical assessment in terms of basic psychological and sociological principles that would be found in comprehensive texts in each area. A construct allows for the testing of hypotheses through the selection of assessment strategies. Most contemporary psychologists currently favor assessing specific constructs that can more easily be translated into direct intervention strategies. For example, one might ask: Does the child have the required social skills to meet the demands of the situation? Does the child value the change in behaviors? What does the child expect to happen in a given situation? What are the child's coping or problem-solving strategies?

Constructs stemming from personality research have been given much less emphasis by contemporary applied psychologists because of the lack of immediate practical utility of theoretical approaches. Personality research, however, helps describe the parameters of human behavior across many different dimensions. Also, global constructs may help initially with organizing the search for meaningful hypotheses. Woody (1980) offers a valuable cross-section of many contemporary constructs related to clinical assessment. One construct that often is stressed with children is the *self-concept*. Specific aspects of the self-concept and various assessment techniques, however, are often overlooked.

Shavelson, Hubner, and Stanton (1976, pp. 411-415) describe important elements of the construct (see also Bandura, 1978). (1) A person's self-concept is structured, and reflects ways of organizing and attributing meaning to experiences. In white middle-class children, four areas may be most important: academic, social, emotional, and physical. (2) Self-concept is therefore multifaceted "and facets represent the category system" adopted by individuals (or groups of individuals through cultural identity). (3) Self-concept may be viewed as hierarchical. "Facets of self-concept may form a hierarchy from individual experiences in particular situations...to general self-concept at the apex" (p. 412). (4) The general self-concept is stable, but less so when specific situations are considered. (5) Self-concept is developmental: "The self-concepts of young children are global, undifferentiated, and situation specific" (p. 414). (6) Self-concept is "evaluative"; individuals judge their performance in specific situations in comparison to ideal standards, peer group norms, etc. (7) Self-concept is "differentiable from other concepts with which it is theoretically related" (p. 415).

Although most people would acknowledge the importance of studying self-concept, the measurement of the construct presents difficult issues (Wylie, 1961, 1974). A number of specific tests have been designed to measure self-concept. The tests, however, are not precisely equivalent. Also, the tests may not have utility in establishing treatment objectives when used in a global way. Further elaboration of person and situation variables would be necessary, in addition to the use of other assessment techniques. Although the tests have mainly been used for research purposes, practitioners would benefit from an awareness of the dimensions of the scales.

The Piers-Harris Children's Self-Concept Scale (Piers, 1969) has 80 items that express concerns, or provide descriptions, along several dimensions (e.g., I am nervous, I am strong, etc.). The children respond by marking the items that reflect how they see themselves. Total testing time is about 15-20 minutes. The test is described by the authors as a research tool. The internal consistency of the items was found to be relatively high (.78 to .93) for various groups of children. Test-retest reliability was moderate (about .70) for three samples over a four month period. The authors have found that, at least by age eight, self-attitudes have "a reasonable amount of stability." Evidence of validity is provided by item selection and by correlations with other instruments. Norms based on 1183 public school children (grades 4 to 12) are included in the manual. Scores can be interpreted by stanines or percentiles. The authors suggest that the test can be used as a part of a test battery, and, when used in this manner, little attention should be given to the total score unless unusually high or low. Responses to individual items of concern can be used "as aids to diagnostic interviewing or counseling" (p. 18). Factor analysis suggests grouping items into six areas: Behavior (e.g., I do many bad things); Intellectual and

School Status; Physical Appearance and Attributes; Anxiety; Popularity; and Happiness and Satisfaction.

A different approach to evaluating a child's self-concept, in contrast to a self-report, is the Inferred Self-Concept Scale (McDaniel, 1973). Thirty items are rated by teachers (or other observers) on the basis of their perceptions of the child's self-concept (e.g., enjoys working with others, is easily discouraged, seems satisfied with level of performance). Normative data are provided by children in 16 elementary schools (16 counselors and 90 teachers; 180 children in grades 1 through 6). In standardizing the scale, a teacher and counselor were asked to rate randomly selected children in order to obtain estimates of interjudge agreement. Representative groups of blacks (n = 81) and Mexican American children (n = 86) were included in the study. A significant difference was found between ethnic groups with whites rated significantly higher than Mexican Americans, but not blacks. The relationship between counselor and teacher rating was .58, statistically significant, but indicating some difference in perceptions. Teacher ratings were, overall, significantly higher than counselors'. Test-retest scores over a six month period suggest moderate stability (r = .66).Minimal validity information is reported in the manual. Of interest are the findings suggesting differences between members of ethnic groups, the apparent differences in perceptions of children's self-concepts, and aspects of the construct of self-concept as measured by the test.

Another construct which parallels one's self-concept involves a person's attitudes towards others. One dimension can be defined as a person's general expectancies about others along a friendliness-hostility dimension (Others-Concept). Barnett and Zucker (1980a, 1980b) review the research contributions of many individuals in areas related to the others-concept. To date, research has involved the prediction of children's cooperative play and in larger studies, the analysis of characteristics of groups of persons across populations (e.g., age and sex differences; differences between groups of Irish children). Significant correlations with stages of moral development and psychosocial adjustment have also been noted. The Paired Hands Test (Zucker and Barnett, 1977) has been used as the assessment device for a number of experiments and studies of clinical usefulness are currently underway. Research has demonstrated, overall, the potential importance of the construct. In addition to one's self-concept, it may be equally important to assess the feelings, attitudes, and expectancies children have regarding persons within their important social environments. Theoretical issues and other dimensions (in addition to the friendliness-hostility continuum) require exploration and different assessment approaches require validation. Most importantly, cooperative behavior and the pro-social aspects of interpersonal behavior generally have been neglected in assessment practices. Moral judgement, roletaking, and empathy, are related constructs stressing positive interpersonal relationships (Mussen and Eisenberg-Berg, 1977).

Cognitive style is a broad term, describing the way the environment is conceptually organized by individuals (Goldstein and Blackman, 1977). Many aspects and dimensions may be of concern with respect to an individual (e.g., impulsivity, complexity, field dependence vs. independence, etc.). Locus Of Control (LOC) (e.g., Lefcourt, 1976; Rotter, 1966) is one example of a cognitive construct that may have functional utility in individual assessments. Generally speaking, the expectancies may relate to perceptions of reinforcement as being either under internal or under external control:

> The generalized expectancy of internal control...[refers to]...the perception of events, whether positive or negative, as being a consequence of one's own actions and thereby potentially under personal control. External control...[refers]...to the perception of positive or negative events as being unrelated to one's own behavior and thereby beyond personal control. (Lefcourt, 1976, p. 29)

LOC has been correlated with important dimensions of adjustment and may be very significant for low socioeconomic status children (Gemunder, 1979). Lefcourt (1976) summarizes studies demonstrating that "perceived control" is significantly related to "access to opportunity" (p. 25). Seligman (1975) states: "Controllability and helplessness play a major role in the child's encounters with our educational system....What is often passed off as retardation or an IQ deficit may be the result of learned helplessness" (pp. 153-154). Dweck and Reppucci (1973), Diener and Dweck (1978) and Goetz and Dweck (1980) have studied learned helplessness in school-age children. Some children, when subjected to continued failure, will still maintain their performance at a high level, but the performance of other children, experiencing the same type of failure, will deteriorate. The results support the hypothesis that children have different beliefs about their "power" or "powerlessness" to "control the outcomes of events" (Dweck and Reppucci, 1973, p. 115). For the children whose performance deteriorates, Dweck and Reppucci hypothesize that: "In essence, they are saying to themselves, that whether they try or not, the consequences will be the same" (p. 115). Diener and Dweck (1978) found that "helpless children made the expected attributions to uncontrollable factors," but the "mastery oriented children engaged in solution-directed behavior such as self-instructions and self-monitoring" (p. 460). Goetz and Dweck (1980) suggest that it is important to study a child's skill in solving problems in difficult circumstances, in contrast to the study of social skills in usual situations. The study of attributional processes may help one understand "the determinants of social behavior." Lefcourt (1976) includes several complete LOC scales in an appendix (e.g., the Crandall Intellectual Achievement Responsibility Questionnaire; the Stanford Peschool Internal-External Scale), but also suggests the advisability of assessing LOC directly, depending on the individual and circumstance.

A related construct is a person's feelings of self-efficacy (Bandura, 1977b). Perceived self-efficacy can influence the choice of activities and also "can affect coping efforts":

> Efficacy expectations determine how much effort people will expend and how long they will persist in the face of obstacles and aversive ex-

periences. . . . Those who persist in subjectively threatening activities that are in fact relatively safe will gain corrective experiencies that reinforce their sense of efficacy, thereby eliminating their defensive behavior. Those who cease their coping efforts prematurely will retain their self-debilitating expectations and fears for a long time. (p. 194)

Assessment Techniques

Interview and observation techniques often generate sufficient information for many interventions. When the child's problems cannot be clearly defined, however, the psychologist may decide to use other techniques such as self reports, behavior rating scales, objective tests, or projective techniques to provide further information. Meichenbaum (1977) and Ellett and Bersoff (1976) describe experimental procedures based on testing approaches. A variety of measures can be used to help evaluate intervention programs.

Interviews. Peterson (1968) describes the first two steps in an interview. First, a "scanning operation" is used, which involves a straightforward inquiry about the nature and circumstances of the problem. Second, an "extended inquiry" follows, requiring a "detailed and individualized study of the client and others most centrally involved" (p. 120). Problem identification and clarification provide the immediate focus. Interview procedures are appropriate throughout the intervention process. Parents and teachers usually provide important perceptions of the child and situation. Often neglected are children's perceptions of the problem, the environment, felt relationships to the significant persons in the environment, and the potential for helping relationships that may be established. Brooks (1979) presents other important perspectives, easily overlooked, relating to the "affective process variables" in assessment. For example, it may be significant to consider: (a) "what testing means to the child"; (b) "the child's sense of 'learning competence,' coping style, and level of resistance when confronted with different test procedures"; and (c) "the child's capacity to form an alliance" (pp. 712-714).

Peterson (1968) further notes that interviews are not necessarily

> regarded as the "truth" about the individual and his environment, but as another form of data whose reliability, validity and decisional utility must be subjected to the same kinds of scrutiny required for other modes of data collection. (p. 13)

Anastasi (1976) warns that "an interview may lead to wrong decisions because important data were not elicited or because given data were inadequately or incorrectly interpreted" (p. 609).

Many resources exist which present guidelines for interviewing. Both Lazarus (1971) and Peterson (1968) include an extensive treatment of clinical interviews. Holland (1976) suggests guidelines for interviewing parents within a behavioral perspective. Special skills are required by psychologists working within the public schools, and Curtis and Zins (1981) provide a comprehensive treatment of consultation techniques from an educational viewpoint. Collaborative consultation creates a framework for psychologist-teacher interaction and is an important prerequisite to assessment and intervention within the school milieu. Ellett and Bersoff (1976) describe interviewing procedures within an educational context. A chapter by Yarrow (1960) discusses interviewing children. Although written from a research perspective, many of the points are widely generalizable:

> The interview is a technique particularly well adapted to uncovering subjective definitions of experiences, to assessing a child's perceptions of the significant people and events in his environment, and to studying how he conceptualizes his life experiences. (p. 561)

Many variables are reviewed (e.g., age, rapport, the meaning of the interview to the child, etc.). Although it may be possible to interview some very young children, Yarrow notes that, between ages four and five, children become more interested in exchanging information and in describing events. However, direct interpretations are often difficult. With younger children, adaptations (e.g., toy telephones, story or sentence completion techniques, the use of clay or crayons during the interview, doll play) can help accommodate for expressive language development, limited verbalization, and motivational problems. Suggestibility may be a problem calling for careful wording of questions. Of course, some children show a great resistance to revealing their feelings. Perhaps the most important point is that the motivation to communicate with an adult is "developed during the course of the interview" (p. 568). Anxiety may be guided by explicitly clarifying the "purpose of the interview," "expectations," and the "interviewer's role." Allowing the child to become familiar with play materials, and having the child bring samples of pictures drawn or painted may be helpful in reducing anxiety.

The eco-map (Hartman, 1978a) can be an important adjunct to the interview process, particularly when faced by the complex networks representative of many contemporary family situations (i.e., divorce, adoption, grandparents raising children, foster parents). The eco-map allows for the visualizing of family and community systems. Hartman (1978a) describes the eco-map in the following way:

> The eco-map portrays an overview of the family in their situation; it pictures the important nurturant or conflict-laden connections....[and] the flow of resources, or the lacks and deprivations. This mapping procedure highlights the nature of the interfaces and points to conflicts to be mediated, bridges to be built, and resources to be sought and mobilized. (p. 467)

Hartman (1978a) comments that the primary value of the eco-map is due to the "visual impact" of the technique, its concurrent organization and presentation of a large amount of factual information, and the depiction of the significant relationships between the variables in a situation" (p. 468). The following procedures illustrate the technique:

1. Within a large circle, a picture representative of the immediate family is drawn. For example, small squares are used for males and circles for females. Ages are placed in the center of the figures.
2. Connecting lines are drawn between family members: dotted lines for ''tenuous connections,'' solid lines for ''strong'' connections, ''x's'' for ''conflicted or stressful connections.''
3. Arrows are drawn where appropriate, along the lines indicating the ''flow of energy,'' ''nurturance,'' ''supplies or support'' (in one or both directions depending on reciprocal relationships).
4. Complex systems may be broken down into different subsystems. (Adapted from a paper by Hartman, 1978b).

The eco-map may be used in the following ways:

1. As a ''thinking tool.''
2. As an assessment tool to be used jointly by worker and clients.
3. As a recording and communication tool.
4. As a measure of change. (Adapted from above source).

Self-report techniques can be used in conjunction with interviews and may aid in the identification of target behaviors. For example, the Mooney Problem Check List (High School Form) has 330 questions across a number of typical problem areas, including health, school, and personal and social adjustment (Mooney and Gordon, 1950). The student is asked to draw a line under the problems that are troublesome. A similar checklist is the STS Youth Inventory (Grades 4-8: Remmers and Bauernfeind, 1968; Grades 7-12: Remmers and Shimberg, 1967). The questions (167) are described across five headings for grades 7-12: My School; After High School; About Myself; Getting Along With Others; Things in General (e.g., social and moral problems). Most students take 30 minutes or less to complete the form. Since ''acceptability by parents and school personnel'' was one selection criteria for items, the present checklist may miss important concerns about child-parent relationships, sexual adjustment, or drug problems. The techniques may be useful to some degree (e.g., with cooperative adolescents having difficulty in openly verbalizing their concerns), but both could profit from revisions.

Observations. Observational techniques are important for helping to establish target behaviors, for defining the significant aspects of situations in which behavior occurs, and, in general, for serving as an indication of the ''completeness'' of information. Observational procedures have been developed for sampling behavior obtained in natural settings, or in ''analogue situations'' designed to provide information comparable to natural settings (Mash and Terdal, 1976).

A number of possible strategies for observational assessment are available (Baker and Tyne, 1980). Kazdin (1975) describes typical dimensions:

Behavior can be assessed by recording the *frequency* with which a response is performed, the *amount of time* (duration) it occurs, the *inten-*

sity... of the response, or its *latency* (i.e., the amount of time until a response is performed). (p. 69)

Possible behaviors amenable to recording by frequency include: number of times a child hits or kicks, number of assignments completed, new words learned, number of times classroom rules are followed, and tantrums. Behaviors appropriate for interval recording include: paying attention, sitting in seat, etc. Recording the duration of the response is useful when it is important to modify the "length of time" a behavior is performed (Kazdin, 1975). Examples would include time working on homework and time spent in appropriate play. Behaviors like tantrums may require the measurement of frequency as well as duration. It is also important to note the stimulus or controlling conditions (e.g., location, time of day, etc.).

Very few opportunities exist for the continuous observation of behavior so that sampling is necessary. Kazdin (1980) discusses three decisions that have to be made when deciding how to sample behavior:

> First, the number of times that data will be collected must be decided.... The frequency of observation depends upon various factors including the variation of behavior over time, the availability of observers, and scheduling exigencies in the treatment setting.
> A second decision... is the length of time set aside for a given observation period.... The guiding... rule is that behavior should be observed for a period of time that will yield data representative of typical performance.
> A third decision... is when the observations are conducted [i.e., a certain time of day, or samples during different parts of the day]. (pp. 85-86)

Another important aspect of behavioral interventions, outside the scope of this section, is that of program evaluation. Many references discuss this topic in depth (e.g., Hersen and Barlow, 1976; Kazdin, 1980; Kratochwill, 1978).

Although natural observations are a necessary strategy, especially with young children, one must not assume that observational procedures circumvent measurement problems and there is a lack of research in this area (Baker and Tyne, 1980). Methodology involved in establishing the reliability of observational data may be questionable (Hollenbeck, 1978; Jones, Reid and Patterson, 1975; Kent and Foster, 1977; Mitchell, 1979). Observer agreement is not necessarily equivalent to reliability and may overestimate the "quality of the data" (Mitchell, 1979). Many factors can influence observer reliability, including "observer drift" (e.g., adopting idiosyncratic definitions of target behaviors), "instrument decay" (e.g., changing measurement operations unintentionally), the complexity of the measurement operations, and "expectation bias" (e.g., seeing improvements that do not exist). Furthermore, children may react to the observers, so their behaviors are not representative. Validity is also a potential problem that is often overlooked. Alternative measures of target behaviors may help in establishing validity (Kent and Foster, 1977).

It may be helpful for those planning intervention strategies to assess potential reinforcers for children. A number of techniques are discussed in Mash and Terdal (1976). Keat (1979) also describes a "Reward Survey," on which the child indicates the degree of preference for a wide range of activities, such as eating, music, reading, and games.

As discussed in Chapter Three, the assessment of covert or private phenomena must take place through self-observation and recording. Thoughts, feelings, sensations, as well as controlling conditions may all be targets for self-monitoring. Bellack and Schwartz (1976) suggest interviewing "combined with imaginal role play" as the most effective assessment approaches for self-control procedures. They include four target areas:

1. *Stimulus control:* Self-generated environmental modifications....[as with]...response prevention....[or the]....restriction of the form or circumstances in which the target behaviors occur.
2. *Self-monitoring:* [Requiring an]...awareness of the environment and one's own behavior.
3. *Self-evaluation:* Comparing performance with some criterion in order to determine the adequacy of the response.
4. *Self-reinforcement:* [including self-reward, self-punishment or refrainment from reinforcement]. (pp. 128-138)

In public schools, behavioral rating scales may serve as important adjuncts to observational data. They are versatile and easy to use, although interpretations should be cautious. Behavior rating scales can be used in the following ways: (1) to help identify target behaviors; (2) to contrast significant behaviors across situations or sets of perceptions (e.g., home-school, between teachers, between parents); (3) to document perceptions of treatment outcomes as an aid in program evaluation; and (4) to help set priorities for target behaviors and to confirm observations. Also, behavior rating scales can be useful as teaching and consultation devices with parents and teachers.

There are many rating scales from which to choose. A sample would include the Burks' Behavior Rating Scales (Burks, 1977), the Walker Problem Behavior Identification Checklist (Walker, 1976), and the Devereaux Child Behavior Rating Scales.

The Burks' Behavior Rating Scale for pre-school and kindergarten children (ages 3-6) is a representative instrument that can be used for the above purposes. (Another scale is available for grades 1 through 9). The stated purpose is "to gauge the severity of negative symptoms as seen by outside persons-ordinarily teachers or parents" (p. 5). Behaviors that are unusual or infrequently observed are included. The scale was standardized on 127 preschoolers and 337 kindergarteners. Test-retest correlations were approximately .70 for 84 kindergarten children rated twice over a ten day period. Extensive validity information is lacking in the manual, but in actual use the specific questions seem to have merit for screening and for identifying target areas.

The Walker Problem Behavior Identification Checklist (Walker, 1976) has fewer items (50) and is limited to grades four through six. Test-retest reliability was .80 over a three week period, but ranged from .43 to .96 for individual teachers. Limited validity information (e.g., content, contrasted groups), is offered in the manual. Scaled scores in five areas are provided: Acting-out; Withdrawal; Distractibility; Disturbed Peer Relations; and Immaturity.

The Devereaux Scales have three separate forms: for adolescents (Spivack, Haimes, and Spotts, 1967); for elementary school children (Spivack and Swift, 1967); and for emotionally disturbed and mentally retarded children (Spivack and Spotts, 1966). The elementary rating scale will be briefly described. Behaviors measured include: Classroom Disturbance (e.g., behavior requiring reprimands); Impatience (e.g., unwillingness to go back over the work prior to handing in); External Blame (e.g., complaining that the teacher doesn't help enough); External Reliance (e.g., seeing how other children are doing something before starting); Comprehension; Inattentive-Withdrawn; Irrelevant-Responsiveness (e.g., giving answers unrelated to questions); Creative Initiative (contributing to classroom discussion); Need for closeness to the teacher; and other miscellaneous items. Normative data were obtained from 13 schools in one district. Thirty-two kindergarten through sixth grade teachers rated 809 children. Ages, IQ scores, and grade levels of children in the sample are given. The groups were relatively heterogeneous. Eighty-eight children included in the standardization sample were black, although the manual does not allow for ethnic comparisons. The median test-retest correlation for individual factors was .87 (n = 128, one week interval). Little validity information is reported in the manual.

Ecological Techniques. Although interviews, observations, self report inventories, and rating scales may all be used from an ecological perspective, several standardized techniques have been designed specifically as "ecological approaches." Brown and Hammill (1978) have developed the Behavior Rating Profile (BRP), measuring six components across home and school ecologies: The Student Rating Scales (home, school, and peer), The Teacher Rating Scale, The Parent Rating Scale, and a Sociogram. All but the last are checklists. The scales may be used independently. The authors describe the uses of the BRP as follows: (a) to identify emotionally disturbed, behavior disordered or learning disabled children; (b) to estimate the "degree" of "deviance" as perceived by different individuals; and (c) to compare perceptions of behaviors in different settings.

The standardization involved 1362 children (ages 6 to 13), 645 teachers and 847 parents in 11 states. They were not systematically selected (although children in special education were excluded). Parents are described in terms of occupation, education level, and urban vs. suburban residence. Minority representation was not identified. The reliability (internal consistency) was found to be moderate to high (.74 – .97). Three types of validity were studied. Concurrent validity was reported by correlations with other major behavior rating scales. The results demonstrate significant relationships, as expected. Construct validity was studied by noting intercorrelations among subtests, and correlations between "ecologically paired scales" as, for example, student and parent perceptions of home behavior. The relationships were moderate to high. Diagnostic validity was studied by analyzing differences between groups of children with different degrees of problem behavior. The results were interesting. Four groups (normal, disturbed-ED, learning disabled-LD, institutionalized) were studied:

1. Normal children were perceived to exhibit appreciably fewer behavior problems [in all settings].
2. Institutionalized emotionally disturbed children were perceived to exhibit appreciably more behavior problems than the public school handicapped children.
3. Though teachers and parents [rated public school ED and LD children similarly]...these children saw themselves to be quite different.... The LD children....rated their home behavior higher....than did the ED children. At school the ED children rated their behavior higher (better).
4. [For all children]..., (a) parents...rated their children lower than teachers and the children themselves, (b) teachers...rated their students higher than parents, though lower than the children's self-ratings, and (c) students...rated themselves better than parents or teachers. (p. 17)

As the authors note, further validity studies are needed. Some problems can be raised about the techniques employed. For example, with the sociogram, potential users may be concerned about the ethics and possible negative outcomes of asking children "whom they would most and least like as a friend." Also, the scoring system may disallow making the best choice for an intervention. For example, a child with two acceptances and twelve rejections is given a lower score than a child with zero acceptances and eight rejections, but the second child may be experiencing greater isolation. Also the use of rating scales often requires an item by item analysis so that the test user becomes aware of specific concerns. Even so, the general assessment approaches are valuable for psychologists.

Moos, Insel, and Humphrey (1974) have developed the Family Environment Scale (FES). Although described as a research instrument, the scale may have clinical utility in certain circumstances. The FES was developed to assess "the social climates of all types of families":

> It focuses on the measurement and description of the interpersonal relationships among family members, on the directions of personal growth which are emphasized in the family, and on the basic organizational structure of the family. (p. 3)

The uses are described as follows: "to derive detailed descriptions of the social environments of families, to compare parent and child perceptions, to assess changes in family environments over time and to compare different families'' (p. 9). Ninety true/false questions cover three major dimensions, including Relationships (Cohesion, Expressiveness, Conflict), Personal Growth (Achievement Orientation, Intellectual-Cultural Orientation, Active-Recreational Orientation, Moral-Religious), and System Maintenance (Organization and Control).

Normative data are limited. The sample included 285 families (three through seven or more family members). Most were from middle and upper middle SES levels, although some families were included from lower and lower-middle groups (not differentiable from the normative information). Means and standard deviations for the ten subscales are included. The internal consistencies of the scales were found to be moderate (from .64 to .79). Test-retest reliability (n = 47) was also moderate for individual scales (from .73 to .86). Of interest is the possibility of determining a Family Incongruence Score which describes "how closely. . .family members. . .agree on the characteristics of the family's social milieu" (p. 7). Recent research has shown a relationship between children's perceptions of family environments and classroom behavior (Murdock, 1979), but further research is needed. Because of ethical concerns involving invasion of privacy, the BRP and FES procedures should be explained to parents prior to use.

One final ecological approach will be briefly described. Wahler, House, and Stambaugh (1976) have developed an assessment system for children described as "incorrigible" (ages 4 to 14). The disturbed behaviors of the children are categorized in the following ways: (1) rule breaking; (2) behavior deficiencies (e.g., autism, retardation, schizophrenia); or (3) unusual behaviors (e.g., hand flapping, head banging). Wahler and his coauthors have developed interview and observation techniques, and a behavior coding system. The categories include the child's important social environments (home and school settings) over five classes of behavior: compliance-opposition; autistic; play; work; and social. Their manual may be of interest to psychologists responsible for developing programs for severely disturbed children.

Traditional psychological tests. Having outlined the numerous concerns relating to the use of personality tests, a serious question arises about when they should be used. Some tests are relatively modern and have been carefully researched. When compared to interview and observation techniques, a standardized test may take little time to administer and score on an individual basis. Tests, subscales, and individual items may aid in problem detection, problem clarification, estimating the severity of a problem, and in broadening the information base about the child in circumstances where elaboration seems necessary. Well researched tests allow for the possibility of normative comparisons. Tests are simply another *method* of personality assessment. Sloves, *et al.* (1979) suggest one safeguard. When following the problem-solving model, decisions about assessment methods are made after the generation of potentially relevant hypotheses about the client's behavior. Weiner (1972) asserts that formal assessment devices should be used when diagnostic questions cannot be answered through the use of other methods.

The Personality Inventory for Children (PIC) (Wirt, Lachar, Klinedinst, and Seat, 1977) has a number of features that make it an important test for school psychologists to know about. The manual, however, requires extensive study and some of the individual subscales (e.g., psychosis) could be potentially abused.

First, it is *not* a self-report measure. Parents respond to true or false questions (600) about their child's behavior, attitudes, and family relationships. Separate forms are provided for boys and girls, ages 6 to 16. Of interest, due to the paucity of instruments for preschoolers, are norms for children from ages 3 to 5, although they are less stable than for older children.

The PIC has three validity scales, an Adjustment Scale (to provide criteria for children in need of further psychological evaluation), and twelve clinical scales (Achievement, Intellectual Screening, Development, Somatic Concerns, Depression, Family Relations, Delinquency, Withdrawal, Anxiety, Psychosis, and Hyperactivity, and Social Skills). A number of supplemental scales are also included (i.e., Aggression, Cerebral Dysfunction, Delinquency Prediction, Introversion-Extraversion, and Learning Disability Prediction, among others). One of the major uses would be to pinpoint the most significant child-related concerns of the respondent (parent) making a referral.

The standardization sample was comprised of 2390 children. The validity of each scale is presented separately. For example, in studying the Adjustment Scale, 600 protocols from normal boys (7-12 years of age) were contrasted to 200 test protocols from "maladjusted boys" obtained from 14 psychiatric centers. Each child in the second group had received a formal diagnosis "indicative of emotional disturbance." Through the use of item criteria analysis, a final cutoff score correctly classified 86.2% of the normal sample and 88.5% of the maladjusted sample. Test-retest reliability averaged .86 in three separate experiments. The test should be used very cautiously. When scales are elevated, an item by item analysis, interviews, and observations of the behaviors represented by the items, may preclude the incorrect assignment of the labels associated with the scales. Knowledge about low scale scores is limited. Users should pay close attention to more recent research on the PIC (e.g., Lachar and Gdowski, 1979).

Two other major scales of interest, both self-report measures, are the California Psychological Inventory-CPI (Gough, 1975) and the Children's Personality Questionnaire-CPQ (Porter and Cattell, 1975). They have been recently reviewed in Buros (1978).

The CPI addresses personality characteristics "important for social living and social interaction." Eighteen scales are distributed between four classes of measures: (1) Poise, Ascendancy, Self-Assurance, and Interpersonal Adequacy; (2) Socialization, Responsibility, Intrapersonal Values, and Character; (3) Achievement Potential and Intellectual Efficiency; and

(4) Measures of Intellectual and Interest Modes. The CPI has been used in research with groups of persons from age 12 and upward. Test-retest correlations of subscales have ranged from low to moderately high (e.g., from .38 to .87). Validity studies of the scale are numerous, and are presented for each subtest through separate, cross-validated research studies. For example, on the Dominance subtest, correlations were obtained between the scale and (1) staff ratings of dominance for medical school applicants (r = .48), (2) staff ratings of dominance in a study of military officers (r = .40), and (3) nominations by high school principals of "most" and "least" dominant students (groups were significantly different at the .01 level). The test has been given to many thousands of persons and a large amount of research has been accumulated. Anastasi (1976) describes the CPI as "one of the best personality inventories currently available" (p. 505). Those seriously interested in the instrument will find the handbook by Megargee (1972) useful.

Projective techniques. Projective techniques are so diverse that they defy simple characterization. Anastasi (1976) notes that the "distinguishing feature" of the techniques is that they are "unstructured" and permit "an almost unlimited variety of possible responses"(p. 558). Rabin (1968) provides a good overview in this area. Several techniques will be described that are almost certain to be maintained in the assessment repertoire of many school psychologists for a long while. They can be used for building rapport, for clarifying aspects of affect as well as behavior, and for generating hypotheses. Continued experimental and creative use of projective-like techniques in individual application is advocated (e.g., Bailey and Green, 1977; Ellett and Bersoff, 1976; Feffer and Jehelka, 1968; Fulkerson, 1965; Meichenbaum, 1977; Ritzer, Sharkey, and Chudy, 1980; and Winter, Ferreira and Olsen, 1965).

The Thematic Apperception Test (Murray, 1943) includes a number of stimulus cards that can be used or adapted to Story Telling Methods. Many derivations have been published. The Education Apperception Test (Thompson and Sones, 1973) provides eighteen pictures that would possibly elicit themes related to a "child's perception of school and the educative process." The pictures are dated, but may serve to expand the range of stimulus situations provided by the TAT. The same may be true of the School Apperception Method (Solomon and Starr, 1968), Symonds Picture-story Test (Symonds, 1948) and the Children's Apperception Test-Human Figures (Bellak and Bellak, 1965). Traditional instructions vary considerably, although typical instructions include reference to the following points: a description of the actions in the pictures, thoughts and feelings, and the outcome(s) of the stories. Interpretations frequently refer to (1) the main theme, (2) the needs of the "hero," (3) the perception of the environment, (4) conflicts, and (5) defenses.

Another category of projectives that are often used with children are drawing techniques. Koppitz (1968) suggests that Human Figure Drawings may reflect a child's level of development...interpersonal relationships, ...attitudes toward himself and toward significant others in his life...attitudes toward life's stresses...and fears and anxieties. (p.3)

Koppitz has analyzed signs indicative of developmental level, emotional and organic problems.

Burns and Kaufman (1972) describe the Kinetic Family Drawing technique. The child is instructed to draw a picture of everyone in their family, emphasizing actions. One modification would be to ask children to draw a picture of their family "doing something together." Reynolds (1978) provides an overview of interpretative methods for the Kinetic Family Drawing (KFD) technique. McPhee and Wegner (1976) describe an empirical study (with 102 emotionally disturbed children) with significant differences apparent in KFD styles, but contradictory of Burns and Kaufman (1972). Differences in style did not seem to be a "defensive component" for emotionally disturbed children, as suggested by Burns and Kaufman. Better adjusted children spent more time and effort on their drawings.

Sentence completion techniques are another popular assessment method. Sentence stems (e.g., I dislike....; My favorite daydream is...; My greatest worry...) can be designed to "elicit responses relevant to the personality domain under investigation" (Anastasi, 1976, p. 571). Rotter (1950) standardized an incomplete sentence form for high school students.

Summary

The assessment of personal and social functioning is an important, but rapidly changing and diverse area of multifactored assessment. Problems associated with the assessment of minorities were briefly discussed. Behavior diagnosis was presented as a major framework, with a corresponding emphasis on interview and observation techniques. The possible utility of psychosocial and cognitive constructs and traditional personality assessment techniques were also considered.

Cognitive and Intellectual Functioning

The use of intelligence tests continues to be controversial. As reviewed in the second chapter, concerns relate to theoretical and measurement problems, as well as the issues associated with the social outcomes of test usage. Despite the concerns and criticisms, it is highly likely that psychologists will continue to use intelligence tests for a number of purposes.

This section has the following plan. First, in response to the questions raised about the value and further use of intelligence tests, reasons for their continued use will be outlined. The Stanford-Binet (Binet) will be introduced and the Wechsler Intelligence Scale for Children (WISC-R) will be described in more detail. Although other scales appear promising and have received positive reviews (e.g., The McCarthy Scales of Children's

Abilities; the Columbia Mental Maturity Scale), most use established tests, such as the WISC-R, or Binet, for diagnostic purposes. In the final chapter, on low incidence assessment, specialized techniques involving the assessment of a full range of skills for severely handicapped persons will be discussed.

Why Use Intelligence Tests?

Kaufman (1979) gives the arguments in defense of intelligence tests, especially the WISC-R. A great number of psychologists would agree with Kaufman's analysis that, although "far from ideal," current intelligence tests are nevertheless still valuable for cognitive assessment (p. 9). Especially with respect to nonbiased, multifactored assessment, psychologists have the responsibility "to be 'better'" than the available tests (Kaufman, 1979). One major reason for using intelligence tests is that they are "known quantities": they have been included in a great number of research studies in the fields of psychology, education, and neuropsychology (p. 9). Clarizio (1979) and Sattler (1974), among others, also review the pros and cons of intelligence testing. A number of studies demonstrate that tests do predict school achievement "effectively" for groups of minority and exceptional children, as well as for other children. Also, individually administered intelligence tests yield opportunities for a variety of observations of a child's functioning, allowing for the generation of hypotheses about psychological processes and skills related to school success. In a global way, intelligence tests may be used to evaluate the degree of support a child might require in designing a special program. The major point is that the IQs should not be used in a rigid manner, independent of other sources of information for classification purposes.

Kaufman (1979) emphasizes that the important role of the examiner is to generate hypotheses from the child's test performance. These results, along with the information obtained by other tests and assessment procedures required by nonbiased multifactored assessment, should attempt to explain low scores and patterns of performance which may be related to learning or behavior problems. Test information may assist with the formation of hypotheses about "learning style," and appropriate "learning environments" for a child. Test sessions create many opportunities to observe a variety of problem solving behaviors and motivational or personality factors across a broad sample of tasks. Test observations also allow inferences to be drawn about the significance of background information (e.g., reason for referral, classroom observations, social-cultural variables), with respect to test performance.

Another area of support for the tests may be somewhat surprising in light of the emotionally charged issues related to the assessment of intelligence with minority group members. As Kaufman (1979) notes, "whatever is being measured...is at least being assessed accurately" (p. 10). This is evidenced by the relatively low test error estimated for the major intelligence scales.

A number of researchers have reported findings indicating that IQ tests are psychometrically sound and that they do provide important information predictive of educational achievement for children of varying cultural groups. Studies exploring the construct validity, and other statistical attributes, of the WISC-R with children from different minority backgrounds, support the interpretations of the major dimensions associated with intelligence tests (e.g., Dean, 1980; Gutkin and Reynolds, 1980; Reschley, 1978; Reschly and Reschly, 1979; Reynolds and Gutkin, in press; and Sandoval, 1979). Sattler (1974) also discusses earlier studies concerned with the validity of IQ tests with ethnic minority groups. Reynolds and Gutkin (in press) examined the predictive validity of the WISC-R for white and Chicano children referred for psychological services and found an absence of bias. Similarly, Reschly and Sabers (1979) explored the relationship between the WISC-R and achievement for white, black, Chicano, and Native American Papago children providing further evidence of a lack of bias in predicting achievement test scores. In many studies using a regression analysis, criterion scores (achievement tests) were underpredicted for white children.

However, varying views exist. Oakland and Feigenbaum (1979) found that item difficulty varied according to SES, ethnicity, and urban acculturation, among other variables. They suggest that evidence for test bias is "mixed." Bias was not found in terms of the construct of intelligence as measured by the test, but was to a small degree evident in the prediction of reading scores (but not math). Sandoval (1979) points out that the *patterns of errors* are similar with children of different ethnic backgrounds. His findings did not support the hypothesis of specific items with radically different difficulty levels for ethnic groups, but do suggest that "general factors" relating to the test as a whole contribute to mean score differences between groups. He found that "a large number of items just slightly more difficult for the minority group children spread throughout the entire test" are responsible for differences (p. 925). There were 80 out of 176 items (45%) more difficult for blacks than whites and 76 (43%) more difficult for Mexican Americans. Fifty-nine of the items were more difficult for both groups. Sandoval argues that evidence for test bias with the WISC-R is not present with respect to how children from different ethnic groups respond to specific items.

In summary, the constructs measured by intelligence tests, predictive of school achievement for white, minority, and handicapped children, may require further study and elaboration rather than abandonment. As Reynolds and Gutkin (in press) note, many other studies of bias, using a variety of criterion measures, must be accomplished prior to concluding that a measure is free of bias. Also, other definitions of bias, as noted in Chapter Two, need to also be explored. Reschly (1979) emphasizes the need to study the social consequences of test usage, in terms of sources of bias, even though it appears that conventional tests predict academic achievement about equally well for groups studied thus far. Although test bias is discussed in Chapter Two, Reschly's appraisal of the "ultimate criteria" for evaluating test bias warrants reiteration: "test use. . . [should lead] to expanded, not diminished, opportunities and competencies for children" (p. 223).

The Stanford-Binet

The Stanford-Binet (Terman and Merrill, 1973), as noted in Chapter Two, has been widely recognized as the "grandfather" of intelligence tests. Sattler (1974) gives extensive treatment of the development, administration, and interpretation of the Binet. Especially helpful is the listing of the numerous validity studies with the Binet, since this information is not provided in the manual. Salvia and Ysseldyke (1978) also provide a critical review. The current edition is based on the earlier work of Terman (1916), who provided the major revision of Binet's original scales in this country. The last revision (1972), however, is severely limited in contrast to the recent revision of the Wechsler Intelligence Scale for Children (1974). Many changes are clearly necessary (Waddell, 1980). Except for testing young children, and children at "the extreme ranges of intelligence," the Binet will probably not be the instrument of choice for most practitioners (e.g., Evans and Richmond, 1976).

The Stanford-Binet requires a trained examiner (psychologist) and involves a clinical interview that allows for the observation of a person's work habits, problem solving approaches, activity level, self-confidence, persistence, and other personality characteristics (Anastasi, 1976). The content of the test uses a wide variety of question formats. Manipulative items are included for young children. At the youngest age levels (the scale starts at the two year level and continues through to adult levels), eye-hand coordination, perceptual processes, and the ability to follow directions are measured by such tasks as building towers with small blocks, stringing beads, comparing the sizes of objects or pictures of objects, matching geometric shapes, repeating digits, answering vocabulary questions, and identifying familiar objects. At older age levels, there is a greater reliance on such skills as expressive vocabulary, word analogies, abstract thinking, and problem solving. The types of questions vary with age level and a person is tested only over appropriate items, not over the complete scale.

Although widely used, the recent revision of the Binet has been criticized for several reasons. Except for the first age levels for preschool children (characterized by diverse tests), skills involving verbal and rote memory are overemphasized. Information is lacking in regard to the representation of minorities in the standardization sample and only one final score is used in referring to the complexity of a child's abilities. Sattler (1974) discusses several approaches involving the analysis of patterns of scores for individual children (scatter analysis). However, the reliability, validity and utility of such systems are questionable. His own approach (Binetgram) involves the classification of the questions and tasks into the following categories: language; memory; conceptual thinking; reasoning;

numerical reasoning; visual-motor; and social intelligence. The scale was not designed to be used in this manner and items measuring the above dimensions appear haphazardly throughout the scale disallowing straightforward interpretations.

The WISC-R

The Wechsler Intelligence Scale for Children-Revised (WISC-R) is used for children from ages 6 years to 16 years 11 months (Wechsler, 1974). (Other Wechsler scales are available for preschool children and adults). The WISC-R is divided into two subscales, *Verbal* and *Performance,* each consisting of the following subtests.

Verbal	Performance
1. Information	2. Picture Completion
3. Similarities	4. Picture Arrangement
5. Arithmetic	6. Block Design
7. Vocabulary	8. Object Assembly
9. Comprehension	10. Coding
*Digit Span (Supplementary)	*Mazes (Supplementary)

Standardization was based on 2,200 children, using six stratification variables (age, sex, race, geographic region, occupation of the head of household, and urban-rural) following the 1970 census. The variable of race involves only the classification of a child as white or non-white, although blacks, American Indians, Orientals, Puerto Ricans, and Chicanos were included. The total sample included 330 non-whites, of which 92.4% were black. The reliability of the scale is good; the test-retest correlation for the Full Scale IQ was .95 for a study reported in the manual.

The WISC-R subtests. To better understand the abilities tapped by the WISC-R and similar scales, a brief description, examples of questions, and comments regarding interpretation of the subtests are given below. Booklets by Cutrona (1976) and Jacobson and Kovalinsky (1976) may be helpful in generating hypotheses and thinking about possible intervention techniques, although the information is not empirically based. Kaufman's recent book (1979) is critically important for users of the WISC-R and will be referred to often. It provides a synthesis of the major research findings with the WISC-R.

As with other types of tests measuring complex abilities, each subtest requires a number of skills, so that many of the subtests overlap. Kaufman (1979, pp. 102-109) lists the abilities for each subtest that are shared with other subtests, and the ones that seem to be generally unrelated to, or not assessed by, other subtests. In the following discussion, the abilities described as "unique" by Kaufman have been included. Some have been modified or expanded slightly. These interpretations are based partially upon factor analytic techniques and are also derived from conventional sources in the literature (Kaufman, 1979).

INFORMATION. This subtest includes specific questions, in increasing order of difficulty, such as "How many feet do you have?,"

"How many months in a year?," "Why does wood float on water?" The "unique ability" is the person's "range of general factual knowledge" in addition to general skills involving verbal comprehension.

SIMILARITIES. By asking questions such as "In what way are potatoes and apples alike?" and "In what way are a guitar and a piano alike?," this subtest attempts to measure the level of a child's understanding of relationships. The "unique ability" measured by this subtest is "logical abstractive (categorical) thinking," along with the requirement of general verbal comprehension.

ARITHMETIC. The questions on this subtest range from simple counting to more complex questions such as: "Three boys had 51 pennies and they divided them equally among themselves. How many did each boy receive?"; "If a taxi charges 25 cents for the first ½ mile, and 10 cents for each ½ mile after that, what would be the fare for a three mile trip?" This subtest requires listening skills and memory, but attempts to measure a child's understanding of numerical concepts, ability to apply an appropriate process, and to use computation skills when the problem is verbally presented. Kaufman identifies the "unique ability" as "computational skill."

VOCABULARY. Verbal expressive ability is required. The child is asked to define words at increasing levels of difficulty. Differential scoring allows for crediting more complete responses that demonstrate a higher level of conceptual thinking. The "unique abilities" are "language development and word knowledge."

COMPREHENSION. Questions similar to "Why is it important for cars to have horns?" or "What would you do if you were sent to the store to buy toothpaste and the person in the store said they didn't have any more?" attempt to measure the child's ability to apply judgement and reasoning when presented with social situations. The "unique abilities" may be considered to be "the demonstration of practical information" and "evaluation and use of past experience."

DIGIT SPAN. The child is asked to repeat a series of digits following the one-by-one presentation of the digits at a one per second rate. The procedure is repeated with a second series of digits recalled in reverse order. This subtest is considered to be a measure of attention, auditory reception, and short-term memory. An example would be as follows: "Please listen to the following numbers and when I am finished I want you to say them back to me—5614. The "unique ability" is "short-term memory (auditory)."

PICTURE COMPLETION. A series of drawings representing familiar items, or pictures of people, are presented, and the child is asked to identify an important part of the picture that was left out. This subtest requires visual attention, and attempts to measure a child's environmental awareness, as demonstrated by the ability to recognize missing details in pictures. The "unique abilities" are "visual alertness" and "visual recognition and identification (long-term visual memory)."

PICTURE ARRANGEMENT. A series of pictures similar to comic strips (without printed words) are presented to the child in a mixed-up order and the child is told that, if they are put in the correct order, they will make a sensible story. Logical reasoning and organization skills relating to social situations are tapped. Bonus points are awarded for rapid performance. The "unique abilities" are the "anticipation of consequences" and "temporal sequencing and time concepts."

BLOCK DESIGN. Blocks with red, white, and half-red/half-white sides are presented and the child is asked to form patterns, first from a model the examiner prepares, and then from pictures. Bonus points are given for a rapid performance. This subtest is thought to assess visual-motor problem solving ability by requiring the child to reproduce the geometric designs. Three "unique abilities" are potentially tapped: (1) "analysis of whole into component parts"; (2) "nonverbal concept formation"; and (3) "spatial visualization."

OBJECT ASSEMBLY. This subtest resembles a series of jigsaw puzzles of increasing difficulty and attempts to measure the child's ability to organize parts into meaningful wholes. It is also a timed test, yielding bonus points for rapid performances. Three "unique abilities" are potentially tapped: (1) "ability to benefit from sensory-motor feedback"; (2) "anticipation of relationships among parts"; and (3) "flexibility."

CODING. A paper and pencil copying test, the child is required to match geometric symbols with a specific numeral or shape provided in a key. Following instructions and a practice exercise, the child must copy the symbol associated with the numeral or shape (for younger children). Time-limited conditions are used. This subtest attempts to measure short-term memory and fine motor speed and coordination. Four "unique abilities" are noted: (1) "ability to follow directions"; (2) "clerical speed and accuracy"; (3) "psychomotor speed"; and (4) "short-term memory (visual)."

MAZES. Also a paper and pencil task, problem solving and visual motor coordination are required. The mazes are shown to the child (demonstrated for younger children). Blind alleys and "walls" are pointed out prior to the child's attempt. A bonus for a rapid performance is awarded. The "unique abilities" are "following a visual pattern" and "foresight."

Interpretation of Results. Although a complete discussion of the interpretation of intelligence tests, particularly the WISC-R, is beyond the scope of this book, a few comments are in order. Kaufman's work (1975, 1979) is of particular importance.

Overall, interpretation involves deriving meaning from a total score (Full Scale Score), a Verbal Score, a Performance Score, individual subtest scores, and patterns of scores. All three major scales have a mean of 100 and a standard deviation of 15, thus adding to the popularity of the test for researchers as well as practitioners. In addition, each subtest (e.g.,

Information, Vocabulary, Block Design, etc.) yields a scaled score with a mean of 10 and a standard deviation of 3, which permits comparable interpretations. The Full Scale Score supports the construct of general or "global" ability because, even though the test is comprised of separate subtests, a common factor is evident, as noted by the correlations between subtests and the total score on the test. Vocabulary, Information, Similarities, Block Designs, and Comprehension are the subtests with the highest correlations with the Full Scale Score (Wechsler, 1974). The Full Scale Score should not be confused with "a theoretical construct underlying human intellect," but as an aspect of the test itself. The "so-called g factor" still has practical significance, "but it should be stripped of the almost magical powers that are sometimes attributed to it" (Kaufman, 1979, p. 110). Kaufman provides important warnings in regard to the interpretation of the Full Scale IQ:

> Large V-P IQ differences, numerous fluctuations in the scaled-score profile, or inferred relationships between test scores and extraneous variables (e.g., fatigue, anxiety, subcultural background) greatly diminish the importance of the Full Scale IQ as an index of the child's level of intelligence. (p. 21)

The division of the WISC-R (and other Wechsler Scales) into Verbal and Performance Scales allows additional flexibility in interpretation. The division has been generally upheld, although, for some children, a three factor approach may be meaningful. As reported in Kaufman (1979), empirical investigations using factor-analytic procedures identified three factors as follows.

Factor I: Verbal Comprehension
Information
Similarities
Vocabulary
Comprehension

Factor II: Perceptual Organization
Picture Completion
Picture Arrangement
Block Design
Object Assembly
Mazes

Factor III: Freedom from Distractibility
Arithmetic
Digit Span
Coding

Kaufman (1979) points out the close resemblance of the first two factors to Wechsler's Verbal and Performance Scales and stresses the following points involving interpretation:

The robust Verbal Comprehension and Perceptual Organization factors for all age groups and for a variety of supplementary samples of exceptional and minority-group children indicate that the Verbal and Performance IQs reflect a child's performance on real and meaningful dimensions of mental ability. Thus, the discrepancy between these IQs may well suggest important differences in the child's learning style and ability to handle different types of stimuli (p. 23).

The third factor, Freedom from Distractibility, is difficult to interpret. It has not always held up with certain populations of children (e.g., Gutkin and Reynolds, 1980). However, Reschly and Reschly (1979) surprisingly found (across three non-Anglo sociocultural groups) that the Freedom from Distractibility factor correlated higher with reading achievement test scores than did the Perceptual Organization factor. The Verbal Comprehension factor had the highest correlation with reading scores, as expected, similar to the Full Scale IQ. The third factor may be related to anxiety, distractibility, or attention. A low score may be related to the skills involved with the task (numerical problem solving, memory, or perceptual-motor speed), but may indicate "behavioral interference." The child's overall performance might be considered as a minimal estimate of intellectual functioning when it seems appropriate to interpret deficits in the third factor for behavioral reasons (Kaufman, 1979). Kaufman points out that if the interpretation of the third factor, Freedom From Distractibility, is not reasonable, the Verbal and Performance IQs remain "excellent factor scores."

A third level of interpretation involves the skills measured by each subtest. By design, the subtests should measure unique abilities, in addition to contributing to the Full Scale and the Verbal and Performance Scores. Kaufman (1979) found that the following subtests could be interpreted in a relatively straightforward manner: Information, Arithmetic, Digit Span, Picture Arrangement, Block Design, Coding, and Mazes (p. 112). The Vocabulary, Picture Completion and Comprehension subtests require more caution. Similarities cannot be interpreted in an unambiguous manner at ages 9½ and above. Kaufman warns that the Object Assembly subtest may not allow a meaningful interpretation in many circumstances.

Clear interpretations of patterns of subtests associated with specific handicapping conditions (emotional disturbance, learning disabilities, mental retardation) have occupied researchers for many years. The best use of subtest analysis results from the generation of hypotheses that require validation through other assessment procedures (Piotrowski and Grubb, 1976). Gutkin (1979) found an absence of predictable scatter indices that would be helpful in determining "a formal diagnosis for special education students," similar to earlier investigations. Sattler (1974) presents a comprehensive review of research with the older WISC (1949).

Special Problems of Minorities

When a child is suspected of having a handicapping condition and is a member of a minority group, extreme caution is in order when traditional instruments like the Binet or WISC-R are used. The foundations for nonbiased assessment have already been discussed with respect to minority groups. There has been, and will continue to be, a search for "alternatives" to intelligence testing. Mercer (1979) argues for the inclusion of the WISC-R in the SOMPA as a Social Systems Measure for a number of reasons. The validity coefficients used in predicting classroom performance are statistically significant for minority groups. The WISC-R is reliable, and the construct validity is "sound" with respect to children with different ethnic backgrounds. She notes that the test appears psychometrically adequate with children of different ethnic groups. The test does not require reading, in contrast to many group IQ measures. The major difference is one of interpretation. Mercer proposes that the WISC-R measures School Functioning Level and can be used to find the Estimated Learning Potential (ELP), which allows the comparison of a child's performance on the WISC-R with those of children from similar sociocultural backgrounds. Inferences about future learning can then be made when the child's past learning opportunities are accounted for (Mercer, 1979).

As mentioned in Chapter Two, the major outcome of using the SOMPA, and interpreting the WISC-R as a social systems measure, is to declassify minority children. It is not a wholistic solution to the problem. Children will still have educational needs that have not been met in traditional programs. Conceptual problems of using IQ tests as measures of "potential" are still evident. The validity of the ELP is unproven. However, the interpretation of IQ tests has been modified drastically, an important outcome in and of itself.

In addition to global cultural influence, language differences may confound interpretations of test scores. Although problems exist with respect to the assessment of Spanish-speaking children, the difficulties are more recognizable, and can be attributed, in part, to general problems of bilingualism. Children must be assessed with instruments in their dominant language. Although not always the case, Kaufman (1979) points out that bilingual Spanish-speaking children with English as the second language, or children who learn both languages simultaneously, are expected to score higher on nonverbal portions of intelligence tests. The verbal scores are probably not the best predictors of academic performance "for Spanish-speaking youngsters in the early school grades" (p. 33). The term "verbal deficit" should be very cautiously applied to bilingual children, although the information obtained from the verbal scores can be used for educational planning (Kaufman, 1979). Problems associated with the understanding of the influence of black dialect have not been as clear, although Kaufman (1979) stresses that, by not knowing black dialect, psychologists may significantly influence obtained scores on the verbal scales.

The booklet by Hewitt and Massey (1969) may be helpful, although based on the older WISC (1949), in that it contains special sections on testing blacks and Spanish-speaking children. Hardy, Welcher, Mellits, and Kagan (1976) found that some inner-city children are penalized for providing reasonable replies for questions when they draw from their own frame of reference.

The Future of Intelligence Testing

While intelligence tests will continue to be widely used, changes are likely to be required in the placement of children, particularly minority children. The major approaches to prevent misclassification of children, in addition to legal safeguards, involve: (a) the use of other measures, including Adaptive Behavior; and (b) interpreting the IQ score as an indication of a child's current school functioning level, taking into account the child's cultural proximity to the American mainstream in terms of primary language and opportunities to learn the skills required by the tests. Overall, many psychologists would argue that intelligence tests have worked remarkably well when viewed as one to one and one-half hour samples of behavior.

Most psychologists recognize that present intelligence tests inadequately measure the full range of cognitive processes and that IQ tests have failed to grow conceptually with new developments in cognitive psychology and neuropsychology. Efforts like Kaufman's (1979) are commendable attempts to apply empirical approaches to existing measures. The responsibility of the psychologist to seek out and apply recent developments in cognitive psychology is an extremely challenging task. New measures will be probably developed, but they will be extremely costly and will take years of research before acceptance. Standardized psychometric approaches may always have inherent limitations as the need to flexibly account for variations in the processes necessary for performance becomes increasingly evident.

One technique currently being developed is the Kaufman Assessment Battery for Children (K-ABC) (Kaufman and Kaufman, 1981). The test represents a distinct break from the Binet and WISC-R, and similar scales, by focusing on processes rather than content. The test in its present form is comprised of two intelligence scales and one achievement scale. The intelligence scales assess abilities related to problem solving and information processing and are theoretically related to recent developments in neuropsychology and cognitive psychology (e.g., Das, Kirby, and Jarman, 1979). The first scale is defined by tasks measuring *sequential processing* whereby:

> Each task. . .presents a problem which must be solved by arranging the input in a sequential or serial order. Each idea is sensibly or temporally related to the preceding one, and the linear concept of time plays an essential role in the outcome. (Kaufman and Kaufman, 1981, p. 3)

The *simultaneous processing* problems "are usually spatial or analogic in nature. The input has to be integrated, and synthesized simultaneously, to produce the appropriate solution" (p. 4).

Although the Achievement Scale was intended to "assess factual knowledge and skills usually acquired in a school setting or through alertness to the environment" (p. 4), many of the tasks themselves are novel. For example, one subtest requires the identification of well-known persons and places through pictures. Reading comprehension requires the child to act out written statements.

Alternative assessment strategies (e.g., Budoff and Hamilton, 1976; Kratochwill and Severson, 1977; Sewell, 1979; Sewell and Severson, 1974) may eventually have more widespread acceptance. Building upon the earlier work of Budoff (e.g., Budoff and Friedman, 1964), Feuerstein (1970), and others, Sewell (1979) has re-emphasized "the need for assessment techniques that will provide additional diagnostic information related to intellectual modifiability, learning styles, and personality/ performance interaction" (p. 330). He found the achievement of middle-class children to be more predictable than that of lower-class blacks. Sewell suggests that "process-oriented assessment" may contribute to the understanding of the lower predictability of achievement for lower SES blacks. Earlier, Sewell and Severson (1974) found diagnostic teaching to be an effective predictor of achievement. Also, the development of additional creative procedures may help in assessing certain children. Piersel, Brody, and Kratochwill (1977) used a "desensitization" procedure that may be of interest in working with some minority children. Children viewed a brief videotape of another child in a testing situation. The model experienced a 60% success rate: "It was evident. . .that the model was sometimes wrong but that no negative consequences followed incorrect answers" (p. 1144). They concluded that "exposing children to an affectively warm and rewarding pretest vicarious experience seems to. . .improve test scores" (p. 1144).

The work of Feuerstein (1979, 1980), especially, is certain to focus attention to the inadequacies inherent in traditional psychometric approaches to assessment and to set the stage for the development of alternative procedures. Feuerstein argues that IQ tests have failed to differentiate between "capacity," "manifest level of functioning," and "efficiency" (1979, p. 29). Traditional measures cannot measure "capacity" and moreover confuse it with the person's "manifest level of functioning," the actual performance as measured by tests (p. 30). Functional or mental efficiency is not considered at all by conventional assessment procedures. Dynamic assessment, as illustrated by the Learning Potential Assessment Device, attempts to estimate cognitive modifiability by presenting the individual with a "focused learning experience" (p. 56). With respect to traditional psychometric approaches, changes are required at four foci: the structure of the tests themselves; the nature of examiner-examinee interaction in the testing situation; the goals and orientation of the testing process; and the interpretation of results. First, the test materials should emphasize tasks which maximize the outcomes of a direct teaching process and the corresponding transfer of skills to new situations. Second, the test situation must become remarkably different from the traditional

diagnostic evaluation. The role of the examiner, usually characterized as "neutral" or "indifferent," is changed into an "active, cooperative role" exemplified by the "teacher who is vitally concerned with the maximalization of the success of his pupil" (p. 102). The examiner directly intervenes in the testing situation through comments, explanations, and summarizations. The examiner may ask for repetitions, and may assist the child in anticipating difficulties. An active goal is to create "reflective insightful thinking in the child" (p. 102).

The third change requires a "shift from a product to a process orientation" (p. 120). The LPAD directs attention to the process by which the child or adolescent produced a particular answer. A cognitive map helps clarify the processes underlying deficient cognitive behavior. The model presented by Feuerstein includes seven parameters: content, modality, phase (i.e., input, elaboration, output), operations, level of complexity, level of abstraction, and efficiency (p. 123). Fourth, cognitive potential may be indicated by "peaks of performance" which may be quite dissimilar from usual or typical performance for a low functioning child. Often, with atypical children, the significance of such behaviors is minimized.

Consistent with the aforementioned development of alternative assessment strategies, the most significant change will probably not be through the development of new standardized measurement devices to improve the classification decisions of children (e.g., Resnick, 1979). Alternative measures will increase the predictability of achievement for certain children and will identify reversible areas of concern. More likely, the application of broad psychological principles will result in assessment strategies to assist with the development of workable interventions for children experiencing, or likely to experience, school learning problems.

Brown and French (1979) review developments based on the work of Vygotsky (1978), which they view as having important implications for the assessment of intelligence. Distinct parallels are evident with the work of Feuerstein, previously described, and the procedures of task analysis. Clinical assessment and corresponding test batteries can be developed based on Vygotsky's concept of the zone of proximal (or potential) development. Two developmental levels may be described. The first is the one tapped by traditional psychometric approaches, "mental functions. . . established as a result of. . .completed developmental cycles" (Vygotsky, 1978, p. 85). Typically, the examiner makes the assumption that skills "indicative of mental ability" are reflected only by what a child can do independent of assistance. Vygotsky theorized, however, that "what children can do with the assistance of others might be in some sense even more indicative of their mental development than what they can do alone" (p. 85). Therefore, a second level can also be described, the zone of proximal development, defined as

> the distance between the actual developmental level as determined by independent problem solving and the level of potential development as

determined through problem solving under adult guidance or in collaboration with more capable peers. (p. 86)

The zone of proximal development helps in understanding a child's learning potential. The focus is not only upon mastered processes, but also on "processes . . . in a state of formation" (p. 87). Vygotsky's work contains many educational implications. One striking proposition is that if instruction is based on normative data usually obtained in testing, then it will be oriented "toward developmental stages already completed" (p. 89). Vygotsky theorized "that the only 'good learning' is that which is in advance of development" (p. 89).

In summary, target areas for the future of cognitive assessment include: (a) the analysis of the basic psychological processes involved in learning for individual children; (b) the evaluation of learning environments; (c) the analysis of individual, social, and cultural determinants of learning; and (d) the evaluation of the outcomes of interventions.

Language and Communication Skills

The importance of assessing language problems is immediately apparent. Language, or the "use of symbolic speech," has the potential for affecting virtually every aspect of behavior.

With respect to nonbiased, multifactored assessment, theoretical and practical issues abound. With minority groups, especially blacks, one hypothesis has been that language usage has suffered through "deprivation," thus requiring extensive remedial efforts. The opposing point of view is that black English deserves due respect as a language and is no less a language system than standard English. While it is perhaps easier to understand the influence of bilingualism on test scores, as with children of Spanish-speaking backgrounds, actual assessment issues are complex. Naremore (1980) describes the problem in the following way:

Some Latino children enter school as monolingual Spanish speakers and must learn English as a second language in the school. Others enter school as monolingual English speakers, with perhaps some Spanish vocabulary, or some phonological interference, but without extensive knowledge of Spanish. Many others come to school with some knowledge of both Spanish and English, usually more of one than the other. (p. 194)

With handicapped persons, the assessment of both spoken language and other communication skills may require extensive and creative study. Sanders (1976) views communication as "adaptive behavior"; verbal language is only one of a number of possible systems. The adaptive view of communication has important consequences for the handicapped. For the deaf or hearing impaired, finger spelling and signing may be forms of adaptive communication. Alternative communication systems, not involving speech, are increasingly being seen as important in a wide range of handicapping conditions.

The major question is how to go about assessing language. Siegel and Broen (1976) comment: "Everyone knows what language is—everybody, that is, except for the psychologists, philosophers, linguists, and clinicians who must deal with it in formal and technical ways" (p. 75). Clark and Clark (1977) provide an extensive introduction to psycholinguistics. Other sources include: Menyuk (1977), a concise summary of theory and research; Hopper and Naremore (1973), a readable introduction to children's communications development; Morehead and Morehead (1976), a book describing normal and abnormal child language development; Nelson (1978, 1980), an expansive treatment of children's language; and Rosenthal and Zimmerman (1978), an updated analysis of cognition from the social learning viewpoint, containing valuable references to language. An excellent overall source is the recent book by Bloom and Lahey (1978). Wiig and Semel (1980) have introduced a comprehensive text oriented toward the learning disabled. Intervention strategies are elaborated upon. The volume edited by Lloyd (1976) is an important reference because of its broad view of communication, especially with regard to more severely handicapped persons. Chapters involving audiology and manual communications are included. A description of the assessment of language from an educational perspective is included in chapters found in Wallace and Larsen (1978) and Hammill and Bartel (1978). A recent issue of *School Psychology Digest* (7 (4), 1978) is devoted to language and communication and the culturally different child, problems with retarded children, and the use of nonvocal communication (e.g., sign and manual communication) with non-traditional populations (severely handicapped *hearing* individuals).

The plan of the present section is to outline assessment approaches, emphasizing the basic dimensions of verbal (spoken) language assessment. In addition, a test of written language assessment is included. Observational assessment, tests measuring language "correlates," and several language assessment techniques are described.

The Need for Different Assessment Approaches

Tests alone may not yield solutions to language and communicaton problems of children. Kretschmer and Kretschmer (1978) suggest the use of two different sources of data for a "comprehensive assessment of linguistic functioning": formal testing and observations of children in spontaneous communication settings.

> Unless formal tests are selected carefully, they may not tap the areas of linguistic or communicative performance intended. Considering only spontaneously generated language...may lead to inappropriate conclusions about a child's knowledge of language. (p. 144)

Sommers, Erdige, and Peterson (1978) found many tests thought to assess discrete language skills do not, in fact, measure specific abilities. Most are intercorrelated from a moderate to high degree, calling into question many of the assumptions of test authors. On the positive side, they note that tests may be clinically useful, or valuable in providing information about language processing variables. In considering specific tests, many problems persist with respect to reliability and validity, especially the validity of tests related to theoretical constructs in language assessment. For example, the Illinois Test of Psycholinguistic Ability (ITPA) has suffered criticism on many grounds; perhaps the most significant is that the constructs measured by the test are not consistent with current linguistic theory.

Another major concern with selecting language tests, not stressed as much with other assessment domains, is the "test response mode": Some tests require imitation, object manipulation, demonstration, identification of objects or pictures, the judgment of grammaticality, or the completion of linguistic units (Kretschmer and Kretschmer, 1978, p. 153). Bloom and Lahey (1978) also stress that individual tests must be selected for the specific information they provide about language functioning.

The Dimensions of Language Assessment

Bloom and Lahey (1978) define a language disorder as "a problem with learning or using the conventional system of signals used . . . as a code for representing ideas about the world for the purposes of communication" (pp. 340-341). Siegel and Broen (1976) refer to four communication dimensions often implicated in severe speech or language problems of children:

> 1) *Articulation* and mastery of the phonologic system . . . ;
> 2) understanding and use of *grammatical* structures; 3) understanding and use of . . . *vocabulary and concepts*; and (4) the functional or *interpersonal* uses of language. (p. 76)

The objectives of language assessment are threefold and include the determination of a language problem, the goals of a language program for a particular child, and the specific procedures for an intervention program (Bloom and Lahey, 1978). Bartel and Bryen (1978) propose the use of three considerations in deciding whether or not to consider a systematic language evaluation for a child:

> Does language usage or lack of it call unwanted attention to the speaker?
> Does the speaker appear to be concerned in any way about his inadequate communication ability?
> Are listeners unable to readily understand the child when he speaks?
> (p. 296)

Finally, in order for a spoken message to be acted upon, it must be heard. As basic as this seems, hearing problems in school-aged children both within regular and special classes are prevalent. Even a relatively minor problem can create distress and learning problems for a child. Detection is often not a straightforward and easy matter. An audiological examination would provide information about a hearing loss (see, for example, Fulton and Lloyd, 1975; Jaffe, 1977; and Martin, 1978). In addition to the awareness of sounds, the child must be able to discriminate between all of the complex variables of speech such as intensity and pitch associated with sounds, words, and phrases.

Special Problems and Issues Related to Language Assessment

The potential list of "special problems" is lengthy. Notable omissions from this section are topics related to non-speech communication (see Lloyd, 1976; Schiefelbusch, 1980; and Schiefelbusch and Lloyd, 1974), and further elaboration on pragmatics and interpersonal communication (e.g., Bates, 1976, and Siegel and Broen, 1976).

A frame of reference is provided by studies of speech development in normal children and by issues that arise from those studies, such as the relationship between speech imitation, comprehension, and production. Also, the practical problems associated with assessing the relationship between language, emotional development, cognition, and problem solving are directly related to multifactored assessment. One will note the extensive overlap in both content and format of the major measurement techniques in the areas of language, intelligence, and certain aspects of adaptive behavior. These three areas should be theoretically related to a significant degree.

One problem that has received considerable attention in the literature is the question of dialect differences between minority, or culturally different children and white, middle-class children. Many sources are available for those desiring additional information (e.g., Anastasiow and Hanes, 1976; Bartel, Grill and Bryen, 1973; Carter, 1977; Hopper and Naremore, 1973; Labov, 1970; Matluck and Mace, 1973; Naremore, 1980; and Samuda, 1975).

Both Menyuk (1977) and Bartel et al. (1973) say that the evidence regarding a deficit in communication competence between members of different cultural groups is, overall, unclear and difficult to research. Mussen, Conger, and Kagan (1974) hold the following opinion:

> A number of prominent...linguists have made meticulous records of the speech of black children in their homes and neighborhoods and have found no strong evidence that these children show any "verbal deficits" or inadequate language or learning ability. With his family and friends, the black child's language is rich and fluent....The language of ghetto black children is no less differentiated, complex, or logical than standard English. (pp. 262-263)

Naremore (1980) summarizes the major differences between black and standard English and phonological and grammatical interference points between Spanish and English. She believes that many of the major problems are not linguistic; the problems are best perceived more broadly in terms of attitudes involving the uses of language for purposes of communication. For example, bilingualism is often associated with some prestige for educated Americans, but usually not for the bilingual Latino (Naremore, 1980). Black English "is simply not that different from standard English" (Hopper and Naremore, 1973, p. 126).

Although many of the authors of tests described in the following section warn about limitations of their instruments with children having dialect differences (e.g., Lee, 1974; Newcomer and Hammill, 1977), the tests may be used in nontraditional ways to assist with educational programming. Naremore suggests that if a "dialect speaker" is accepted for speech or language training, the goal of the training should not be "to eradicate the dialect of the black child or the Spanish of the Latino child. Rather, it should present the child with useful alternatives for certain situations" (p. 214).

Language Assessment Techniques

References for specific language assessment techniques can be found in Bloom and Lahey (1978), Cicciarelli, Broen, and Siegel (1976), Irwin, Moore, and Rampp (1972) and Wiig and Semel, 1980. Several techniques will be described, including observation, testing, and speech sample analysis, that either through direct use or adaptation, may help clarify language problems. A general awareness of the available assessment techniques may help non-specialists with the referral process. One comprehensive assessment technique emphasizing an environmental approach will also be described. Certain tests such as the Boehm Test of Basic Concepts (Boehm, 1971) and the Slingerland Screening Test for Identifying Children with Specific Language Disability (Slingerland, 1970) cannot be considered "pure" language tests. The procedures they suggest, however, may be helpful in everyday informal assessment because of close parallels to educational tasks. The Reading Miscue Inventory, described in the section on Academic Assessment, can be considered in the same way. Many other instruments (e.g., intelligence tests, adaptive behavior scales) provide information about language functioning, especially evidence of language competence in different situations. There is a lack of emphasis in this section on the assessment of specific skills relating to phonetics (e.g., articulation, auditory perception, and discrimination). An illustrative test is the Goldman-Fristoe-Woodcock Auditory Skills Test Battery (Goldman, Fristoe, and Woodcock, 1976).

Observation. The importance of natural observation in language assessment can be attributed to two broad factors. First, natural observation provides a necesary context:

> Since language is a form of communication and essentially a social interaction, its use can only be described in a social context—ideally one that is representative of the child's usual interactions. (Bloom and Lahey, 1978, p. 315)

While noting the limitations of observational approaches, Dale (1978) suggests:

> There is something approaching a consensus that the child shows best what he knows when allowed in a familiar and unconstrained situation to express himself on a topic of his own choosing in a manner he favors. (p. 219)

A sampling of possible target areas for observation in a wide range of situations appropriate for young children has been adapted from Cohen and Stern (1978). Because of the descriptive and narrative style, the book may be of special interest to those who have not worked with young children.

The first observation is the manner in which the child interacts with the daily routines in the classroom. The following questions might be asked: Does the child need visual cues from other children after the teacher announces to the class that it is time for a usual activity? Do particular games or problem situations elicit anxiety or frustration as a reaction, as indicated by gestures, body posture, quality of the child's voice, and other mannerisms, or by withdrawal or avoidance reactions? Especially evident may be problems of socialization, basic concepts, or vocabulary (e.g., being "first" in line, language skills involved in games), and communication for the purpose of making one's needs known (e.g., bathroom, eating).

The second area is the child's use of materials. If playing with blocks, does the child know "on top of," "behind," "red," "large," or other vocabulary words, basic language concepts and grammatical structures similar to other children of the same age? How rich and descriptive is the child's vocabulary and use of structures when telling a story, or discussing a picture or photograph?

A third area involves peer and adult interactions. Are frequent repetitions of requests or instructions necessary, possibly implying hearing problems? Do misinterpretations occur? Do questions require rephrasing, thereby implying that vocabulary, basic concepts, syntax, or language structure are not properly understood? How are contacts between children made? (e.g., "What does the child say?" "How does the other child respond?")

Another area involves the dramatic play of children. Observing children when they assume various roles (e.g., father, mother, police officer, bus driver) may allow teachers and parents the opportunity to gauge the use of language for social and interpersonal purposes and for the expression of fantasy and creative thought.

In making observations, it is important to be able to define the particular stimulus for the child's reaction, the setting for the activity, and the range of behaviors elicited by the child. Also, through the use of observation techniques, appropriate contexts for spontaneous language samples will be made more evident.

While Cohen and Stern (1978) give an excellent description of overall targets for observations that yield opportunities for the development of hypotheses across a wide range of child development, Bloom and Lahey (1978) develop a more complete outline, involving the assessment of language through observations. Low structured observations are carried out in "settings that are familiar and comfortable and that involve as little manipulation of language behavior as possible" (p. 342). Description of current language behaviors in naturalistic settings would include:

> [The] amount of verbalization, intelligibility of speech, comprehension, words, length of utterances, completeness of sentences, variety of sentences, gestures, [and] manual signs. (adapted from Bloom and Lahey, 1978, p. 344)

In summary, the content of language, and the use of language involving objects, events, affect, relationships between objects, between people, and between people and objects, all may yield important observations regarding language and language usage (Bloom and Lahey, 1978).

Specific tests. The Boehm Test of Basic Concepts (Boehm, 1971) can be used as a criterion, or norm-referenced technique, to help determine whether a child in the primary grades has the basic vocabulary concepts prerequisite for academic success. Fifty concepts and language structures relating to space (left, right, top, next to), time (beginning, after) and quantity (few, every, equal), as well as other areas, are assessed. A set of pictures is shown to the child and the child is asked to mark the picture that illustrates the concept. Two forms of the test are available. It is most useful for kindergarten and first grade. Remedial procedures include fifteen teaching units, each developing a basic concept area (e.g., Top-Bottom, Near-Far, Forward-Backward) along with support materials (concept cards, duplicating masters, game cards, etc.) (Boehm, 1976).

The Slingerland Screening Tests for Identifying Children with Specific Language Disabilities (Slingerland, 1970) includes forms for preschool through elementary school children. Reliability and validity information are not provided. The tests, however, have "content" validity because they represent common tasks requiring mastery for successful school achievement. The subtests may suggest diagnostic procedures that could be used by teachers with greater ease on an informal basis. As with all educational tasks, the Slingerland requires skills from many areas to be integrated; it is not a "pure" test of any one area.

Two subtests (for elementary school children) involve simple copying (distance and close work). Problems with handwriting can be observed, a neglected, but often remediable problem of communication, especially with learning disabled children. One useful observation is whether or not the child is copying the word automatically. If the child has to think about the manner in which letters are formed (e.g., "which way does the *b* and *d* go," or has to frequently recheck and look up from the work that is being copied), the performance is inefficient (Early, 1969). It would be easy for a child to lose the deeper meaning involved in writing or copying because of the time spent discriminating the surface features of the letters and words. Other subtests require visual or auditory perception, and memory, both with and without a motor response (e.g., cards with letters, letter combinations, words, phrases, and series of digits are briefly shown to the child and the child has to write the correct symbol or phrase from memory, or letters, series of digits, words, and phrases are spoken out loud to the child and the child has to remember and write the correct symbols). Additional subtests require the correct identification of beginning and ending sounds in words. One can see that by varying everyday tasks, a teacher can note many types of problems that might occur as in modality problems, sound-symbol difficulties, and writing problems. The test suggests methods for examining everyday school work.

Hammill and Larsen (1978) have developed specific assessment strategies for identifying written language problems (the Test of Written Language) including mechanical skills (e.g., forming letters), productive components (e.g., quantity of meaningful units), conventions (e.g., using rules for punctuation, etc.), linguistics (e.g., syntactical and semantic structures), and cognitive components (e.g., logical, coherent, and sequenced writing). Some innovative procedures are used (e.g., vocabulary items are selected from a spontaneously written story; "thematic maturity" is judged by 20 criterion statements applied to a story written by the child). Graded examples of handwriting are offered as scoring guides. Scaled scores can be derived from the subtests and the norms are based on 1,602 children (ages 8-6 to 14-5). Grade equivalents are derived from data on 1,712 children, grades 2 through 8. Internal consistency of subtests are moderate to high (most above .80). Test-retest correlations vary from .74 to .96. Validity information (content and face) is impressive. Also, other sources of validity are derived from correlations with teacher ratings and another test (Picture Story Language Test, Myklebust, 1965).

The Peabody Picture Vocabulary Test (PPVT) (Dunn, 1965; Dunn and Dunn, 1981) is a popular measure of receptive vocabulary, potentially useful for a wide range of exceptional children (e.g., orthopedically handicapped, mentally retarded, and verbally inhibited children). The revised test consists of a series of 180 plates (including 5 training items), each with four pictures (one on each quadrant of the page). A stimulus word is given orally and the person indicates by pointing, or some other prearranged signal if physically impaired, to the picture that illustrates the stimulus word. Persons from age 2½ to 40 were included in the sample. Parallel forms are available. The PPVT is well designed, but some potential cautions should be noted. Although the first edition of the PPVT yielded both a mental age and deviation IQ, the interpretation of the scores is perhaps best accomplished by noting a child's relative skill in receptive language or "hearing vocabulary," as recommended in the revised edition. The PPVT should not be considered "interchangeable" with the WISC-R and Stanford-Binet (Sattler, 1974), and the older form led to some confusion. The standardization sample of the first edition was restricted to an all white population in Nashville, Tennessee. The revised edition was normed on a national basis including 4,200 children and 828 adults. Black (n = 422) and Hispanic (n = 143) persons were included.

Validity studies with the original PPVT have varied considerably (Sattler, 1974). The correlation between the PPVT and IQ tests has been moderate to high, while correlations with achievement tests have ranged from low to high. Sattler (1974) has an excellent review of the older PPVT, including a bibliography of research studies.

The Illinois Test of Psycholinguistic Abilities (ITPA) (Kirk, McCarthy, and Kirk, 1968) has been a fascinating but controversial assessment technique. The test is difficult to administer and interpret. Potential users are advised to read Kirk (1974), Paraskevopoulos and Kirk (1969) and at least some of the critical writings that have appeared (e.g., Hammill and Larsen, 1974; Mann, 1971; Newcomer and Hammill, 1975, 1976; Waugh, 1975).

The ITPA is comprised of twelve subtests (two of which are supplementary) intended to measure discrete skills in terms of a three dimensional model. Components of the model include: (1) channels of communication (auditory and visual input, verbal and motor responses); (2) psycholinguistic processes (receptive, organizational or associative, and expressive); and (3) levels of organization (representational or mediational, and automatic) (Paraskelopoulos and Kirk, 1969). The following description of the major subtests has been adapted from Paraskelopoulos and Kirk (1969, pp. 16-23).

Auditory Reception: Assesses the child's ability to derive meaning from questions requiring a yes or no response. Syntax has been minimized.

Visual Reception: Parallel to the first subtest, this subtest assesses the child's ability to derive meaning from picture items. A pointing response is required, eliminating the need for expressive language.

Auditory Association: Measures ability to analyze orally presented concepts through the completion of analogies.

Visual Association: Analogies are presented visually. The child views four pictures, along with a stimulus picture, and has to point to one in response to the question "What goes with this?" The format is expanded at upper levels: "If this goes with this. . .then what goes with this?"

Verbal Expression: The child is asked to describe familiar objects (e.g., ball, button); the child examines the object and is asked "Tell me all about it."

Manual Expression: The child is shown pictures of common objects and the child's understanding of the use of the object is noted by appropriate gestures or pantomimes.

Grammatic Closure: This subtest taps the redundant or overlearned aspects of syntax and grammatical inflections through an incomplete sentence format accompanied by pictures (e.g., "Here is a pan; here are two _____.").

Auditory Closure: (Supplementary) Words with deleted syllables are presented and the child is required to say the complete word (e.g., "airpl_____"; "/ype/iter").

Sound Blending: (Supplementary) Words are spoken so that a half-second interval separates the sounds. At younger levels, pictures are used; nonsense words are included at upper levels. The child has to synthesize the sounds.

Visual Closure: Complex scenes are presented with a specified object in various stages of concealment. The child is asked to quickly (a timed subtest) locate as many of the objects as possible.

Auditory Sequential Memory: This is basically the same subtest as is found on the WISC-R, except that the digits are presented at a two per second rate, rather than one per second, and two trials are allowed.

Visual Sequential Memory: Non-meaningful geometric designs on plastic chips are used to reproduce, from memory, a sequence of designs presented by the examiner.

Although children included in the standardization ranged in age from 2 years 4 months to 10 years 3 months, a more useful age range is from 3 to 9 (Kirk, 1974, p. 81). The norms are restricted to middle class children *not* having school learning problems. Four percent of the standardization sample was black. The test manual provides adequate information on reliablity, but validity is a questionable issue. Waugh (1975) criticizes the ITPA as not being a test of psycholinguistics: It "does not reflect current knowledge of the development of natural language systems" (p. 203). Further, Waugh elaborates upon the major criticisms:

> The factor structure is dominated by verbal comprehension and indeed the test may find use as a measure of general ability.... The premise that specific abilities can be identified and remediated has not been supported by research evidence. (p. 206)

Hammill and Larsen (1974) and Newcomer and Hammill (1975, 1976) review a number of studies relating to the second criticism based on deficit skill training of the ITPA model. They point out the limitations of the ITPA in establishing training objectives in psycholinguistic skills and question the efficacy of psycholinguistic training and the educational relevancy of the ITPA constructs.

> For school-aged children, the existence of any specific psycholinguistic difficulties as determined by the ITPA has not proved to be related to the achievement problems which they may currently exhibit or which they may develop in the future.... The ITPA's value is limited to gathering broad, descriptive information regarding certain...learning characteristics; use for individual diagnosis is neither supported nor recommended. (Newcomer and Hammill, 1975, pp. 739-740)

Language Samples. A very different approach, becoming increasingly popular, is the analysis of spontaneous language. Bloom and Lahey (1978) and Kretschmer and Kretschmer (1978) provide extensive reviews of various procedures, the latter oriented towards hearing impaired populations. The procedure has advantages over formal testing; it is more natural than direct testing methods and much normative data is becoming available. Some of the limitations, or drawbacks, include the possibility of examiner influences, variability related to the situation or topic, and the size of a language sample required (Kretschmer and Kretschmer, 1978).

Many different approaches can be used in analyzing the language samples including the Mean Length of Utterance (MLU), grammatical complexity, and semantics. Kretschmer and Kretschmer (1978) note that research has shown the MLU "to be the best single indicator of language growth in children with MLUs of five morphemes or less" (p. 175).

One popular method is Lee's (1974) Developmental Sentence Analysis which is a method for evaluating a child's use of standard English grammar. A sample of spontaneous speech is tape-recorded in conversation with a clinician. The standardization sample precludes use with children from bilingual homes, or children with different dialects, if one is using the test to identify a child with delayed language. Of general interest are Lee's suggestions for obtaining a language sample:

> The adult must be willing and able to subordinate his own interests and personality to those of the child. He must follow what the child sees and

> thinks and does rather than direct the conversation. . . .[The adult should]. . .be stimulating, encouraging, and approving. He must be able to. . .respond. . .in vocabulary and grammatical forms that the child will understand. He must not try to be clever or funny. . . .He should be willing to look silly. . .and wrong himself and to let the child correct and instruct him. (p. 57)

Toys and pictures are used for motivational purposes, but also to ensure that speech and creative thought are maintained as much as possible. The clinician should try to elicit "complete sentences" and "high-level grammatical forms." When the clinician uses a variety of grammatic forms, such as past tense, plural pronouns, etc., it increases the opportunities for the child to use them in response (Lee, 1974).

The Developmental Sentence Analysis (Lee, 1974) is comprised of two procedures allowing for the analysis of spontaneous language samples. The first, Developmental Sentence Types (DST), aids in the classification of "pre-sentence utterances and indicates. . .whether grammatical structure is developing in an orderly manner prior to the emergence of basic sentences" (p. 65). Utterances are analyzed through the use of the DST chart, organized horizontally (single words, two-word combinations, multi-word constructions) and vertically (showing a variety of sentence types). The second procedure, Developmental Sentence Scoring (DSS), "is used to analyze and evaluate the child's syntactic development after he is speaking in complete sentences at least 50 percent of the time" (p. 73). The DSS is restricted to "eight categories of grammatical forms. . .showing the most significant developmental progression in children's language":

> (1) indefinite pronoun or noun modifier, (2) personal pronoun, (3) main verb, (4) secondary verb, (5) negative, (6) conjunction, (7) interrogative reversal in questions, and (8) wh-questions. (p. 136)

Reliability and validity are extensive, but restricted to middle-class children. Although comprehensive and well researched, the DSS emphasizes syntax and excludes semantics and pragmatics, and "deviations from normal linguistic usage" are not specified (Kretschmer and Kretschmer, 1978, p. 178).

An Environmental Approach. Another approach to language assessment and intervention is provided by MacDonald and his associates. One basic question, given that a "technological base" has been established for language intervention, is "who is to do the training?" MacDonald (1976) stresses that both assessment and training should take place within the child's natural environment where the communication occurs. The approach attempts to integrate the fields of psycholinguistics, child development, and behavioral psychology to establish "functional generalized communication." The target population is children who do not use sentences, or children with even more severe language deficits involving the absence of prelanguage skills (e.g., eye contact, attention, etc.). The program has been used with severely handicapped children and is applicable to low incidence assessment procedures (Chapter Six) over a wide range of communication disorders. Parental participation is a crucial part of the model consistent with naturalistic research that stresses social and cultural variables and the role of mothers (or caretakers) as active language teachers (e.g., Moerk, 1976; Snow, 1977; and Whitehurst, Novak and Zorn, 1972).

The Environmental Language Intervention (ELI) model consists of three Diagnostic Training Batteries. The first, The Parent-Child Communication Inventory (MacDonald, 1973), is designed to provide "home-based communication assessment." It has educational as well as diagnostic value. The parents become aware of the behaviors related to "prelinguistic" and beginning "expressive language" by making observations and through direct testing themselves.

The Environmental Prelanguage Battery (EPB) (Horstmeir and MacDonald, 1975) assesses behavior necessary for the development of communication (e.g., attending, sitting, responding) and more advanced behaviors (e.g., receptive language, motor imitation, etc.) The Environmental Language Inventory (ELI) (MacDonald and Nickols, 1974), focuses on the assessment of "early expressive language in imitation, conversation and play."

MacDonald (1976) stresses four essential features of the model for "establishing a generalized functional communication system":

> First, the content for expressive language training must come from those meaning units first expressed by normally developing children....Second, generalization training should be designed into the program from the beginning. Third, the parallel use of linguistic and nonlinguistic cues appears to be necessary to alert the child to the full meaning of the language units being taught. Fourth...significant persons in the child's environment...[should]...conduct the training in order to effect transfer of learning to the child's natural environment. (pp. 27-28)

A Language Screening Technique

The Test of Language Development (TOLD) (Newcomer and Hammill, 1977) is likely to receive wide recognition for its design, standardization, and psychometric qualities. Because it takes only 35 to 40 minutes to administer, and is not overly technical in its procedures, the TOLD may be used by people without extensive linguistic background.

The TOLD follows a linguistic model and includes subtests tapping semantics, syntax, and phonology over both receptive and expressive functions. Even though theoretically based, the specific items were chosen to be consistent with everyday "language behavior."

One important feature of the test manual is the reporting of evidence for concurrent validity. The manual provides correlations, by age level and for each subtest, with other accepted language assessment devices. The following is a description of the subtests, including reference to the independent criterion test used to establish concurrent validity across age levels.

Picture Vocabulary: A receptive subtest not requiring verbalization, similar to the Peabody Picture Vocabulary Test (Dunn, 1965). The correlation between measures was .80.

Oral Vocabulary: The child is asked to define common words requiring expressive ability, similar to the vocabulary subtest of the Wechsler Intelligence Scale for Children (Wechsler, 1949). The correlation between measures was .79.

Grammatic Understanding: A receptive subtest, not requiring verbalization, assessing the comprehension of syntactic forms and grammatic markers. The criterion-test was the receptive subtest of the Northwestern Syntax Screening Test (Lee, 1971). The correlation was .70.

Sentence Imitation: The child repeats a sentence spoken by the examiner assessing familiarity with appropriate word orders and grammatical markers. This subtest was correlated with the Expressive subtest of the Northwestern Syntax Screening Test (Lee, 1971) and the Auditory Attention Span for Related Syllables subtest from the Detroit Tests of Learning Aptitude (Baker and Leland, 1967). The correlations were .77 and .84 respectively.

Grammatic Completion: This subtest requires both expressive and receptive usage. The examiner reads a sentence with a word omitted which the child is asked to verbally identify thus measuring skills related to morphological forms and inflections (e.g., plurals, possessives, verb tenses, etc.). The criterion measure was the Grammatic Closure subtest from the ITPA (Kirk, McCarthy and Kirk, 1968). The correlation between the two measures was .78.

Word Discrimination: A supplemental subtest, the child is required to recognize similarities and differences in specific speech sounds. The criterion measure was the Auditory Discrimination Test (Wepman, 1958) with the resulting correlation coefficient of .69.

Word Articulation: Also a supplementary test, the child's ability in producing important speech sounds is assessed. The criterion measure was the Templin-Darley Test of Articulation (Templin and Darley, 1960) and the obtained correlation was .84.

The TOLD was normed on children from ages 4-0 to 8-11 (n = 1014). All spoke standard English. Geographic areas were sampled (including 15 states). Fifteen percent of the population was black, 49% of the children were from the South, and 61% were children of white-collar families. Reliability (split-half and test-retest) of individual subtests and total test are adequate to high. The test yields a spoken language quotient with a mean of 100 and a standard deviation of 15.

Diagnostic validity was demonstrated by an empirical study that differentiated between groups of children with deviant language, articulation problems, and a control group of normal children. Statistically significant results were achieved for all subtests, based on comparisons between the children with identified language problems and the control group. The children with articulation problems predictably scored higher than the children with more severe language problems on all subtests except Word

Articulation and Sentence Imitation. The results are very encouraging, but require replication since the total sample was relatively small (n = 27). The authors caution that the test is not specifically designed for diagnostic use, but can be used to determine areas of language deficits. A program involving further criterion testing and diagnostic teaching would be necessary. Also, the authors advise that individual subtests can be given apart from the rest of the test battery.

There is a serious lack of assessment approaches for adolescents. The Test of Adolescent Language (TOAL) (Hammill, Brown, Larsen, and Wiederholt, 1980) was developed to help meet this need. The TOAL was standardized on a population of 2,723 students (ages 11 to 18) from 17 states and three Canadian provinces. Information about race, ethnic background, or SES was not available and handicapped students were not included in the sample. Vocabulary and grammatical skills are tapped in four areas—listening, speaking, reading, and writing. Scores are represented in the same manner as the TOLD; subtests have a mean of 10 and a standard deviation of 3. Composite scores (e.g., Receptive Language, Expressive Language, Vocabulary, Grammar) and a Total Adolescent Language Score yield quotients with means of 100 and standard deviations of 15.

In contrast to many available tests, detailed information about reliability and validity is reported, although some of the validity studies are based on small samples and require replication. In one study, the reliability of the subtests ranged from .60 to .90, with 70% of the results .80 or higher. The reliability of the composite scores is greater with almost 80% in the .90s. The test-retest correlation (n = 52, 2 weeks) for the total Adolescent Language Quotient was .97. Information about criterion-related validity is provided by correlations between the TOAL subtest and other language tests. Issues involving construct validity are explored (e.g., Are the skills measured by the TOAL developmental in nature? Are they interrelated? Can the test differentiate between "language deficient and language able students?"). To address the last question, the TOAL was administered to mentally retarded students (n = 61) and learning disabled students (n = 35). The learning disabled group scored higher (mean = 74) than the mentally retarded students (mean = 62) on five of eight subtests, both groups scored less than the established mean quotient of the test (100). The groups were about equally deficient in written skills. Also, the performance of the mentally retarded students yielded a flat profile, in contrast to the learning disabled group which showed greater variability. Such findings are usually thought to be characteristic of those groups.

Another positive feature of the manual is reference to "adaptive testing." The authors point out the need for interviews and probing questions to fully understand the meaning of low scores. Low scores may represent "deficits, differences, or...creativity"; adaptive assessment aids the clinician in understanding the student's responses to various tasks.

Also of interest are the Screening Tests and Diagnostic Battery comprising the Clinical Evaluation of Language Functions (CELF) (Semel and Wiig, 1980), designed to be used by a variety of professionals for identifying children with suspected language disabilities and for "probing" specific language processing and production variables. The Diagnostic Battery includes thirteen subtests (two of which are supplementary). The processing subtests contain questions related to knowledge of word and sentence structure, word classes, linguistic concepts (requiring logical operations), verbal relationships and figurative language, and facility with oral directions and spoken paragraphs. The production subtests tap skills involved in naming series of words (days, months), visually presented colors and geometric forms (for detecting fluency in the rapid retrieval of common words), making word associations to common classes of nouns (e.g., foods, animals), repeating sentences, and formulating sentences. The supplementary subtests involve the processing and production of speech sounds.

The total estimated time for administration is 76 minutes. The standardization of the Diagnostic Battery involved 159 children. The manual presents information pertaining to intertest correlations (i.e., between subtests; between the screening and diagnostic components), internal reliability (e.g., K through 5th = .82; 5th through 12th = .78 for the total test) and test-retest reliability (r = .96 for the total test over a six week interval; n = 30). The internal consistency of individual subtests is not reported and validity information is minimal. One study is described that compared the performance of 30 learning disabled children tested with both the Diagnostic Battery and subtests from other speech and language measures. Concurrent validity coefficients are reported. For example, the total CELF had a correlation of .87 with the verbal subtests of the ITPA for the learning disabled sample.

The Diagnostic Battery has a clear and easily administered format. The materials are attractive and durable. The manual includes guidelines for error analysis and "extension testing" (further testing to "explore the variables which seem to be primary in contributing to the child's error response," p. 79). For in-depth assistance with error analysis, the authors recommend their more comprehensive text (Wiig and Semel, 1980). Overall, the CELF represents an interesting approach to language assessment. However, further development is necessary, especially in areas associated with criterion-related validity and diagnostic utility. Individual subtests and question formats should provide skilled clinicians with useful hypotheses regarding language dysfunction and potential targets for remediation.

Summary

The objectives of language and communication assessment are three-fold and include the determination of a language problem, the organization of goals and objectives of a language program for a particular child, and the specification of procedures for an intervention program (Bloom and Lahey, 1978). In depth language and communication assessment requires the skills of a highly trained speech, hearing, and language clinician, special educator, and psychologist well trained in communication disorders. Other members of the multidisciplinary team, including parents, teachers and school psychologists, can make important contributions through screening procedures. Observational assessment remains one of the most versatile and powerful techniques. When communication skills are defined as adaptive behavior, the importance of naturalistic settings for assessment and intervention takes on additional significance. Specific testing techniques were described for the assessment of basic concepts (Boehm), skills related to language (ITPA, Slingerland), receptive vocabulary (Peabody Picture Vocabulary Test), Syntax (Developmental Sentence Analysis) and general language functioning (TOLD, TOAL, CELF). An environmental assessment and intervention system (Environmental Language Intervention) was also described. Resources for other tests and for theoretical and developmental perspectives were suggested.

Assessment of Academic Skills
With a Special Emphasis on Reading

Techniques used to assess academic skills may be classified in several ways. Some tests may be norm referenced or "standardized." Large groups of children are given the tests and the scores are transformed into *grade equivalents*, *percentiles*, or *stanines* which enable comparisons of a child's performance to local and national reference groups. Most tests developed in this fashion do not examine the processes involved in reading, but serve as measures of prior learning, or *achievement*. Salvia and Ysseldyke (1978) point out the major function of achievement tests is for screening purposes. They can assist with educational decision-making by providing a "global index" of a child's academic level, whether unusually high or low. Achievement tests are important for identifying exceptional children in the areas of learning disabilities and mental retardation. Valuable information, however, about learning and performance processes may be lost through group administration (Salvia and Ysseldyke, 1978).

A great number of achievement tests are commercially available. The most popular tests used in the public schools include the Wide Range Achievement Test (Jastak, Bijou, and Jastak, 1978), the Peabody Individual Achievement Test (Dunn and Markwardt, 1970), and the Stanford Achievement Test (Madden, Gardner, Rudman, Karlsen, and Merwin, 1973). All are relatively well standardized. Although traditionally achievement and aptitude tests have been developed in this manner, diagnostic tests that are also norm referenced have been developed. Most diagnostic tests stress either the processes involved in reading, the specific skill prerequisites to reading, or both, and are somewhat limited in normative characteristics in comparison to achievement tests.

Criterion (or domain) referenced tests should also be used in assessing academic skills. They are very important to nonbiased, multifactored assessment because, by intent, the use of criterion referenced tests results in a specific outline of an individual child's instructional needs. Samuda

(1975) views the criterion referenced movement in testing as one of the principal trends in developing alternative strategies for one group of children isolated from the mainstream of education—American minorities. Many criterion referenced tests are commercially available. Also, they can be effectively developed by an individual teacher or a team of educators within a school district. Most important to the development of criterion referenced testing is the sequencing of specific skills, and an adequate sampling of the academic domain (e.g., reading, math). The kind of responses a child has to make (e.g., writing the correct response, answering orally, marking an "X" on the correct item), and the instructions given to the child (e.g., oral, written) are important (Cronbach, 1970). For example, in designing a math test, an almost infinite number of possible questions would exist even over a narrow range of math facts. In math, written word problems require different skills than oral word problems or computational problems and care must be taken to design questions that tap intended skills.

Many references exist in the area of academic assessment. For a more complete discussion of the parameters of teacher made tests, Gronlund (1976) offers valuable suggestions. The book by Martuza (1977) is helpful for an in-depth analysis of the differences between normative and criterion referenced testing, as well as other measurement issues. Hively (1974) believes that the term "criterion" may be easily misinterpreted. His book presents a readable view of domain referenced testing, a more general term. For children with specific learning problems, Salvia and Ysseldyke (1978) provide a critical review of many commercially available tests as well as an overview of basic measurement concepts. Wallace and Larsen (1978) stress informal and standardized approaches to educational assessment. Faas (1980) and Hammill and Bartel (1978) integrate informal approaches to assessment with suggestions for educationally based intervention techniques.

The assessment of reading is perhaps the most critical problem because of the high incidence of reading failure and because of the dependency on reading for school success. In this section, the diagnostic assessment of reading will be stressed.

Theoretical Perspectives: The Reading Process

Many perspectives are required to understand the reading process. For example, the study of language, visual processing, perception, word recognition, cognition, and cultural influences are all necessary for a complete treatment of reading (Singer and Ruddell, 1976). Sensory screening and assessment (visual, auditory) is essential for any child experiencing learning difficulties. Although, for practical reasons, it is important to divide reading into specific component skills, there are conceptual problems in doing so, because of the complexity of the reading process. To provide an overview, aspects of the perceptual processes in reading, the necessary skills from the child's viewpoint, and an ecological approach will be briefly introduced.

Perceptual Skills. Haber (1978) defines the reading process as "a continuous visual language context" enabling the reader to draw forth meaning (p. 47). Haber continues by pointing out that the following component skills, often tapped by reading diagnostic tests, are *not* reading: "identification of singly presented letters, identification of singly presented words, matching pairs of letters, pairs of words. . . . naming of sequentially presented words" (p. 47). Haber characterizes reading as a continuous process, whereby meaning is extracted "on-the-fly" from the written language context (p. 52). The context, and the redundancy built into written systems of language, are important considerations. The written context allows the reader to apply the "rules of language," word knowledge, content, etc.; redundancy provides the "mechanism" that restricts choices while reading (increasing expectancies) and expands the field of vision. The process of reading involves the "integration of successive fixations."

> As long as theories of reading treat single fixations as the unit of processing, they will not be able to account for either the reader's awareness of seeing a whole line of print rather than a disjointed list of sequentially viewed words or phrases, nor, more importantly, for his ability to process whole segments of text simultaneously. (p. 54)

Component Skills. Carroll (1976) notes the probability of a number of different ways of learning to read, as well as different skill sequences. He lists eight components of reading skills:

1. The child must know the language that he is going to learn to read.
2. The child must learn to dissect spoken words into component sounds.
3. The child must learn to recognize and discriminate the letters of the alphabet in their various forms.
4. The child must learn the left-to-right principle by which words are spelled and put in order in continuous text.
5. The child must learn that there are patterns of highly probable correspondence between letters and sounds, and he must learn those patterns of correspondence that will help him recognize words that he already knows in his spoken language or that will help him determine the pronunciation of unfamiliar words.
6. The child must learn to recognize printed words from whatever cues he can use—their total configurations, the letters composing them, the sounds represented by those letters, and/or the meanings suggested by the context.
7. The child must learn that printed words are signals for spoken words and that they have meanings analogous to those of spoken words. While decoding a printed message into its spoken equivalent, the child must be able to apprehend the meaning of the total message in the same way that he would apprehend the meaning of the corresponding spoken message.
8. The child must learn to reason and think about what he reads, within the limits of his talent and experience. (pp. 13-14)

The Ecological Perspective. Gillespie-Silver (1979) presents a rather complete ecological analysis of the reading process. The major point is the necessity of relating assessment (and intervention) to the needs of the child, the task of reading, and the unique patterns of interactions between the child, task, teacher, and the child's environment.

A major area of assessment is the child's "interaction" with the reading process. Assessment may include reading readiness, language, cognitive and experiential development, and the child's reading strategies. A wide variety of formal and informal assessment procedures may be used. Most importantly, Gillespie-Silver includes an excellent discussion of diagnostic-prescriptive approaches. Behavioral or task analytic approaches are considered important methods appropriate for the assessment-intervention process. Behavioral assessment allows for information beyond that obtained by standardized or criterion referenced tests; it allows the direct assessment of

> the child's responses to each progressive task....Direct, continuous observations of the child's behavior gives more functional information that the teacher needs to plan and evaluate instructional programs. (p. 235)

However, Gillespie-Silver (1979) also warns that behavioral approaches are not a complete solution to the complex process of reading. There may be a bias towards more direct behaviors in terms of "which reading behaviors to observe, teach, and analyze" (p. 243).

Also important from an assessment point of view are qualitative approaches stemming from anthropological and ethnographic research—all becoming increasingly important to the analysis of educational problems. The book by Gillespie-Silver (1979) provides a comprehensive review of practical, as well as theoretical, issues and approaches to reading.

Diagnostic Approaches to Reading Assessment

As with the other domains of multifactored assessment, many continuities exist between various assessment strategies, such as interviewing, observations, and direct test methods. All may be necessary with individual children. Despite the dangers of "over" or "under" testing, a combination of strategies using a variety of methods is usually required to assess the special learning needs of children making inadequate progress in school. The skills measured by most reading tests include word recognition, phonetic analysis, oral and silent reading, comprehension, and reading speed (Gillespie-Silver, 1979).

Wallace and Larsen (1978) and Salvia and Ysseldyke (1978) critique popular reading diagnostic approaches, with a few differences of opinion being evident. Wallace and Larsen (1978) consider the Gates-McKillop Reading Diagnostic Tests (Gates and McKillop, 1962) to be the "best overall measure of specific word-analysis skills" (p. 311). In addition, they recommend the widely used Durrell Analysis of Reading Difficulty (Durrell, 1955) and The Diagnostic Reading Scales (Spache, 1972) for evaluating specific reading problems (p. 311). Salvia and Ysseldyke (1978) cautiously point out that the Gates-McKillop battery requires "considerable sophistication to interpret," although it is easily administered (p. 178). They recommend the Gates-McKillop as a useful instrument, given an awareness of its limitations. Salvia and Ysseldyke note the absence of normative data on the Durrell, but suggest that the test generates useful "qualitative information" allowing insights into the possible nature of the reading problems (p. 182). Salvia and Ysseldyke (1978) critique the Stanford Diagnostic Test (Karlsen, Madden, and Gardner, 1977) and note the "exceptional standardization" and find it useful for identifying specific areas of reading problems (p. 186). Another popular test is the Woodcock Reading Mastery Test (Woodcock, 1973). The standardization included over 5,000 children in kindergarten through twelfth grade. Because of relatively high reliability, strengths and weaknesses in specific skill areas may be identified.

There are four general criticisms that may apply to many standardized diagnostic tests (from Gillespie-Silver, 1979). First, the grade levels they yield may be of "little diagnostic value," because the tests do not necessarily correlate well with available reading material. The diagnostic tests require "considerable practice and study," more than may be generally recognized. Many of the tests are very time-consuming. Most significantly, standardized diagnostic tests do not usually provide sufficient diagnostic information, because they ignore key reading processes (pp. 119-121).

One method that is helpful in analyzing a child's reading strategies is the Reading Miscue Inventory (Goodman and Burke, 1972). Miscues are defined as "deviations in oral reading." Through the analysis of reading miscues, teachers can assess the differences and interactions between the language of the reader and the written language in terms of three language systems: phonological, syntactic, and semantic. Goodman and Goodman (1977) further explain that "miscues reflect the degree to which a reader is understanding and seeking meaning" (p. 320). Very briefly, the steps can be outlined as follows (Goodman and Burke, 1972, pp. 6-7). (1) The child is asked to read a new passage orally and the performance is taped in as natural a setting as possible. (2) After reading, the child retells the story and the teacher "probes" for "details of plot, character, and description." (3) The tape allows for the confirmation of the teacher's marking of miscues made as they occurred. (4) A number of inventory questions (relating to graphic similarity, sound similarity, grammatical function, meaning change, etc.) are asked about each miscue and a "Reader Profile" is prepared showing the student's strengths and weaknesses in reading. (5) A reading program is then planned.

Tortelli (1976) offers a shorter version of the Reading Miscue Inventory. The child reads an unfamiliar story and the teacher notes everything the child reads "not contained in the text." On a four column piece of paper, the teacher notes "unexpected readings," "intended readings," "language," and "meaning" (p. 638). Guidelines for questions are provided: "The teacher asks himself if the unexpected readings sound like language.... Is each reading grammatically correct?," and the "unexpected reading" is examined in terms of "meaning" (p. 638). The focus is on "how well the reader is applying his intuitive knowledge of oral language to the written language" and also on "the extent to which the reader is comprehending the thoughts expressed in the text" (p. 639).

Boyd and Bartel (1978) provide a word of caution consistent with Haber's earlier description of the reading process as extracting meaning "on-the-fly." Competent readers do not use every available cue (e.g., letter-by-letter or word-by-word) when reading. Teachers should be concerned if the reading miscues begin to interfere with comprehension. This is dependent upon the type and frequency of the miscue. Miscue analysis can assist with the discovery of "faulty strategies and consistently misleading patterns or rules...that interfere with...reading performance" (Boyd and Bartel, 1978, p. 55).

Another helpful and straightforward approach to diagnosing reading problems is through the use of informal reading inventories. The child is asked to read aloud from graded passages, usually from 100 to 150 words, and errors and patterns of errors in sight word recognition, word attack skills, and problems with reading rate are recorded by the teacher. Comprehension questions are asked at the end of the passage. A determination is made of the child's reading level in terms of independent, instructional, frustration and hearing comprehension level (Wallace and Larsen, 1978). Graded passages also may be read silently, an important addition to reading diagnostics after the primary grades.

Two examples of published reading inventories are those by Silvaroli (1976) and Ekwall (1979). The Classroom Reading Inventory (Silvaroli, 1976) takes twelve minutes (or less) to administer. Three alternate forms are included. The recommended grades for usage are two through ten. Graded word lists, passages for oral reading, and a spelling survey are included. Optional reading selections are available for the assessment of silent reading comprehension or for the evaluation of the child's progress in remediation.

Ekwall (1979) similarly has developed a very usable reading inventory. Oral and silent reading, phonetic analysis and comprehension skills are assessed in passages ranging from preprimer to ninth grade. The passages were intended to be interesting to children regardless of age level, which is extremely important for older children with reading problems. Independent, instructional, frustration, and listening comprehension levels can be derived. Another advantage is the provision of four alternative forms and a graded word list. The average time for administration is generally less than thirty minutes.

Ekwall (1977a) designed a one page "Reading Diagnostic Sheet," outlining twenty-eight problem areas including oral reading (e.g., word-by-word reading, incorrect phrasing, use of context cues), oral-silent reading (e.g., comprehension), silent reading (e.g., speed, voicing-lip movement, inability to skim), and other related abilities. The book (Ekwall, 1977a) is organized around locating and remediating a wide range of problems outlined on the reading diagnostic sheet. Suggestions are brief, but would provide an overview of possible approaches.

A final approach to reading assessment is through the use of *criterion referenced tests*. Gillespie-Silver (1979) offers an excellent overview of the area and notes that this type of test is "an outgrowth of the behavioristic or task analytic approach" and the corresponding individualization of instruction (p. 228). There are a great number of published tests available as criterion referenced instruments; they also can be teacher made. Only a few are listed as samples.

The Woodcock Reading Mastery Tests (Woodcock, 1973) may be used as a criterion or norm-referenced test. Other tests include Diagnosis: An Instructional Aid (Shub, Carlin, Friedman, Kaplan, and Katien, 1973); Criterion Reading (Hackett, 1971); the Fountain Valley Teacher Support System in Reading (Zweig Associates, 1971); and the Basic Educational Skills Inventory (1972).

Another representative instrument is the Diagnostic Inventory of Basic Skills (Brigance, 1977). The purposes include the assessment of readiness and academic skills (reading, language arts, math) in kindergarten through sixth grades and the provision of a "systematic performance record" for monitoring student achievement. Key instructional objectives are defined. The author points out that many of the tests were "text-referenced." The grade level in children's texts where the skill was first introduced was determined. The format is very usable; all of the tests are contained in one compact spiral bound book.

Since a great many criterion referenced instruments are available, a brief evaluation of this approach is warranted. Salvia and Ysseldyke (1978) provide the following perspective:

> Criterion-referenced assessment, observation, and diagnostic reading are the preferred techniques to use when deciding appropriate educational interventions for individual students or when evaluating the extent to which they have profited from instruction. (p. 473)

The criterion referenced approach to reading is not without criticisms. Problems exist in agreeing about "a clear-cut progression of skills in the reading process" (Gillespie-Silver, 1979, p. 234). Also, Gillespie-Silver notes that the "process" of reading is not evaluated by tests that measure isolated skills. "The reading process is 'frozen' into bits that lose their meaning when divided into small discrete steps" (p. 234). Oakland and Matuszek (1977) point out that criterion referenced tests are not immune from cultural bias. They warn: "The tendency to use these tests to establish standards of excellence or desirable instructional goals should be vigorously avoided" (p. 57). Some test users have attempted to interpret norm referenced tests as criterion referenced techniques. Gillespie-Silver (1979) points out that "many of the concepts or skills necessary for instruction do not exist in norm-referenced tests'' (p. 22). Items are included that differentiate between the skills of individual children and these do not necessarily indicate the most significant areas of instructional objectives.

One of the major problems with both criterion referenced and informal reading approaches is the assessment of reading comprehension. In developing the Test of Reading Comprehension (TORC), Brown, Hammill, and Wiederholt (1978) have tried to address four major concerns:

> Assessment strategies, especially for older students, should ...differentiate ...general reading comprehension from a lack of experience with a specific content area.
> Reading comprehension...[is] ...an interactive process... [one]...must consider both author and reader variables within a framework of language and cognition.
> [A reading comprehension test should] ... minimize the possibility of obtaining ''correct'' responses solely as a result of general information, memorization, or guessing.
> Silent reading is... usually more appropriate. (pp. 8-13)

The TORC has a general reading comprehension core involving vocabulary, paragraph reading, and syntactic similarities (designed to measure ...meaningfully similar, but syntactically different sentence structures). Diagnostic supplements are included (e.g., content area vocabulary in math, social studies, science; a subtest assessing the ability to read the directions involved in school work).

The standardization sample consisted of 2,520 unselected children varying in ages from 6-6 to 14-6 from 10 states. A ''reading comprehension quotient'' with a mean of 100 and a standard deviation of 15 can be derived, as well as grade equivalents. The reliability of subtests (from second grade on) are mostly above .90. Sources of criterion related validity (e.g., correlations with other measures such as the Peabody Individual Achievement Test) are available.

Ekwall (1977a, 1977b) provides practical suggestions for everyday use in the classroom. Ekwall's (1977a) outline of the important procedures in remediation helps maintain the balance between assessment and intervention.

1. Ensure that the remedial reading program is highly individualized.
2. Start with the student's strongest area.
3. Help the disabled reader to recognize and verbalize his or her problem.
4. Make the disabled reader aware of his or her progress.
5. Make the learning process meaningful to the child.
6. Use materials appropriate to the needs of the child.
7. Continue the diagnosis while you teach.
8. Make use of the teaching method with which the child is most successful.
9. Maintain a relaxed attitude.

10. Do not be too authoritative.
11. Have confidence in the student's ability to learn.
12. Direct the child toward self-instruction.
13. Begin each period with a summary of what you intend to do; and end each period with a summary of what you did and why.
14. Provide for a follow-up program. (pp. 5-10)

Ekwall's points concerning remedial approaches are consistent with the expanded scope of multifactored assessment. He stresses the need to identify the child's problems and resources in relationship to the task to be learned, teacher and environmental characteristics, and the possible interactions between variables.

Summary

The problems associated with the assessment of reading were stressed in this section. Key references were pointed out that would provide direction for in-depth academic assessment. For the area of reading, a brief theoretical overview was provided emphasizing three aspects: (1) perceptual processes, (2) the skills necessary for a child to learn how to read, and (3) the ecological perspective. Examples of diagnostic approaches and a sampling of specific instruments were offered. A language based approach (The Reading Miscue Inventory) and two recent informal reading inventories were included. Approaches to criterion referenced testing were introduced and limitations noted. Normative approaches help to define global deficiencies, but provide little insight into the processes of reading or the specific skill deficits of the child. Both diagnostic reading tests and criterion referenced approaches serve to fill the gaps. Ecological approaches attend to the complex variables and interactions between the child and the task.

Adaptive Behavior

The importance of assessing adaptive behavior has recently been emphasized because of its major role in nonbiased assessment with respect to mental retardation. This section will provide definitions of adaptive behavior and will describe some of the more popular and promising measures from the perspective of identifying mildly handicapped children within a nonbiased, multifactored framework. Adaptive behavior measures have also been developed for severely mentally retarded or developmentally disabled persons, and are described in Chapter Six.

Definitions and Theoretical Perspectives

Adaptive behavior has been defined as "the effectiveness or degree with which the individual meets the standards of personal independence and social responsibility expected of his age or cultural group" (Grossman, 1973, p. 11). Mercer and Lewis (1977) provide a socioecological view:

> Increasing levels of adaptive behavior are measured by (1) the number of social groups in which the child participates, (2) the number of different roles played in those groups, (3) the extent to which the child demonstrates internal control and independent behavior, and (4) the complexity of role behavior. (p. 84)

Mercer (1979) and Robinson and Robinson (1976) note the absence of much theoretical work on the concept of adaptive behavior, and diverse points of view exist. Logically, adaptive behavior should be related to intellectual growth (e.g., Piaget), and other aspects of a child's development involving coping skills (Leland, 1978). Adaptive behavior is related to many issues and techniques discussed in the section on personality assessment. In contrast to many items on intelligence tests, the items measured by adaptive behavior scales should be practical, related to the day-by-day independence of the person, and they should be potentially modifiable (Leland, 1978). This last point involving the modifiability (or reversibility) of the skills on an adaptive behavior scale constitutes a significant departure from intelligence tests. Behavior analytic techniques are strongly implicated.

The theoretical aspects of adaptive behavior require translation into operational skills. Leland (1978) suggests that adaptive behavior can be described by three key facets:

1. *Independent functioning:* Tasks or activities demanded...by the general community both in terms of...critical survival...and...in terms of typical expectations for specific ages.
2. *Personal responsibility:* The willingness of individuals to accomplish those critical tasks they are able to accomplish...and their ability to assume individual responsibility for their personal behavior.
3. *Social Responsibility:* The ability of the individual to accept responsibility as a member of a community and to carry out appropriate behaviors in terms of group expectations. (p. 40)

Important Issues and Uses of Adaptive Behavior Scales

One major issue of theoretical and practical significance involves the implications of varying perspectives in defining adaptive behavior. Leland presents the problem in the following manner: "The overall objective remains one of achieving a generalized view of society's observations of the manner in which an individual copes" (p. 42). Lambert (1979) argues that "for school children, teachers or parents can provide reliable observations and assessment of adaptive behavior" (p. 4). Mercer and Lewis (1977) offer a different view. A measure of adaptive behavior is important as an "independent assessment of the child's current functioning level from the perspective of the child's family" and that it "may or may not coincide with the perspective of the school" (p. 7). Mealor and Richmond (1980) found that parents and teachers did not always agree on the level of adaptive functioning of moderately or severely retarded children. They suggest that both parents and teachers may exhibit bias in their ratings. The second strategy appears most consistent with the intent of P.L. 94-142 in reducing sources of bias for minority children, although a combination of approaches will be appropriate for certain children.

Another issue involves conceptual problems in the identification of children as mentally retarded, especially minority group children. Mental retardation is a relativistic term. Goodman (1977) argues for descriptive approaches in mental retardation, as pointed out in Chapter Two. Although many of the scales include adequate descriptive information of a child's overall functioning, the psychometric approach is fraught with difficulties. Even with very recent measures (e.g., Mercer and Lewis, 1977), evidence suggests a need for establishing local norms indicating that what constitutes retardation in one community may not in another.

Although the use of adaptive behavior measures for the classification of children as mentally retarded looms as one of the larger issues (along with a corresponding search for psychometric adequacy), other potential uses of adaptive behavior scales may be warranted. Because of the focus on coping skills related to overall functioning in multiple settings, adaptive behavior measures can possibly yield increments in understanding adjustment problems of not only children suspected of being retarded or developmentally disabled, but with children having other handicapping conditions. For example, adaptive behavior scales may expand information about a child with an emotional problem in terms of home adjustment, personal responsibility, and community adjustment, when used in an individual clinical manner. Also, Oakland (1979) reports that about 84% of the Adaptive Behavior Inventory for Children (ABIC) items were judged to be appropriate with institutionalized blind children. Additional research may demonstrate adaptive behavior measures to be flexible and important indicators of overall adjustment.

Another potential use seems critically important in light of descriptions of special classes as "dead end placements" for certain children. Mercer (1979) warns that special classes may result in a "disabling trajectory," whereby the child is moved away from pathways "leading to broader vistas of social participation" (p. 90). The major issue is not classification but ensuring that educational decisions result in "enabling rather than disabling trajectories" for children (p. 90). Adaptive behavior scales may be useful in tracing the impact of institutional decisions when used over time (Mercer, 1979).

Measures of Adaptive Behavior

The Vineland Social Maturity Scales (Doll, 1953) is perhaps the first adaptive behavior measure that comes to mind and it is still widely used. The standardization sample included persons from birth to age 30; however, the sample was highly restricted, and the scale is in the process of revision. Questions distributed among the following eight domains comprise the scale: self-help involving general skills, eating, and dressing;

self-direction; communication; occupation; locomotion; and socialization. The Vineland yields a social age and social quotient.

Perhaps one of the least known instruments, but deserving of wider recognition, is the Developmental Profile (Alpern and Boll, 1972; Alpern, Boll and Shearer, 1980). Robinson and Robinson (1976) describe it as "one of the most useful and best standardized instruments," achieving a "compromise between age-level" (e.g., the Vineland) and inventory approaches (discussed in Chapter Six) (p. 358). The Developmental Profile was standardized on over 3,000 subjects, including blacks (the only minority included) and can be used with infants through age 9. One of the goals in developing the scale was "to provide an inventory which has no significant bias as a function of the sex, race, and social class" (Alpern and Boll, 1972, p. 2). A total of 186 items are divided among the following five scales:

1. *Physical Scale:* (large and small muscle coordination, strength, stamina, flexibility, and sequential control skills)
2. *Self-help Scale:* (ability to cope independently with the environment...eating, dressing, working)
3. *Social Scale:* (interpersonal relationships...emotional needs for people,...manner in relating to friends, relatives, and various adults)
4. *Academic Scale:* (skills prerequisite to readiness functioning...to actual academic achievement)
5. *Communication Scale:* (expressive and receptive communication skills with both verbal and non-verbal languages...spoken, written, and use of gestures)

The Adaptive Behavior Inventory for Children (ABIC) is one of the social system measures of the SOMPA, System of Multicultural Pluralistic Assessment (Mercer and Lewis, 1977). Adaptive behavior relating to the social role in the family, peer group, and community are measured by six scales:

1. *Family:* (e.g., relationship with brothers and sisters, supervision of younger siblings) 52 items
2. *Community:* (e.g., religious and recreational activity, movement about community, trouble with police, play with other children, knowledge of neighborhood, and beyond neighborhood) 41 items
3. *Peer Relations:* (e.g., relationships with children and school mates, including play and handling disputes, club memberships) 36 items
4. *Nonacademic School Roles:* (e.g., relationship with teachers, helping in classroom, taking care of school supplies, playground behavior) 37 items
5. *Earner/Consumer:* (e.g., knowing value of money, saving, buying gifts, clothes) 26 items
6. *Self-Maintenance:* (e.g., caring for physical needs, persistence, lack of irrational fears, avoiding dangers, using telephone) 49 items

In addition to the above scales, three ancillary measures are included: "Not allowed" and "no opportunity" responses may be indicative of role boundaries. A "Veracity" scale (24 items) may help check on the "inflation of a child's adaptive performances." "Don't Know" responses are also counted and may suggest the need for another source of information. A Spanish translation is available.

The ABIC is well standardized in terms of the selection of questions, and item analysis. Local norms are probably necessary (Buckley and Oakland, 1977; Gridley and Mastenbrook, 1977). In contrast to most scales, a large proportion of minorities were included (696 black; 690 Hispanics; and 699 whites), but subjects were from only one state, California.

Mercer (1979) has found sex differences on individual items, but not by total score. Also, she found socioeconomic status differences on items but argued that SES differences between high and low-status families balanced each other. Items are included that "favor" both high and low status families. The magnitude of the relationship between SES and the ABIC Scaled Scores is very low. When analyzed by ethnic group (perhaps confounded by SES), 114 questions (out of 218) were significantly different. Overall the reliability (split-half) is moderate to high; .95 or above for the ABIC Average Scaled Score and above .75 for the subscales. The ABIC is not highly correlated with either school achievement or intelligence (e.g., Tebeleff and Oakland, 1977; Mercer, 1979), thereby providing some evidence for construct validity. All of the standardization information (e.g., sex differences, SES differences, ethnic differences) is clearly reported, item by item, in the manual.

Oakland and Feigenbaum (1980) examined the ABIC for possible sources of bias. Four hundred thirty six children were stratified on racial-ethnic and SES dimensions. The groups included white (n = 180), black (n = 119), and Mexican American children (n = 137) from both middle and low SES levels. They concluded that the ABIC was relatively free from sources of bias in most respects, especially in terms of the internal characteristics of the test. The construct validity of the ABIC was found to be very similar across the three racial-ethnic groups and two SES levels. The items were generally easier for middle SES children, children from more usual family structures (e.g., biological parents caring for child, both spouses present), and for first or second born children. Kazimour and Reschley (1981) question the use of the ABIC for children of other sociocultural groups such as American Indians. They also state that questions concerning validity of the ABIC have not been answered. Further research is needed.

Another major instrument is the public school version of the Adaptive Behavior Scale (Lambert, Windmiller, Cole, and Figueroa, 1975), developed as an outgrowth of the American Association on Mental Deficiency Adaptive Behavior Scale (Nihiri, Foster, Shellhaas, and Leland, 1969; 1974). The public school version is comprised of two parts, concerned with independent living and "maladaptive behavior related to personality and behavior disorders" (Lambert, 1979, p. 4). The domains and subscale titles give a global view of the assessment dimensions.

Part I Domains (56 items)
Independent Functioning
Physical Development
Economic Activity
Language Development
Number and Time Concepts
Vocational Activity
Self-Direction
Responsibility
Socialization

Part II Domains (39 items)
Violent & Destructive Behavior
Antisocial Behavior
Rebellious Behavior
Untrustworthy Behavior
Withdrawal
Stereotyped Behavior and Odd Mannerisms
Inappropriate Interpersonal Manners
Unacceptable Vocal Habits
Unacceptable Eccentric Habits
Hyperactive Tendencies
Psychological Disturbances
Use of Medications

Most of the domains are self explanatory; Part I is generally consistent with other measures previously described. Part II is different from the other adaptive behavior measures because of the emphasis on social and emotional development. Lambert (1978) describes the scale in terms of four clusters: (1) Functional Autonomy (Independent Functioning, Language Development, Economic Activity, Number and Time Concepts, and Vocational Activity); (2) Social Responsibility (Self-direction, Responsibility, and Socialization); (3) Interpersonal Adjustment (Destructive Behavior, Antisocial Behavior, Rebellious Behavior, Untrustworthy Behavior, and Psychological Disturbances); and (4) Intrapersonal Adjustment (Stereotyped Behavior, Inappropriate Manners, and Unacceptable Vocal Habits) (pp. 170-171). The factor dimensions have been renamed in a Second Edition. For Part I, they are Personal Self-Sufficiency, Community Self-Sufficiency, and Personal Responsibility. For Part II, they are Personal Adjustment and Social Adjustment.

Many of the domains have one or only a few items. The standardization sample contained 2,800 children, representing three major California ethnic groups (black, white, and Spanish). Sample selection involved approximately equal numbers of children in regular classes, and in EMR (mildly retarded) classes. A smaller number of TMR (trainable retarded) children and EH children (similar to a learning disability classification—children with learning problems and average measured intelligence) were also included. Children in the second through sixth grades were represented (ages 7-12).

Children can be compared to peers in EMR or TMR programs by using percentile ranks. Part II has separate norms because of ethnic or cultural differences found in response to items. Validity studies show that the scale can differentiate regular students from those in EMR classes (Lambert, 1978).

Although an important and well standardized instrument, some issues exist with the AAMD Adaptive Behavior Scale-Public School Version. As Lambert and Nicoll (1976) note, the scale measures adaptation to school. Though recognizing the many dimensions of adaptive behavior, the approach to scale construction may neglect some of the implied purposes of the scale, including the measurement of a child's performance of independent ''everyday living tasks'' in the home environment and in the broader community (Salvia and Ysseldyke, 1978, pp. 372-373). Lambert (1978) argues that either parents or teachers may act as observers of adaptive behavior, and advises that parents can rate adaptive behavior through an interview and the use of the scale (p. 177). Lambert reports no differences between parent and teacher ratings and a lack of evidence to suggest significant systematic bias with respect to either ethnic status or sex on Part I domains. Significant differences were found on Part II domains. Since normative information for ethnic groups is provided in the manual, Lambert suggests that users of the scale may interpret the results if cultural factors are taken into account (p. 166). Even so, the family and community emphasis given to the ABIC (Mercer, 1979) seems to be closer to the intent of P.L. 94-142 with respect to nonbiased assessment with the culturally different (Mastenbrook, 1977). The AAMD Adaptive Behavior Scale may be useful for designing interventions. Research is needed on the effects of using different adaptive behavior scales for decision-making and for instructional intervention.

Another measure has recently been published, the Children's Adaptive Behavior Scale (Richmond and Kicklighter, 1980). The domains are similar to the other previously mentioned scales: Language; Independent Functioning; Family Role Performance; Economic-Vocational Activity; and Socialization. One major difference is that the child is used as the respondent, not a parent or teacher. The CABS may be administered to children ranging in age from five to ten. Unfortunately, the normative data are severely limited, obtained from 250 mildly retarded children in two southern states. The use of local norms is suggested by the authors. Data concerning validity is also very limited. Test scores appear to increase with chronological age, and can differentiate groups of slow learners and educable mentally retarded children. Test bias may not be a factor; a sample of black children scored slightly higher than white children. Correlations between the CABS and the Adaptive Behavior Scale are reported (n = 120; overall r = .42) and between the CABS and the WISC-R (r = .51 for total CABS and WISC-R Full Scale IQ). One should expect that adaptive behavior scales would have higher correlations with each other than with an intelligence scale. Although the authors state that the domains of the scale are relatively independent, and suggest that domain scores may have diagnostic and instructional utility, further research in this area appears necessary.

Still other measures may be forthcoming because of difficulties inherent in using the published instruments. For example, Mastenbrook (1978) and Scott (1978) describe the development of the Texas Environmental Adaptation Measure (TEAM). The TEAM has sections comprised of Environmental Measures (Sociocultural History and Family Dynamics), Personality Adjustment, and Adaptive Behavior Assessment.

Summary

Adaptive behavior is a concept of emerging and critical importance. Two separate influences relate to nonbiased, multifactored assessment and the process of normalization. Although not necessarily mutually exclusive, the two influences are broad enough to have encouraged the development of instruments that should be defined by either function, not by both. Mercer's ABIC, developed as a part of the SOMPA, is designed to meet the need from a social systems perspective independent of school functioning. Also, the Developmental Profile appears to have utility for nonbiased multifactored assessment when a parent or guardian is interviewed.

The AAMD Adaptive Behavior Scale-Public School Version, is a well-standardized measure that may have utility in understanding a child's problem with school adjustment. It can be used with members of different ethnic groups; however, aspects relating to adjustment outside of the school situation may be overlooked. Other measures (e.g., Mastenbrook, 1978; Scott, 1978; and Richmond and Kicklighter, 1980) may eventually be sufficiently developed to give practitioners more choices. Adaptive behavior measures, because of the emphasis on objectives related to broadbased coping skills, may prove to be versatile clinical instruments. Research with other applications should be encouraged.

Vocational Assessment

The topic of vocational assessment is of critical and increasing importance for handicapped and minority individuals. It is also a very diverse topic, with threads from many related areas. Although there are dangers in discussing the two different groups together, the reasons for doing so are because both require related, extensive skills, a critical reexamination of traditional models, and both have been neglected to a marked degree in past reviews of vocational and industrial psychology. From the viewpoint of psychology as practiced in the shools, this has been true to a great degree.

The Bureau of Education for the Handicapped makes the following predictions for handicapped children who will leave the schools in the next four years:

1,000,000 (40%) will be underemployed and at the poverty level.

200,000 (8%) will be in their home community and idle much of the time.

650,000 (26%) will be unemployed and on welfare.

75,000 (3%) will be totally dependent and institutionalized. (Federal Programs for Career Education of Handicapped Individuals, 1979, 6, p. 11)

It is difficult to find clear predictions for ethnic minorities. Neff (1977) discusses the problems with such an appraisal and emphasizes the danger of attempting to think in terms of stereotypes for such diverse groups as blacks, Puerto Ricans, Chicanos, American Indians, and smaller numbers of recent immigrants from underdeveloped countries. Certain commonalities between groups do exist:

high rates of unemployement, restriction for most to the lower and more poorly paid occupations, inadequate and interrupted schooling, and inordinately large numbers of people at poverty and near poverty levels. (p. 277)

The unique problems of handicapped persons with sensory limitations (e.g., vision, hearing) or motor problems (e.g., crippled, cerebral palsied, quadriplegic) and the innovative technological breakthroughs allowing handicapped individuals mobility and communication capability make the collaboration of many specialists necessary. From the viewpoint of minority group members, the need for access to opportunity, elimination of test bias, and special training programs for vocational skills have been stressed (e.g., Backer, 1973) as have been the reconsideration of vocational theories (Smith, 1980).

Although vocational assessment has a distinct focus and is characterized by many specialized techniques, continuities exist with other assessment areas. Anastasi (1976) states: "Nearly every type of available test may be useful in occupational decisions" (p. 435). The statement could be expanded to include other assessment techniques, such as interviews and observations.

Vocational assessment can be approached in many ways. A brief overview of the traditional, as well as emerging, directions will be presented. Especially noteworthy are recent trends which include (a) the social learning viewpoint of career counseling, (b) the career education movement, and (c) the task analysis approach.

The Assessment of Work Potential

Industrial psychology traditionally has stressed the methodology of personnel selection and the evaluation of personnel decisions (e.g., Horst, 1966; Fleishman, 1967; McCormick and Tiffin, 1974). An industrial psychologist may examine the necessary requirements of various jobs and the relationship of the abilities and interests of applicants to job success. As one would expect, efficiency and cost effectiveness have been the guiding parameters which, historically, have served to limit opportunities for handicapped or culturally different individuals.

The special problems of minority and handicapped individuals have not been addressed until quite recently. Crites (1969), for example, excluded topics pertaining to handicapped and minority individuals from his major review of vocational psychology for the following reasons:

> First, it is a disparate body of knowledge, which does not meaningfully lend itself to any one organizational scheme and hence is better treated separately; and second, it is marked by many lacunae [gaps] in both research and theory, which indicate that it is not ready for review at this time. (p. 24)

The Crites analysis is important because it emphasizes that despite legislative changes (as well as good will on the part of many industries), the scientific study of vocational assessment of the handicapped and members of minority groups has an extremely short history. More recently, in the major edited work by Dunnette (1976), discussions of vocational preferences of minorities and discrimination in personnel selection of minorities are included. Other cross-cultural issues are presented, and problems related to handicapped populations are briefly treated.

Backer (1973) reviewed assessment approaches and concluded that traditional aptitude, interest, and personality tests have limited utility in seriously "disadvantaged populations." Major advances (e.g., work samples) still may have only limited potential and modest validities.

Neff (1977) outlines the four major approaches to the "assessment of work potential": (1) the mental testing approach; (2) the job-analysis approach; (3) the work-sample approach; and (4) the situational assessment approach (p. 197). The four approaches are basic to the evaluative phase of vocational rehabilitation (e.g., Bitter, 1979).

The *mental testing approach* has already been described in other contexts. Anastasi (1976), Bitter (1979), McCormick and Tiffin (1974), and Super and Crites (1962) survey a number of tests that have been used in occupational testing. These have involved the measurement of aptitudes and interests.

A second approach, originating in industry, is *job analysis*. The focus is on a "description of the work to be performed. . .what workers actually do and what they have to know" (Neff, 1977, pp. 201-202). A third approach is the *work-sample:* "a 'mock-up'. . .of an actual industrial operation" (p. 204). The fourth approach is *situational assessment,* oriented toward "work behavior in general" or "the general work personality" including:

> the meaning of work to the individual, the manner in which he relates to important other persons on the job, his attitudes to supervisors, peers and subordinates [and acceptable] roles. (p. 206)

Bitter (1979) includes examples of specific techniques within each approach and notes advantages as well as disadvantages. Neff (1977) also describes well known techniques and discusses appropriateness of various applications. Ghiselli (1966; 1973) reviewed the results of numerous studies involving measures of specific abilities (e.g., intellectual, spatial, mechanical, etc.) related to various occupations. The validity studies were considered within two broad criteria: the ability to predict the success of novices in training, and the "proficiency level" of trained workers. Ghiselli's summary of the results, compiled from many different studies, is important. He found that "for all occupations the average of the validity coefficients for training criteria is .30, and for proficiency criteria is .19" (1966, p. 115). The 1973 results are slightly higher, although when the best test is selected for each job, the ranges are considerably greater. Although generally low, many of the correlations were statistically significant, especially those relating intellectual, spatial, and mechanical abilities to "general occupational trainability" (1966, p. 124).

Despite statistical significance, the overall predictive power for individuals is quite low. For handicapped or minority individuals, the tests may not be very useful for screening and decision-making purposes. Gold, (1973, 1975, 1976) has been an influential critic of the use of such tests with mentally retarded people: "Prediction and testing promote a reliance on screening out individuals who are difficult to train instead of developing training procedures with sufficient power to meet the needs of all trainees" (1975, p. 259). Gold (1973) further states: "The extensive literature on vocational evaluation and prediction is full of *statistical* significance but devoid of *practical* significance" (p. 105).

In summary, until recently, traditional methods in industrial and vocational psychology have neglected the problems of minority and handicapped individuals. Errors have occurred in job selection because of the limited validity of tests used to predict successful adaptation to work. Another problem has been the difficulty in predicting the potential of minority and handicapped persons, especially in light of new technological advances and training methods. Despite the fact that some industries have major assistance programs to aid handicapped and minority members in career possibilities and work adjustment, it still is quite a new field. Many times an initial job has to be individually negotiated between school support staff, the adolescent or young adult, and the industry or business. Techniques that have evolved through industry (e.g., job analysis) and vocational rehabilitation (e.g., work-sample, situational approaches) although still limited, have much to offer handicapped and minority individuals in terms of assessment and intervention.

Career Counseling

Another perspective in vocational assessment is provided by the field of counseling psychology. Krumboltz, Becker-Haven, and Burnett (1979) comment that assisting people with career decisions is one of the important roles of counseling psychologists. The authors review five areas that provide an important framework for vocational assessment and counseling of mildly handicapped, minority, and other persons. For a broader introduction to career counseling, the book edited by Whitely and Resnikoff (1978) would be helpful.

The first area reviewed is that of *decision-making skills* including the

> ability to learn about oneself, learn about career opportunities, consider many alternatives, seek information, clarify values, make plans, see oneself in control, engage in exploration process with satisfaction, or overcome indecisiveness and its accompanying anxiety. (Krumboltz, *et al.*, 1979 pp. 577-578)

Krumboltz, et al. note that certain adolescents may need an "expert approach" involving, for example, modeling decision making behaviors, guided practice, anxiety management, and problem solving (p. 579). For some students, *interest inventories* and *aptitude tests* may be of help. Examples are the Strong-Campbell Interest Inventory (Campbell, 1974), the Kuder Occupational Interest Survey (Kuder, 1975), the Reading-Free Vocational Interest Inventory (Becker, 1975) and the Minnesota Vocational Interest Inventory (Clark and Campbell, 1965). Popular aptitude tests include the General Aptitude Test Battery (U.S. Department of Labor, 1970) and the Differential Aptitude Test Battery (Bennett, Seashore, and Wesman, 1969). Interest inventories and aptitude measures are useful for exploratory, rather than for decision-making purposes. Sundberg (1977) notes that interests and abilities are not highly correlated.

Designed specifically for educable mentally retarded students in secondary programs, the Social and Prevocational Information Battery (Halpern, Raffeld, Irvin and Link, 1975) assesses nine areas of importance for community adjustment: purchasing, budgeting, banking, job related behavior, job search skills, home management, health care, hygiene and functional signs. The domains and content areas would be very useful for many individual and programmatic decisions, although the true-false format would require additional time for individual task analysis in order to determine specific competencies in skill areas. The test has been revised for use with lower functioning EMR and trainable students (Irvin, Halpern and Reynolds, 1979).

Wallace and Larsen (1978) review many tests and inventories from a "career-education" assessment point of view. The Mooney Problems Check List (Mooney and Gordon, 1950), and the STS Youth Inventory (Remmers and Shimberg, 1967) also present questions in a self-report format in the areas of vocational preparation and post high school plans. Samuda (1975) has compiled a number of tests that may be useful for minority or educationally disadvantaged adolescents and adults. He includes work-related aptitude tests, occupational preference inventories, and non-reading interest inventories. The use of tests or questionnaires to assess interests and one's orientation to the future must be viewed as only one aspect of assisting with the decision-making process as Krumboltz, *et al.* (1979) point out. Merachnick (1970) and Brolin and Gysbers (1979) have described the effect handicapping conditions have on preparation for work. Handicapped students do not have the same "opportunities for exploration" and "pre-work activities" (e.g., part time jobs, helping around the house, social interactions with a cross section of persons). Also, parents of handicapped adolescents (or the adolescents themselves) may have overprotective attitudes. For these reasons, specialized testing may not be that helpful because interest and aptitude measures are dependent upon "familiarity and practice with activities in daily living" (Merachnick, 1970, p. 227).

The second major area is *career maturity*, defined as "activities, knowledge, and attitudes about occupations, planning, and career decision making that tend to show development over the adolescent years" (Krumboltz, *et al.*, 1979, p. 58). Super (1953, 1980; Super and Hall, 1978) has been one of the most influential writers in this area.

The third area reviewed by Krumboltz, *et al.* involves the *nature and quality of vocational choices.* In order to assist with vocational choices,

> counselors may provide appropriate role models, provide occupational and sex-role-destroying information, reinforce "congruent" choices, and give accurate self-knowledge feedback. (p. 583)

The fourth and fifth areas involve the potential value of training in *employment seeking skills* (e.g., "job finding" steps and interviewing) and *occupational adaption* (including occupational success and satisfaction).

Social Learning and Career Decision Making

Krumboltz (1979) describes a social learning theory of career decision making. Of importance is the analysis of the complex interactions between genetically determined characteristics, learned behavior, and environmental circumstances that can determine one's "career path." In addition to the assessment of special abilities and interests, the social learning approach includes an analysis of "environmental conditions and events," such as the number and nature of opportunities, differences and availability of training approaches, and social policies and procedures (Krumboltz, 1979, pp. 20-22). Extremely important for assessment of the career potential and decision making patterns of handicapped individuals are technological developments (e.g., for blind, deaf, or hearing impaired, or people with impaired motoric functioning) and family resources. As Brolin and D'Alonzo (1979) point out, important technological advances have allowed "handicapped individuals to be more mobile and to interact and communicate more effectively within their environment" (p. 248). Many of the innovations require special expertise and make collaboration between families, job seeking individuals, specialists in the handicapping field, and industry representatives essential.

Another characteristic of the social learning approach is the priority given to broad based interventions, especially important with ethnic minorities. Jones and Gelatt (1979) explore the possibilities of various interventions that would (a) assist in career decision making, and (b) possibly improve the "outcomes" of the decisions. For example, interventions may address the effects of sex, ethnic, and handicapped stereotypes, as well as specific handicapping conditions. Social learning interventions might address "environmental conditions and events," the learning of specific job related skills via methods appropriate for the individual, and self-assessment skills, among others (Jones and Gelatt, 1979, pp. 67-75).

With respect to minorities, Oakland and Matuszek (1977) note that criterion referenced measures are being used increasingly in vocational, as well as educational, settings. "Vocational aptitude and ability tests are being constructed which permit a more direct assessment of a person's actual ability and desire to perform effectively certain jobs than is available through paper and pencil instruments" (p. 57).

Vocational Assessment: Other Important Trends

Several additional perspectives are important for minority and handicapped individuals. The first relates to legislative trends, outside the scope of this book. Razeghi and Davis (1979) review the federal laws relating to vocational education for handicapped individuals. (For a discussion of legislation relating to discriminatory testing practices within industry, see Anastasi, 1976, pp. 62-64 and Appendix B.) Two other aspects of critical importance will be mentioned: the career education movement and the task analysis approach.

Career Education. Although there have been many definitions of career education, Wallace and Larsen (1978) note four common aspects:

> Career education...(1) relates to preparing students for the world of work, (2) involves more than teaching vocational skills, (3) should be part of the curriculum for all students, and (4) is the responsibility of other community agencies as well as the school. (p. 469)

Career education includes the early childhood years through the retirement years. The focus is on "the full development of all individuals" (Brolin and Kokaska, 1979, p. 104). Skills are conceptualized by three areas: daily living, personal-social, and occupational. The family and community, in addition to the school, are expected to share in responsibility for career education. In their comprehensive text, Brolin and Kokaska (1979) define career education as "the process of systematically coordinating all school, family and community components together to facilitate each individual's potential for economic, social and personal fulfillment" (p. 102). Schools with comprehensive career education programs, as discussed by Brolin and Kokaska (1979), may significantly recast the traditional role of vocational assessment.

Smith (1980) suggests that compensatory vocational programs for minorities should be an integral part of the "entire educational experience." A major objective of the schools should be preparing youth for work. This would include not only "facts and skills," but also values and attitudes concerning careers. Smith continues by stressing that the above objectives would be insufficient without addressing current problems with the "occupational opportunity structure" (p. 354).

Clark (1975) and Brolin and D'Alonzo (1979) review the implications for career education for handicapped students. Career education may be helpful for determining "the least restrictive career development experiences" (Brolin and D'Alonzo, 1979, p. 251). Further, they point out that

> because of the wide range of learning styles, ability levels, sensory motor development, and social-emotional development of handicapped students, career education experiences will need to be personalized and tailored to meet their special needs. (p. 251)

Task Analysis. Ysseldyke (1978) views task analysis and specific skill training as alternatives to ability assessment and training.

> Task analysis consists of breaking down a complex terminal behavior into its component parts (enabling behaviors), teaching those enabling behaviors that a pupil does not yet demonstrate, and integrating those behaviors into a terminal objective. (p. 128)

With more severely handicapped individuals, the work of Gold (1973; 1975; 1976; and Gold and Pomerantz, 1978) has been extremely influential. Gold (1973) offered criticisms of various ability measures and approaches using tests to predict vocational success with mentally retarded individuals. He pointed out that the "mentally retarded population...is perceived by almost everyone as being far less capable than is really the case" (p. 140).

For example, Gold (1976) illustrated a task analysis approach with moderate, severe, and profoundly retarded blind and deaf blind people (the mean age was 33 years; the mean IQ was 32). The task involved the assembly of a complex coaster brake. The hypothesis relating to the feasibility of developing training procedures for blind retarded persons based on task analysis work with sighted retarded individuals was upheld. By emphasizing a commitment to apply an appropriate training strategy (e.g., Gold, 1980), all subjects reached the criterion level on the task. Gold offered three generalizations, summarized as follows:

1. The more difficult it is...to acquire a task, the more a trainer must know about the task.
2. The more the task analyst knows about the task, the less prerequisites are needed by the learner.
3. The decision to teach or not to teach any task to the severely and profoundly handicapped must be based on whether that task can be analyzed into teachable components rather than force analysts to rely on some general feeling about the difficulty of the task. (pp. 82-83)

Gold (1976) calls for a "reconceptualization of the severely handicapped," viewing them as individuals requiring "powerful training procedures" for learning, rather than considering them "as individuals who can learn very little" (p. 84). Rusch and Mithaug (1980) apply a behavior analytic approach to the vocational training of mentally retarded adults. Chapters on "Community Mobility Training," "Social and Vocational Survival Skills" and sections on conducting a job analysis survey and job task analysis are certain to have broad applicability.

Vocational School Psychology

In March, 1979, the National Association of School Psychologists unanimously approved the subspecialty of vocational school psychology. Hohenshil (1975) and Hohenshil and Warden (1977) have described the possible roles and training of specialists in this area. They argue that "it is especially critical that school psychological services be expanded in vocational programs for handicapped and disadvantaged youth" (Hohenshil and Warden, 1977, p. 16). In addition to traditional techniques, direct and consultative service would require that psychologists have competencies in the areas discussed in the present section.

A number of resources exist for school psychologists who want more information about vocational school psychology. Hohenshil and Warden (1977) outline competency domains and an example of a university training program. Hohenshil (1980) has also compiled a bibliography, *Vocational School Psychology/Vocational Education for the Handicapped.* The text on vocational rehabilitation by Bitter (1979) gives an introduction to specific disabilities and describes a number of vocational evaluation techniques. Another important perspective is given by recent texts on career education (e.g., Brolin and Kokaska, 1979; Brolin and Kolstoe, 1978) and a recent issue of *Exceptional Children* (47, 8, 1981). Other sources of information are the newsletter "Programs for the Handicapped ," published by the Office for Handicapped Individuals, 200 Independence Ave., S.W., Washington, D.C. 20201, the Division on Career Development, Council for Exceptional Children, 1920 Association Drive, Reston, VA 22091, and the document *Resources for the Vocational Preparation of Disabled Youth,* U.S. Government Printing Office, Washington, D.C. 20402.

Summary

The topic of vocational assessment draws from many areas and disciplines. Industrial psychology has, in the past, emphasized selection procedures that have limited the opportunities for handicapped and minority group members. Vocational psychology has contributed to the scientific study of vocational behavior, but has neglected the problems of special groups of individuals. Neither field has addressed the complexities of assisting individuals with career choices. Many significant evaluation techniques have been developed in the field of vocational rehabilitation. Counseling psychology has been directly concerned with assisting individuals in making career choices. Most notable are recent trends in applying the principles of social learning theory to career choice. Theories of career development and maturity are also applicable. Even more specialization is required to counsel handicapped individuals due to the difficulties in recognizing potential and the complexities of technological advances, allowing new career choices. The career education movement has been an important trend. With severely handicapped individuals, a task analysis approach to learning has clearly changed the perceived limits of performance in work related tasks. Vocational school psychology offers great promise as an important area of specialization.

The Assessment of Visual-Motor and Gross-Motor Skills

The use of perceptual-motor assessment techniques has been severely attacked in recent years (e.g., Hammill, 1978), especially in the diagnosis and remediation of children considered learning disabled. Three major criticisms stand out, with the first two being closely related.

The first concerns the basic assumption that academic problems are caused by underlying perceptual disorders (Wallace and Larsen, 1978). The second criticism is that the efficacy of a curricular approach based on perceptual-motor assessment and remediation has not been demonstrated. Salvia and Ysseldyke (1978) comment:

> In short, the devices currently used to assess children's perceptual-motor skills are extremely inadequate. The real danger is that reliance on such tests in planning interventions for children may actually lead to assigning children to activities that do them absolutely no good. (p. 303)

A third criticism concerns the use of perceptual-motor tests for the "differential diagnosis" of children who may be brain injured. A number of perceptual-motor tests (and also various subtests on intelligence scales such as the Wechsler) have been explored in terms of their usefulness in identifying children with hypothesized central nervous system dysfunction.

This section will provide an overview of theoretical assumptions and examples of perceptual-motor techniques stressing the visual modality. A discussion of indications for accepted usage will also be presented.

An Overview of Perceptual-Motor Assumptions

Frostig (e.g., Frostig and Maslow, 1973) and Kephart (1971) best illustrate the application of motor skills to educational tasks. The major assumption Kephart makes is that higher levels of learning are dependent upon a motor base of achievement as represented by earlier stages of development. The three dimensions of space, time and space-time are also considered in relationship to the child's functioning. Spatial aspects involve the knowledge and internal representation of up-down, front-back, and left-right (the three dimensions of Euclidean geometry). Time is a complex dimension having many aspects such as rhythm, past, present, future, pace, sequence, and simultaneity. Simultaneity refers to the relationship between space-time. For example, writing requires the rhythmic movement of the hand in such a way as to satisfy the spatial requirements of the letters and the drawing surface. The movement occurs over time. The academic problems of children, especially those considered to be learning disabled, are explored for "low level functional deficits." For example, confusion with "b" and "d" might indicate a problem with laterality. A child with a reading problem may have difficulty visually tracking an object, which leads to an inability to acquire consistent visual information from the environment.

Representative Techniques

The Purdue Perceptual Motor Survey (PPMS) (Roach and Kephart, 1966) is an informal test that permits a trained observer to assess the quality of an elementary school child's perceptual-motor development. The child is observed during the performance of a number of activities that require skills related to laterality (left-right awareness), directionality (internal automatic functioning associated with laterality and other space-time movements), and the perceptual-motor match (when perceptions and movements become integrated). Activities include the Walking Board (requiring balance), Identification of Body Parts, an Obstacle Course (relating visual cues to motor movements and allowing for objects outside the visual field), Angels-in-the -Snow (requiring the child to move arms and legs singly or in combination in an automatic smooth fashion in response to commands), Chalkboard Activities (circles, and lines; copying repetitive geometric motifs and letters such as cursive mmmmm's, bbbbb's, ppppp's, lllll's) and Ocular Pursuits (requiring visual tracking).

A related and complementary evaluation technique has been developed by Miriam Bender to assess even lower levels of problems in motor functioning. In an experimental study (n = 69), Bender (1976) found a "significant relationship...between persistent immaturity of the Symmetric Tonic Neck Reflex and the presence of learning disorders among children of elementary school age" (p. 38). Bender hypothesized that if the Symmetric Tonic Neck Reflex (facilitative for the infant in learning to walk) persists, it would have the effect of restricting voluntary movement and normal motor development. For example, evidence of abnormal reflex activity can be found in a creeping task by noting (a) the position of the head (not held erect), (b) the use of arms and hands (e.g., bent elbows, hands turned sharply in or out), (c) the position of hips and knees (i.e., cramped movements, trunk lowered), and (d) tension and lack of rhythm in movements. It is surprising to observe the restricted voluntary movement of seemingly normal children on this test and on similar tests (e.g., the PPMS). Based on her study, she proposed that "about 75 percent of the children with disorders of learning may be expected to show behavioral signs of Symmetric Tonic Neck Reflex immaturity persisting without regard for CA or IQ" (p. 39). The Bender Purdue Reflex Test (Bender, 1976) offers assessment and intervention strategies for children with this problem. The manual, however, does not provide validity information relating to the efficacy of the training approach with children having academic learning problems.

The Developmental Test of Visual-Motor Integration, or VMI (Beery, 1967), is widely used in the public schools. The test is comprised of a series of twenty-four geometric drawings beginning with simple lines and forms (vertical, horizontal, circle) and ending with complex patterns. The test may be given either through the use of a booklet, on which the child is asked to copy the forms in a space immediately below the drawing, or the forms may be presented one-by-one, with the designs presented on small cards. The test is easy to administer and score and may be used in screening groups of children. In contrast to many other perceptual-motor measures, reliability is adequate. Norms are provided from ages 2 to 15. The VMI is perhaps most appropriate for preschool and primary aged children.

The Bender-Gestalt is a popular test consisting of nine geometric forms that a child is asked to copy in an unstructured fashion on a sheet of paper (more paper can be used if the child desires). The Koppitz (1964, 1975) system of scoring is frequently used. Shape distortions, perseveration of the designs or features of the designs, integration problems, rotations of the designs and qualitative aspects of the drawings (e.g., organization, line quality) are noted. The test has been used as a predictor of academic achievement and for the differential diagnosis of brain injury. Also, characteristics of the child's performance. Although widely used for all the above purposes, the reliability and validity of the technique does not support use, in isolation, for either decisions concerning placement or for differential diagnosis of brain injury (Salvia and Ysseldyke, 1978). The use of the Bender-Gestalt for assessing emotional problems has often been challenged (e.g., Trahan and Stricklin, 1979).

Comprehensive reviews of other techniques (e.g., the Lincoln-Oseretsky Motor Development Scale, Frostig Developmental Test of Visual Perception, Ayers' Southern California Sensory Integration Tests), as well as the critical issues involved in the assessment of perceptual and gross-motor skills from an educational viewpoint, can be found in Hammill and Bartel (1978), Salvia and Ysseldyke (1978), and Wallace and Larsen (1978). Coles (1978) summarizes the use of popular tests with respect to the diagnosis of learning disabilities from the ''minimal brain dysfunction'' perspective and similarly offers a critical review. In a recent text edited by Rie and Rie (1979), many of the myths about minimal brain dysfunction are explored. They point out that many existing assumptions and beliefs cannot be adequately supported by research evidence. The above sources serve as especially important reading for psychologists and educators providing services to children categorized as learning disabled. Anastasti (1976) and Buros' Mental Measurement Yearbooks contain references to a number of techniques (e.g., vocational aptitude) that could similarly be categorized as perceptual-motor tests. Also, tests described in other sections of this chapter tap skills relating to perceptual-motor development (e.g., the Wechsler Scales, the Binet, the Slingerland, etc.), as do popular reading readiness tests.

Indications for Use

The severe criticisms directed toward perceptual-motor assessment serve as warnings to practitioners who have either made educational decisions based on unvalidated assumptions of perceptual-motor development, or have used certain tests to hypothesize constructs relating to the etiology of academic problems, especially constructs such as minimal brain dysfunction. With the criticisms in mind, what are the possible uses of perceptual-motor tests?

Although the value of perceptual and gross-motor training relative to academic learning has not been established, the skills can be often improved and this may serve as an end in itself. Teachers, parents, and psychologists may decide that a child would benefit from training in this area independent of academic concerns. For example, improved perceptual-motor skills may contribute to a child's positive self-image. Consistent with the ethical viewpoint expressed by the normalization principle, Hammill (1978) states:

> If...the decision is made to provide perceptual-motor training, teachers should be urged to implement the programs on a remedial basis only in those few cases where improvement in perception is the goal and to consider even these efforts as being highly experimental. (p. 373)

Earlier, Cratty (1967) noted the lack of direct evidence with respect to the correspondence between perceptual-motor activities and intellectual functioning, but argued that "there are *certain components* of the overall educational program to which movement activities can contribute in a positive way" (p. 3). Many references exist containing suggestions for the development of perceptual-motor skills in children. Examples are Frostig and Maslow (1969, 1973), Mourouzis, et al. (1970), and Kephart's (1971) classic text. It is important to note that academic tasks can be combined with perceptual-motor games and activites (Early, 1969). Perceptual-motor training and academics are not necessarily mutually exclusive, and may be significant, when combined, in developing interventions for young children. The major points to keep in mind are the empirically demonstrated advantages of the direct task analytic and behavioral approaches in the remediation of severe academic problems.

A second area of potential use, the differential diagnosis of brain injury or minimal brain dysfunction, is still quite problematic. School service personnel are obligated to provide comprehensive services to children, which often necessitates evaluations by medical specialists (e.g., neurologists, ophthalmologists, pediatricians). The observations of severe performance deficits in perceptual-motor functioning have often been the basis for referrals by parents, teachers, and psychologists. Informal observations of motor performance (e.g., child's gait, balance, stair climbing skill), analysis of patterns of successes and failures on tests previously described in the cognitive areas (e.g., the WISC-R), delays in language functioning, marked deviations and distortions in perceptual-motor tasks (e.g., the Bender-Gestalt), and problems in classroom behavior all have, singly or in combination, led to medical referrals. Referrals to specialists based on careful observations are important and medical evaluations can be a significant aspect of multifactored assessment. Unfortunately, the potential contributions have been often misunderstood, particulary for children having relatively mild learning and behavior problems. Feuerstein, Ward, and LeBaron (1977) review the literature on neuropsychological and neurophysiological assessment batteries with learning disabled and behavior disordered children. They report:

> While the use of these techniques may be appropriate in selected cases, clinicians may refer children for these types of evaluations more frequently than is warranted. In fact, it is often recommended that the child with learning or behavior problems referred for assessment of "brain damage" be sent back to the referring psychologist for evaluation of "cognitive and behavioral" difficulties because no clear evidence of neurological damage was actually observed. (p. 242)

Neurophysiological assessment (especially with regard to attention and arousal deficits) appears to be promising, but techniques are in the research stage and not available "for direct clinical application" (Feuerstein, et al., 1977). Neuropsychological and EEG techniques are helpful in the identification of serious brain abnormalities; the usefulness of such techniques in assessing children's learning and behavior problems has not been sufficiently demonstrated (Feuerstein, et al., 1977). Their summary of contemporary approaches is important for practitioners working with learning disabled and behavior disordered children (including those considered as hyperactive) because, "from a practical-clinical perspective," the techniques appear to be "no more useful than what is generally completed in a standard psychological behavioral evaluation"(p. 274).

Boll (1977) describes the rationale for neuropsychological assessment. Trupin and Townes (1976) argue for the inclusion of an analysis of neurological functioning in an ecological approach to assessment, while Oakland and Goldwater (1979) view psychoneurology as an "emerging" area of assessment. It will be important for school psychologists to follow the development of neurophysiological techniques. Suggestions for further reading include Braud (1978), John (1977), Lezak (1976), Knights and Bakker (1976), Reitan and Davison (1974), and Rie and Rie (1979). Brown's (1980) text provides a background understanding of neuroanatomy, neurophysiology, and neurology, and is intended for use by professionals in health fields. Especially helpful is the edited *Handbook of Clinical Neuropsychology* by Filskov and Boll (1981). The expense and low probability for meaningful assessment information pertinent to educational programming, however, make such referrals a difficult decision. The following techniques may provide parameters for practitioners. It is important, however, to note that the techniques require further validation to assist with referral decisions.

In developing the SOMPA (System of Multicultural Pluralistic Assessment), Mercer (1979) included a number of measures that, while not comprehensive, may facilitate decision making regarding the need for medical evaluations. Among the "Medical Model Measures" related to perceptual-motor functioning are the Physical Dexterity Tasks and the Bender-Gestalt. Other measures include the Health History Inventory, vision and hearing screening, and weight standardized by height (a global measure of health). "Children who score in the lowest 16 percent [of the Medical Model Measures] are considered to be at risk of organic anomaly" (Mercer, 1979, p. 83).

Another approach is the Screening Scale for Neurological Dysfunction, "designed to aid the professional examiner in determining whether a child should be referred for a neurological evaluation" (Kuhns, 1978, p. 7). The strategy is potentially important, but requires additional standardization and research. The technique is presently validated only on professional opinion. The amount of agreement was determined between a psychologist and medical specialist, as to the appropriateness of referrals over a small number of cases. Referral clusters relate to the following specialists: Ophthalmologist, Audiologist, Pediatrician, Speech Specialist, and Pediatric-Neurologist. The comprehensive description of a neurological evaluation contained in the manual may be of interest to practitioners.

Similarly, the Quick Neurological Screening Test (Mutti, Sterling, and Spalding, 1978) is comprised of fifteen tasks adapted from a pediatric neurological exam and takes about twenty minutes to complete. The authors state that a "neurologically intact" child should be able to complete the tasks with little difficulty after age seven, while persons with organic brain syndromes "will almost certainly fail multiple tasks" (p. 8).

Summary

The severe criticisms of the utility of perceptual-motor assessment provide an important context for this section. Concerns relate to (a) curriculum development for children with academic problems, based on perceptual-motor assessment and remediation techniques, and (b) the construct of "minimal brain dysfunction" with children characterized as learning disabled, hyperactive, and behavior disordered, as identified by neuropsychological techniques. Because of the vehement criticism, valid reasons for use may be overlooked. Perceptual processes and motor skills can often be successfully trained and may be an end in themselves for a child with a severe problem. With young children, perceptual-motor games and activities can be combined with cognitive tasks. Hammill's earlier warning serves as a cautious reminder for those who want to provide such assistance. To balance the issue, perceptual-motor assessment techniques and informal observations of such skills may assist the psychologist, parent, and teacher in making referrals for comprehensive medical evaluations.

One could argue that references concerning neuropsychological and neurophysiological assessment do not logically belong in a section describing the assessment of perceptual-motor functioning. The reasons for doing so involve the traditional attempts to tie learning disabilities to brain functioning (e.g., minimal brain dysfunction, minimal brain injury, neurologically impaired, etc.), and the strong historical association between learning disabilities diagnosis and perceptual-motor tests. Neuropsychological assessment includes more than perceptual-motor tasks. Sources of evidence may include personality or behavior changes, problems with cognition, language disturbances, problems with reflexes, as well as with sensory and sensory-motor systems. The major point is that neuropsychological and neurophysiological approaches have not been proven to be useful, thus far in their development, for the educational problems of children with relatively mild learning and behavior problems. The techniques are generally useful in screening for gross abnormalities involving serious problems.

Chapter 6

PROCEDURES IN THE EVALUATION OF CHILDREN WITH LOW INCIDENCE HANDICAPPING CONDITIONS

Nowhere have the impact of P.L.94-142 and the urgency of procedural changes been more evident than with low incidence handicapped children. They comprise a group that was generally excluded from school, but which now must be served within the public school domain under the zero reject philosophy of the new laws. This chapter will examine the historical perspectives, major issues, and practical methodology associated with the provision of school psychological services to the low incidence population.

Historical Perspectives

The term "low incidence" refers to a group of several types of exceptionalities that were served in public school settings very infrequently prior to the 1970's. Although large city schools occasionally had their own programs for the deaf and the blind, these groups were generally provided educational programming at specialized state schools. Deaf, blind, severely and profoundly retarded, physically handicapped, and emotionally disturbed children were usually institutionalized if their families could not care for them. Conditions at state facilities were often poor and dehumanizing with little in the line of educational or therapeutic programming. Parents who decided to keep their children at home bore a heavy burden, since virtually no services were provided in most communities. With the passage of P.L.94-142, all low incidence groups have become the educational responsibility of local school systems and the evaluation responsibility of school psychologists.

In the past, many children in low incidence groups were described as "untestable." For them, the outcomes of a traditional evaluation might, at best, include a rather hopeless description of intellectual or physical impairment, and a label selected from the classification system most

162

familiar to the examiner. The evaluation processes basically verified what was already obvious—that the youngster was severely handicapped. The result was that the child was certified as having a specific impairment (diagnosis) and could then be excluded, institutionalized, admitted, committed, etc. In this sense, the evaluation was of no direct benefit to the child. Little pertinent educational information was obtained and instructional programs were often not offered to the handicapped. Wolfensberger (1972) provides an excellent historical overview of social services. He illustrates how predominant attitudes toward the handicapped have affected social and educational policies in the past, as well as the present.

With the mandated changes, two points have become clear. First, school psychologists are now expected to provide information of direct relevance for preparation of the Individualized Educational Program (IEP). Second, traditional evaluation tools and techniques are incapable of statifying the requirement of the first point. Although many professionals may have felt dissatisfied with evaluation outcomes for the severely handicapped, there was little impetus for change prior to the recent legislation. Most now recognize the need to locate new materials and procedures that will permit meaningful and effective contributions by psychologists involved with the low incidence handicapped individual.

Trends and Issues

The majority of school psychologists have not been formally trained in assessment of either severely handicapped or pre-academic skills. Thus, understanding of the proposed procedures may be facilitated by consideration of several theoretical and practical issues related to the task. One problem involves the type of evaluation tools selected for low incidence cases. A second issue is related to the acquisition and use of educationally relevant information.

Traditional evaluation procedures are based on normative comparisons, but this approach is of little value for the severely handicapped. The profoundly retarded child may be totally unable to perform the lowest items on a standardized instrument. Less severely impaired youngsters may still function at levels below minimum requirements for normative comparison. One must question the value of extreme or derived scores (an extrapolated IQ of 10, for example) in terms of educational programming (Brown, Branston, Hamre-Nietupski, Pumpian, Certo, and Gruenwald, 1979). An over-reliance on norms and standardization has made psychologists somewhat rigid in their orientation to low incidence assessment, and the traditional approach has been widely criticized (Bennett, Hughes, and Hughes, 1979; DuBose, Langley, and Stagg, 1977; and Salvia and Ysseldyke, 1978).

In contrast, one may view evaluation as the first step in the educational process (Sailor and Horner, 1976). In this context, evaluation information is used in the development of the child's IEP and must be pertinent to skill planning. Pressure for psychologists to change their approach appears to have come from special educators charged with responsibility for program planning in the absence of appropriate data. The demand has been for information that will facilitate the selection of educational goals, objectives, teaching activities, and materials. The result has been the development of criterion referenced assessment strategies to permit evaluation of the individual's relative standing with respect to mastery of sequence of skills. The procedure is based on direct measurement of educationally relevant tasks and is closely tied to teaching objectives.

Criterion referenced systems have been used in different ways. One approach has been based on information from developmental approaches. Haring and Bricker (1976) have described three assumptions which characterize this technique: (a) behavior changes follow a developmental hierarchy that is relatively fixed in sequence; (b) behavior acquisition moves from simple to complex activities; and (c) more complex behavior is the result of the modification or coordination of basic component behaviors. These principles seem quite logical and straightforward and many assessment tools frequently used with low incidence children incorporate them. A child's developmental status is specified exactly, and the next sequential skill is identified for teaching emphasis. Questions, however, have recently been raised about the appropriateness of the developmental model for the severely handicapped.

Developmental schedules are constructed and validated on the basis of normative standards, such as the average age of skill emergence, and the sequential steps of development. The problem is that little evidence exists to support the assumption that the severely handicapped develop in the same manner or sequence as suggested by a normative model (Switzky, Rotatori, Miller, and Freagon, 1979). Furthermore, empirical validation of teaching programs based on developmental concepts has yet to be accomplished. Given the levels of impairment of many children, an inordinate amount of valuable instructional time might be required to insure sequential and uniform skill acquisition at such low levels.

Brown, Nietupski, and Hamre-Nietupski (1976) have expressed concerns about developmental and educational activities that promote specific skills that either have no relevance for, or do not generalize to, the post-educational setting where the individual must function. They have proposed "the criterion of ultimate functioning" as a vehicle for evaluating educational (and assessment) activities with the severely handicapped.

> The criterion of ultimate functioning refers to the ever changing, expanding, localizing, and personalizing cluster of factors that each person must possess in order to function as productively and independently as possible in socially, vocationally, and domestically integrated adult community environments. (p. 8)

They further state:

> The criterion of ultimate functioning should be the standard by which educational activities are judged as they relate to severely handicapped students. Any activity, however episodic or apparently inconsequential, must be related to the criterion of ultimate functioning, or that acitvity should be terminated. (p. 8)

Despite criticism, developmental scales are not being totally abandoned as new uses are being advocated. Several authors (Cohen and Gross, 1979; Cohen, Gross, and Haring, 1976; Somerton and Meyers, 1976; Switzky, *et al.*, 1979) have suggested that developmental information can be combined with a task analysis format to produce individualized instruction programs for low incidence children. After the general assessment of the child's developmental status, analysis is directed toward the identification of skills that will improve the child's ability to interact with the environment. Each required ability can then be broken into components through task analysis. Missing areas can be translated into immediate instructional objectives (Guess, *et al.*, 1978). Evaluation and teaching become closely linked in a test-teach-test format (DuBose, *et al.*, 1977). The psychologist and teacher may contribute jointly to the initial assessment, but the teacher assumes responsibility for on-going evaluation and reprogramming. The psychologist's role then becomes that of a consultant to the teacher and other educational staff. Given the instructional problems with the low incidence population, the task analysis assessment approach appears likely to grow swiftly in popularity. The procedures that follow are intended to promote development of new perspectives for psychologists as an avenue to expanded professional functioning and utilization of a broader range of skills.

Low Incidence Evaluation

Prior to the consideration of the processes that constitute a low incidence evaluation, the areas of professional preparation and service delivery, assessment objectives, and evaluation domains will be reviewed.

Professional Preparation and Service Delivery Options

Low incidence evaluations are very difficult to learn and perform because virtually no emphasis is directed to the task in the traditional training of school psychologists. For those interested in developing assessment skills, little information or training has been available. With the influx of severely handicapped children into the public schools, practices have ranged from the assignment of all cases to one person to the distribution of the caseload equally among staff. Since all psychologists, particularly those in rural areas, are likely to encounter low incidence cases sooner or later, familiarity with a framework for assessment is highly recommended. Specialization, however, is the advocated method of service delivery for several reasons.

No psychologist can become comfortable or proficient in low incidence evaluation while seeing only ten or fifteen children each year across handicapped groups. Direct experience with large numbers of low incidence children is important for training and maintenance of skills. Furthermore, in districts or counties where large numbers of handicapped individuals reside, specialization within various exceptionalities is possible and desirable. To this end, regionalization of services might be explored in order to generate an adequate caseload to justify specialized services. The rationale for development of expertise with specific handicapping conditions can be understood when one considers the demands of the job in each separate low incidence area. The psychologist must become extremely familiar with the characteristics of the population to be served in order to facilitate interpretation of behavior and evaluation data. Psychologists must keep abreast of the literature related to the area from both an educational and a psychological perspective. The responsibilities imply long hours within school settings for the target population, frequent evaluation experiences, additional training, plus membership in organizations specific to the handicapping condition (i.e., American Association on Mental Deficiency, Autistic Society). The inappropriateness of the generic "low incidence psychologist" is apparent when one considers the vastly different skills required in the evaluation of two diverse groups such as the severely retarded and the hearing impaired. Manual communication skills are essential in working with the hearing impaired and must be kept up through practice. In most severely retarded cases, however, communication factors do not place major impediments in the way of skill documentation or interpretation of behavior.

Even though such descriptions might tend to reinforce preexisting fears of many psychologists about low incidence evaluations, the purpose has been to heighten awareness that the task should not be taken lightly. The specialization position represents the ideal and may not always be feasible. In those areas where administrative or practical arrangements will not support specialization, psychologists performing the assessments will at least have an understanding of the complexity of the task as well as a framework for approaching evaluations. Awareness of specialized instruments and procedures will help school psychologists identify those cases appropriate for referral to clinics and agencies better prepared to perform the evaluation.

Objectives of Evaluation

Since the objectives of low incidence assessment are directly related to educational practices, the process should satisfy several objectives. Forcade, Matey, and Barnett (1979) have suggested the following functions: (a) determination of a global approach or program for the child through identification of required services; (b) definition of objectives for intervention and instruction; (c) recommendation of appropriate environmental, behavioral, and instructional strategies; and (d) provision of a basis for program evaluation through repeated measurement. The psychologist does not have sole responsibility for accomplishment of all the objectives, since evaluations are conducted by multidisciplinary teams. The role of team members will vary, depending on professional composition of the team, and each member must endeavor to make significant contributions to the process of meeting the evaluation objectives. Therefore, psychologists should be prepared to select materials and to formulate strategies that will enhance their participation.

Evaluation Domains

Low incidence evaluations can be conceptualized as the formal and informal collection of data necessary to satisfy the above objectives. The seven domains identified in Chapter Five are important in the selection of materials, organization of information, and planning of services. The value of the domain concept is enhanced for low incidence evaluation because observational and developmental assessment tools are usually organized around several categories. For low incidence cases, not only must specific information be provided under each heading, but habilitation issues must also be addressed in planning programs in the various domains.

Sensory and motor evaluation has special pertinence for the physically handicapped children in determining their educational and vocational training potential. Planning of physical and occupational therapy, or development of programs that circumvent physical limitations, are important goals of sensory and motor assessment. For people with visual or hearing impairments, residual sensory skills must be determined in order to identify the degree of supportive services that will be required. Sensory and motor limitations may also present practical evaluation and progamming problems for low incidence children.

Evaluation of communications skills becomes particularly difficult with multiply handicapped children, such as those with cerebral palsy. The documentation of the presence or absence of skills may not fairly reflect a child's potential or abilities. A major goal would be to realistically suggest approaches that would attempt to maximize communication skills for further assessment or training.

For the severely retarded, the evaluation of social skills may include observation of areas such as environmental awareness, recognition of others, or social interactions. Behavior problems that have a potential for disrupting programming should be identified so an appropriate intervention can become part of the child's IEP. Socialization can be limited severely in persons with sensory impairments despite interpersonal abilities. For example, a blind individual may be socially isolated outside of school or work regardless of appropriate social skills. Thus, evaluation should take place in a broader perspective than that found in a classroom setting or the one-to-one evaluation. For higher functioning individuals, social and self-help skills are often interpreted as "adaptive behavior." The adaptive behavior concept, however, encompasses all evaluation areas for more severely impaired children and should not be narrowly defined. The evaluation should address the impact of all domains on the individual's ability to function in an educational or vocational placement.

The evaluation of self-help skills should go beyond documentation of specifics such as dressing, feeding, and toileting. The degree to which these skills exist directly affects the child's potential for independence and integration into the least restrictive environment. Assessment should attempt to address questions regarding the need for related services, such as physical therapy to improve functioning. For severely physically handicapped children, potential environmental barriers to skill acquisition must also be identified.

Vocational assessment is more important for older handicapped individuals, but must be kept in mind even with younger children. The criterion of ultimate functioning demands that children be challenged to advance. The philosophy implies realistic assessment of future opportunities and placements, so that appropriate skills will be developed. For example, there may be a tendency to overlook the evaluation of skills directly relevant to workshop placement (manual dexterity, work orientation, attention span, etc.) with a sixteen year old severely retarded youth if his program has an academic emphasis. Acquisition of job related skills is equally important for deaf or blind people, and the potential for such skill development is a legitimate focus for the evaluation.

Cognitive/academic skills are sometimes included within other headings or completely left out of many scales used in low incidence evaluation. Tasks that tap cognitive abilities might need to be acquired from instruments such as the Bayley Scales of Infant Development in the evaluation of younger, more severely handicapped children. Assessment of specific cognitive skills of the profoundly retarded, however, is not emphasized within a task analysis approach. Therefore, the examiner will need to be prepared to select appropriate materials and strategies depending on the type and severity of the handicapping condition.

No single developmental scale or test instrument can possibly provide information across the broad range of areas covered in low incidence assessment. Therefore, the task of evaluation becomes one of gathering comprehensive information through several related and overlapping activities, including interviewing, formal and informal observation, and adaptive use of tests and scales to pinpoint specific skills (Forcade, *et al.,* 1979). The on-going interaction process between the psychologist and the child and family should also be considered as facilitative. These strategies are not independent or sequential and will often be performed simultaneously by members of the assessment team. The approach must be highly individualized and seeks to recognize the interactive effects between the child, the handicapped condition(s), and the environment. Despite the interrelationship and overlap, each component of the evaluation process will be considered separately for the purposes of illustration and discussion.

Establishment of Rapport

The initial activities of a low incidence assessment are crucial to successful completion of all tasks which follow. Two major preliminary goals are the establishment of rapport and familiarization with the child.

With respect to rapport, the psychologist attempts to establish interest in the welfare of the child that goes beyond the completion of the evaluation. The family must be made to feel part of the assessment and intervention process from the outset and, to this end, professional jargon and condescension should be avoided. Communications are conducted on a warm and personal level, as professional distance may work against efforts to obtain accurate information or to later involve the family in programming. For some families, the evaluation may be a novel process associated with intense anxieties. Others may have extreme reservations based on previous unpleasant, impersonal professional encounters. The focus of initial activities should be less concerned with gathering of specific information than with facilitation of a relationship conducive to such tasks in subsequent meetings. Therefore, a face-to-face meeting (often in the home) is much more appropriate than a phone contact. Rapport building should also be seen as an on-going process that characterizes all evaluation activities.

From the outset, the psychologist must maintain an empathic perspective through which family feelings about the handicapped member are sought and recognized. Levels of guilt and acceptance may vary depending on the coping strategies of individual families. The adjustment process is just beginning to be appreciated and understood (Buscaglia, 1975; Drotar, Baskiewicz, Irving, Dennell, and Klaus, 1975; Waisbren, 1980).Generally, the psychologist should be prepared to begin assessment of family factors during the first contact and empathy is essential to this task.

During the first meeting, parents will be oriented to the general evaluation team process. In accordance with the legal requirements of P.L. 94-142, the nature, purpose and possible outcomes of the assessment will be reviewed. Due process procedures and parental rights must be explained and informed consent obtained before formal evaluation is initiated. Regardless of how straightforward these activities may appear, extreme caution must be exercised in their completion for low incidence cases. The immediate presentation of legal forms accompanied by technical explanations of "rights" and "due process" will only add to the anxiety associated with the evaluation, especially for initial evaluations. While families need to be informed, care should be exercised to introduce the required information in a manner that will not induce suspicion or defensiveness. Rapport and trust may be facilitated by the informal review of materials in the context of parental awareness of the process. Depending on circumstances, forms can either be completed near the end of the first meeting, or left with the family for review until a subsequent session. In either case, rapport will not be enhanced if the family is rushed or pressured to sign a consent form.

In addition to rapport building, familiarization with the child will help set the stage for the evaluation. Factors such as age, school experience, and type or severity of disability must be considered in determining the setting(s) that will maximize the child's performance for evaluation purposes. Young children and the severely handicapped may lack adaptive flexibility and become extremely upset in unfamiliar surroundings. In such cases, as in the evaluation of mobility skills in the blind, evaluation should take place in a familiar environment such as the home, school, or day care center. The physical condition of many handicapped children may make it impractical to move them outside of the home for evaluation. Ideally, the examiner should observe the child in a variety of settings in order to assess adaptability and consistency of behavior. The feasibility of such an objective must be determined quite early. Accuracy of information, not convenience, is the criterion for determination of the setting for various activities.

Preliminary contact with the child will supply valuable information for the anticipation of evaluation procedures. For example, special handling problems must be identified to avoid accidentally hurting physically handicapped children during repositioning. Medication information is important, both for the interpretation of behavior and for anticipation of emergencies such as seizures. Where medication is used to control behavior, the examiner may wish to consult the child's physician about the feasibility of observation in the absence of drugs. Finally, initial observations of the child will help determine which assessment materials and procedures to use. Awareness of communications systems for deaf or non-verbal children will prepare the examiner in advance. Subsequent observations and interviews, however, will furnish more precise information upon which to base further evaluation activities.

Interview Procedures

In many low incidence cases, the parent interview will produce some of the most important and valid information obtained during the entire evaluation (Freeman, Malkin, Hastings, 1975). Interviews with additional significant persons in the child's environment (babysitter, grandparents, teachers, etc.) will enhance information gathering. The psychologist must carefully develop interviewing skills and have a context for organizing the interview and obtained data in order to maximize returns from the process.

The interview should generally be conducted in an informal conversational format and, with permission, might even be tape recorded for later analysis. Use of open ended questions such as, "Describe the way Mary is fed" will provide more information than a series of questions that can be answered by single affirmative or negative responses ("Can Mary feed herself?"). Estimation of the informant's reliability is simplified when questions require details and elaborations, that can later be verified by a second person, or thorough observation. Forcade, et al., (1979) have also pointed out that parents may be more truthful and receptive if they perceive the interviewer as seeking to understand the child, rather than trying to determine if specific items of a test will be passed or failed.

Given the open-ended questioning method, the examiner should devise a system for formulating question content. At the most general level, the interview should furnish ample opportunity for parents to express feelings of acceptance or to discuss concerns about their child's future. The interview will produce information about family history, the child's medical history, etc. that lends itself to organization along the lines of socio-familial interview (i.e., Nichols, 1960). In addition, specific developmental data will be gathered through an interview and should be organized around the various domains, as well as related to adaptive behavior in general. Several assessment tools are characterized by domains and the examiner will need to become familiar with the general format of one or two as a basis for questioning. The type and extent of required information will vary depending on the stage of the evaluation.

At the screening level, global knowledge about the child is sought and tools such as the Vineland Social Maturity Scale are often sufficient. The scale provides gross estimates of development in six areas (self-help, locomotion, occupation, communication, self-direction, and socialization) as only a few items sample each area across the span of birth to adulthood. The tool is useful in establishing a foundation necessary for planning subsequent activities, but more detailed skill description will be required in the majority of low incidence evaluations. One widely used instrument is the Adaptive Behavior Scale (ABS), which assesses ten general skill areas, nine of which are further broken down into subgroups. Individual items generally provide descriptions of observable behaviors ranging from no skill to highly developed ability. Despite the extensive information available from the ABS, even more behavioral specificity may be necessary for skill analysis pertinent to instructional planning in more severely impaired individuals. Thus, the Adaptive Behavior Scale may reflect the subject's relative strengths and weaknesses and provide a broad estimate of adaptive behavior, but the use of the instrument is not a substitute for observational or direct assessment approaches. Related discussions may be found in Halpern, Irvin, and Landman (1979) and Millham, Chilcutt, and Atkinson (1978).

A third area often initially investigated through interviewing involves maladaptive behavior. Educational interventions will require detailed planning in the behavioral domain, although the area is often overlooked. The degree of behavioral specificity required for programming will not be achieved by the use of terms such as "psychotic" or "self-abusive." The Adaptive Behavior Scale covers fourteen different maladaptive areas, but examiners must be aware of the need to move beyond the simple descriptions that characterize the scale. Positive and negative behaviors should be objectively defined and the necessary conditions under which the behaviors occur should be systematically investigated. For example, knowledge that a child is self-abusive only begins the interview process.

The specific behavior must be clearly identified and defined and those situations most likely to be a stimulus for the behavior should be determined. Intervention approaches that have either succeeded or failed are also investigated through the interview. Furthermore, many severely impaired children may lack attentional skills, which are a prerequisite for instructional program development. In such cases, the examiner will need to identify reinforcement preferences, response characteristics, and generalization factors to facilitate instructional planning. Behavioral interview methods suggested by Bergen (1977) may be helpful in organizing an approach, while Haring (1977) and Miller (1980) offer excellent perspectives on behavioral analysis.

Since the interview process is expected to provide substantial knowledge, several sessions may be required over the course of the entire evaluation. The interview is a gradual and continuous process of information collection, followed by verification through observation or assessment. Although time consuming, home visits are highly recommended for low incidence evaluation, for they provide an excellent framework for acquisition of information without upsetting the child. In the home, children can be left alone to engage in their daily routines, which the examiner can observe while interviewing the parents. This is often not the case in an office setting, where children become bored and restless during lengthly conversations between adults. While there may be value in observation of the child and parents under office conditions, an element of stress is introduced in the interview when it becomes rushed and impeded as the child's agitation increases. Since the examiner needs to maintain a relaxed atmosphere while building rapport, parents who have reservations about a home visit should be seen without the child during initial interview efforts.

The interface between the interview and other evaluation phases is perhaps best illustrated by a brief example. During an initial interview, Mary's mother reported both that the child could speak in full, intelligible single words and had an estimated vocabulary of ten to fifteen words, primarily nouns. During observation and evaluation, the examiner was unable to elicit any verbalizations in response to objects that were reportedly familiar to Mary. In a subsequent interview, Mary's mother admitted that only family members had produced such behavior. Thus, when mother was permitted to administer the language items, a different response pattern was observed. The gradual refinement of information through interviewing eventually led to more accurate assessment, as well as the precise documentation of the necessary conditions for Mary's verbal behavior.

Observation

Two observational strategies yield a substantial amount of information for low incidence evaluation. First, observations may be informal and spontaneous, as when the examiner witnesses a temper tantrum or other natural interaction between the child and environment. Such observations provide impromptu opportunities to verify interview information and impressions, or to add data not clearly covered by other activities. Another type of observation is that which is structured intentionally for the express purpose of assessing behavioral status. Given the observational nature of the majority of assessment tools for severely impaired groups, a substantial percentage of the evaluation process is composed of observational data collection.

The opportunity for incidental observation occurs as early as the first time the examiner sees the child and parents together. Interaction patterns in such circumstances provide direct information about behavior management style, parental attitudes, and the type of reinforcers parents provide or the child seeks. The examiner must plan for the occurrence of unanticipated events and be prepared to record such information. The importance of informal observational notes can be demonstrated from an actual experience. During assessment of motor skills, a child was asked to throw a ball to the examiner in a direct test of accuracy and distance. Instead, the youngster tossed the ball into a part of the room well away from the examiner. Since the task was not refused by the child and his accuracy was poor, the item could have been scored as failed. Yet, before a previous session at the clinic the child had been observed throwing a block at his mother quite accurately during a tantrum which resulted when a noisy toy was removed. Information from an informal observation, which took place ten days before, enabled the examiner to rate the skill area accurately. Furthermore, the observed parental reaction to the child's behavior (toy was returned during the tantrum) was of great value in assessing parental style of behavior management.

General observations increase familiarity with the child and facilitate the selection of structured observation and assessment devices. They may also permit the examiner to become accustomed to unusual or unanticipated situations. One or two informal sessions may be necessary before an evaluator is at ease with a child with a severely disfiguring physical anomaly or unpleasant medical disorder. Both communication and behavior patterns are easier to understand after extended observation. For instance, a child's heightened activity and excited laughter might appear quite bizarre to the examiner at first. However, the teacher could explain that the child reacts in the same way each time a new person enters the classroom. Thus, most observational rating activities are facilitated when performed by, or with the assistance of, someone who is familiar with the child.

Direct rating of behavior through observation fulfills an important role in low incidence assessment. Sackett (1978) discusses techniques to enhance descriptive information with the mentally retarded. Observational measures are also essential in classrooms, since many popular rating scales have been developed for, or have been incorporated into, curriculum guides focusing on programming for the severely, profoundly, and multiply handicapped (e.g., The Pennsylvania Training Model Assessment Guide). Some tools (e.g., Learning Accomplishment Profile) have drawn items from a combination of standardized developmental assessments, while others (e.g., Behavior Characteristics Progression Chart) have emphasized a task analytic approach. In either case, the purpose is to document the presence or absence of specific behaviors to facilitate program planning. Although certain scales do provide norms that enable comparisons with other handicapped persons, their practical value lies in usefulness in identifying the child's educational and adaptive behavior needs.

Controlled observation is a type of formal assessment where the examiner attempts to elicit a behavior through presentation of the appropriate stimulus conditions. In this context, all standardized tests are highly controlled observations of behavior. In low incidence assessment, the observational process does not always require standardized materials. The child is given an opportunity to perform a specific behavior (self-feeding) and the response is observed and recorded. Millham, et al. (1978) caution that this type of observation may not typify the subject's behavior in the natural environment. Contrived situations may elicit optimal, but not usual, performances. This problem should not be new to school psychologists, as most have probably examined children with adequate academic skills who were unproductive in the classroom. Discrepancies, however, are of great concern for low incidence children and often may reflect isolated skill training or failure to program for generalization of learning (c.f., Brown, et al., 1976; Millham, et al., 1978; Switzky, et al., 1979).

A good example of the discrepancy problem is the case of a sixteen year old, who was observed both in a classroom and in a pre-workshop setting. His classroom teacher rated him as capable of performing all toileting activities. She was observed sending him to the toilet when she noted increased activities and other behaviors that had come to be identified as signs of his need. Moreover, she would also cue him about personal care, although he did usually perform all separate skills without physical assistance. In the pre-workshop, such structure was not available and the result was frequent toileting accidents, as well as almost total inability to care for himself in the absence of supervision. Another young woman was totally independent in using a bathroom within her classroom. Yet, she had regular accidents in a workshop, until taught to leave the work area to use a facility well removed from the group.

Psychologists need to be aware of the complex issues illustrated by these examples when planning or conducting observations, as well as during the resolution of discrepancies in evaluation data. Observational assessments require a high degree of familiarity with the child, so that a test-teach-test, continuous progress monitoring format is used for children who are already in an educational setting. Therefore, psychologists and teachers should work collaboratively to complete such assessments.

In all low incidence evaluations, observations should include repeated samples of behavior in familiar environments during the performance of the child's preferred activities. Naturalistic observation is particularly important during initial evaluations and a home visit often provides the best opportunity. Another useful method is to permit the parents to observe and comment on the examiner's interactions with the child. DuBose, *et al.* (1977, p. 4) have recognized the fact that parents "possess far more knowledge about many aspects of the child than any team will ever know." They further advocate the use of family members as participant-observers in the evaluation. Through such involvement, parents feel accepted and are more likely to appreciate their child's needs, as well as understand the importance of programming recommendations resulting from the evaluation.

Selection of assessment and observation devices depends, in part, on the general level of functioning of the child. For higher functioning groups of children (non-retarded sensory impaired), formalized evaluation procedures are possible and will be discussed in the following section. Diebold, Curtis, and Dubose (1978) recommend the use of testing and observation together because they appear to yield non-redundant information. For less impaired children, observational and developmental scales may be used essentially for screening and for evaluating adaptive behavior domains. The assessment team may need to depend almost exclusively on observation-based techniques for severely impaired children.

New assessment tools are regularly being introduced. Selection depends on a number of factors, including the theoretical perspective of the examiner, functional objectives of the evaluation process, situational appropriateness, and both the cooperation and flexibility of the assessment team. Several devices are presented for the purpose of illustration.

The Learning Accomplishment Profile (LAP) is a criterion referenced record of a child's developmental skills in the age range of six to sixty-six months. Compiled from several normative schedules, items are organized around six domains: gross motor, fine motor, self-help, social, language, and cognitive skills. An infant edition (birth to thirty-six months) is available and would be more appropriate for severely and profoundly handicapped youngsters. The TARC (Topeka Association for Retarded Citizens) Assessment is similar to the LAP in that observable behaviors are stressed. Behaviors are organized into four domains (self-help, motor, communications, and social). Neither tool is a substitute for the comprehensive assessment required for programming decisions, but both provide more complete information than can be derived from the Vineland Social Maturity Scales or the Bayley Scales of Infant Development.

On an extremely detailed level, the Behavior Characteristics Progression Chart (BCP) has over fifty strands, or task analyzed sequences of specific skills. The BCP provides information directly keyed to the classroom, but the items are so specific that many could only be realistically assessed through diagnostic teaching and repeated measurement of skills. Although not as extensive as the BCP, the Pennsylvania Training Model Assessment (PTM) is also based on a task analytic model and yields relevant educational information. Both the BCP and PTM provide the level of assessment necessary for program planning. However, somewhat less specific information available from instruments like the LAP or TARC may be adequate for initial evaluations and placement decisions. A list of additional assessment devices and their publishers is presented at the end of this chapter.

To assist in the process of gaining a perspective for the selection of observation tools, several references are available. Somerton and Meyers (1976) discuss practical considerations associated with the development of the Pennsylvania Model. Cohen, et al. (1976) argue for the use of "developmental pinpoints" (objectively stated developmental skills) and task analysis in educational programming. Sailor and Horner (1976) review educational assessment strategies in the context of seven of the more popular global evaluation tools. The Kansas State Department of Education (1979) has put together an excellent review of twenty-four instruments ranging from simple checklists to full curricula. The document is very useful for those just becoming familiar with the methods and materials of low incidence assessment. Other reviews include Faris, Anderson, and Greer (1976), Stern (1975), and Gerken (1979).

Adaptive Use of Tests

Formalized evaluation plays different roles for various low incidence populations. Up to this point, the reader may have felt that the advocated model was incompatible with standardized assessment, but this is not so. The basic purpose of evaluation has been presented as the acquisition of information that will facilitate educational planning and provision of services. This rather broad objective can have very different meanings, depending on the individual child. For the profoundly retarded, standardized measures have generally been of little demonstrable value, as they have basically led only to classification outcomes (Itkin, 1972; Ross, 1974). Such results, based on meager assessment information, are incompatible with the goal of identification of a child's behaviors and the conditions under which they occur (Faris, et al., 1976). In these cases, the previously described observational assessment methods are more likely to provide the desired data.

For other populations, standardized measures may have great value. For example, severely physically handicapped children may have average or better cognitive potential, which could be masked by their disability. In these cases the evaluation team has a responsibility to provide information that will reflect the child's potential as well as facilitate the development of the IEP. Assurance of an appropriate educational placement is very important and generally necessitates documentation of estimated potential via standardized or accepted measurement procedures. The next paragraphs will address the role of adaptive use of standardized measures with various low incidence handicapped groups.

The evaluation of severely and profoundly retarded children is complicated by their usual inability to perform consistently on tests standardized for their chronological age group. Yet, they may be able to succeed on instruments developed for younger populations. In selecting evaluation procedures, the psychologist must consider the purpose and anticipated outcomes very carefully. If functional value cannot be tied to the use of a tool or technique, there is serious reason to question its inclusion in the assessment. Developmental age-referenced description ("the child was functioning at the two year level in language skills") does not provide information about skills that are present, or those that are needed for daily living. Outcomes are likely to be more descriptive than educational, unless additional information is drawn from the instruments.

Two different examples illustrate the point that the adaptive use of standardized instruments is best considered on a case-by-case basis. In one situation, a non-verbal nineteen year old was unable to perform any items on the Wechsler Adult Intelligence Scale. Scattered successes were noted for motor items through the four year level on the Stanford-Binet, although a basal level could not be established. In order to assess the overall developmental level, an infant scale (i.e., Cattell Infant Intelligence Scale or Bayley Scales of Infant Development) would have been necessary. Yet, the profound nature of his developmental impairment was already apparent, and attempts to describe functioning in terms of a mental age would have been an inappropriate substitute for the "missing IQ". Therefore, after several attempts to use various standardized tools, observation based assessment was used to complete the evaluation.

A second example involved the evaluation of a five year old child with Down's Syndrome. Observational assessment indicated the presence of many skills, which led the examiner to believe the child would be able to succeed on standardized measures. Therefore, the Peabody Picture Vocabulary Test was used to estimate receptive language (and circumvent this child's poor speech). The Developmental Test of Visual Motor Integration was also administered to measure copying skills. Furthermore, he passed numerous motor items on the Stanford-Binet, although his articulation problems precluded the administration of verbal tasks. Despite the fact that an IQ score was not derived, the use of standardized tests for this child provided important evidence to support inferences about cognitive functioning. Knowledge about general abilities permitted placement in a program for the moderately handicapped, as opposed to a setting for more severely impaired children. The crux of the problem in the use of formal tests with retarded children is the need to obtain useful descriptive data while avoiding the inclination to stop with only a numerical summary of the child's functioning. While certain tests may be required by state standards, the actual value of the assessment is determined by factors such as how the tools are structured, the selection of additional procedures, and how obtained information is summarized.

Evaluation of non-retarded low incidence groups, such as the blind, deaf, and severely physically handicapped, presents a somewhat different challenge for the school psychologist. Traditional goals of determining cognitive and educational strengths and weaknesses, identifying learning style, and assessing personality constructs are added to assessment of adaptive behavior areas for vocational and habilitation planning. Assessment must be accomplished through techniques that circumvent the particular handicap of the subject. There are two general approaches available for these evaluations and they may be used separately or together, depending on circumstances.

One strategy requires directing attention to the type of materials selected for the assessment. *Response fair* tests can be administered through the non-handicapped modality (Harrington, 1979). In selecting evaluation materials, the examiner will need to consider either the use of "response fair" parts of certain tests (i.e., use of verbal subtests of the WISC-R for blind children), or instruments developed for special problems or populations. A second approach concerns the methodology through which the test is administered. Test modifications, non-standardized administration, and altered response requirements are but a few of the procedures that have been used. These general approaches will be considered in more detail within the context of specific types of handicapping conditions.

Children with cerebral palsy and other physical disabilities will require test selection adjusted to their specific problems. This is determined through careful observation. As a general rule, timed motor tasks are not appropriate and the usefulness of untimed devices such as the Leiter International Performance Scale will depend on the child's motor control for block manipulation. The Leiter requires the subject to grasp small blocks and to place them in specific stalls, which are only slightly larger than the blocks. Severely spastic children are not able to perform such tasks. Verbal scales will also be difficult if speech and language are impaired or extremely arduous. Ideally, instruments that require minimal, non-verbal responses are best suited to the task, but there are few to choose from. Two possible measures involve non-verbal, pointing responses. The Columbia Mental Maturity Scale requires the child to identify the one different stimulus from a group of three or more. For the Peabody Picture Vocabulary Test, the child must pick one of four pictures in response to a stimulus word. Both tasks may be within the physical abilities of certain children, but, for others (e.g., completely paralyzed), only procedural alterations or non-standardized administrations will permit their use in evaluation.

In the consideration of test or administration modifications, one must realize that *any* alterations to the original materials or standardized procedures technically precludes the use of established norms, except in an informal manner. Obviously, certain procedures deviate less from standardization than others and would appear to preserve the true intent of the items, but the question cannot be answered intuitively. On the practical side, the decision is between maintenance of standardization in the acquisition of no information versus a more experimental approach designed to yield data that requires professional judgment and interpretation. Modifications have become acceptable in light of the critical need for information and the low probability that many instruments will ever be restandardized due to cost factors. When alterations take place, they should be justified by the handicapping condition and fully described in the report. Derived scores should be interpreted very cautiously, and presented as estimates of functioning acquired through experimental procedures.

A number of modifications have been described for children with cerebral palsy (Allen and Jefferson, 1962; Sattler, 1972; and Sattler and Anderson, 1973). At the most basic level, the establishment of a communication system will permit several different options. For example, when evaluating a paralyzed child who is also non-verbal, eyeblinks, head nods, or tongue clicks will permit the child to respond to simple yes/no questions or allow the child to make multiple choice responses. Many tests, such as the Peabody Picture Vocabulary Test, lend themselves to such approaches. The examiner might also perform motor responses for the child. An example for the Leiter International Performance Scale would require the examiner to slowly move blocks along the form until the child signals that the block should be positioned. Sattler (1972) designed test modifications to accommodate non-verbal response capabilities. Both the Wechsler Intelligence Scale for Children and the Stanford-Binet were altered to permit multiple choice and yes/no responses. Another source of ideas for assessment practices with the physically handicapped is Sattler and Tozier (1970).

For the deaf and hearing impaired population, several tests circumvent their sensory limitations. Most notable is the Hiskey-Nebraska Test of Learning Aptitude which has norms for both groups and covers the 3 to 17 year age range. The Hiskey consists of twelve subtests, although only selected tests are used, depending on the child's age. The emphasis on memory may be a limitation. Pantomimed directions may be used with children who are not proficient in manual communications. The test requires an experienced examiner for administration and interpretation. The performance section of the Wechsler Intelligence Scale for Children is also useful when administered via total communication (Sullivan and Vernon, 1979). One should not, however, assume that any non-verbal performance scale is appropriate. For example, Sullivan and Vernon (1979) point out that the Wechsler Preschool and Primary Scale of Intelligence is very difficult to explain to young children. A key feature in the selection of appropriate techniques with the hearing impaired is the communication factor. For examiners who cannot use manual or total communication, assessment becomes virtually impossible with higher functioning children. Pantomime or the use of an interpreter are possible as a last resort, but these techniques are not advocated. Rather, the evaluation requires specialized communication methods by an examiner trained specifically to work with the hearing impaired (Levine, 1974). With such skills, a wide range of instruments are appropriate across all evaluation domains. Sullivan and Vernon (1979) provide a comprehensive review and critique of materials for hearing impaired assessments. Other sources of information include Levine (1974), Lloyd (1976), and Matkin, Hook, and Hixson (1979).

For evaluation of blind and visually impaired children, specialization is also appropriate to properly interpret behavior. Bauman and Kropf (1979) have surveyed assessment instruments commonly used by field practitioners and conclude that the verbal subtests of the Wechsler Intelligence Scales have remained both popular and useful. One specialized device is the Haptic Intelligence Scale for the Adult Blind. The Haptic Test has six subtests which require the integration of a sequence of touch sensations experienced as an object is explored by the hands. Unfortunately, the test is limited to adults, the kits are not standardized, the norms need improvement, and the tasks are difficult for the newly blind, who have not refined the haptic sense. In contrast, the Blind Learning Aptitude Test (BLAT) is a well standardized untimed performance test for the functionally blind from ages 6 to 16. The instrument is a cognitive test and requires the subject to progressively discriminate, by touch, blocks that do not belong. These two devices represent the most up-to-date efforts in test development specifically for the blind. Enlarged versions of certain devices (e.g., Wide Range Achievement Test) are now available for the partially sighted, but cost factors make the probability of additional modifications of tests very low. While academic progress can be assessed verbally in many areas, materials are not typically available to probe more complex abilities of the blind without special resources on the part of the examiner (ability to translate reading passages into braille, for example). Further discussion of assessment problems and practices with the visually impaired may be found in Bauman (1973), Coveny (1976), and Scholl and Schnur (1976).

A final area is the evaluation of children who are both deaf and blind. At younger ages the deaf/blind may appear to be severely retarded. Observational assessment and intensive educational intervention may help distinguish those children with higher potential, as they will respond actively to stimulation. The Callier-Azusa Scale, designed for low functioning deaf and blind children, is essentially a developmental schedule, with norms from birth to nine years (Vernon, Bair, and Lotz, 1979). Although the norms make the scale unique, it is not as complete as assessment devices with a criterion referenced format. Use of tools specific to either the deaf or the blind will generally not work for this population. An experimental intervention approach is the best method to ascertain a child's ability to profit from instruction. Strategies suggested by single subject research (Kratochwill, 1977) have relevance for evaluation of the child's learning progress under such teaching methods.

After the processes of interviewing, observation, and adaptive use of tests have each been undertaken, the evaluation process is not necessarily completed. There may continue to be a need to reconcile discrepancies or clarify certain aspects of the child's behavior through additional interviews or observation. Assessment is ongoing for the teacher who uses periodic reappraisal to evaluate effectiveness of instruction. The psychologist, however, eventually reaches a point where sufficient information has been obtained to permit a shift in activities. A wide range of outcomes is possible upon the completion of data collection activities.

Evaluation Outcomes

The development of reports by various team members to summarize evaluation information is one important outcome of the assessment process. In addition to describing special procedures or test modifications, the psychologist's report will need to pinpoint the child's developmental status across various domains with a high degree of behavioral specificity. Information related to adaptive behavior and educational objectives must be consistent with the criterion of ultimate functioning. In other words, the psychologist will want to make suggestions that are most likely to be of benefit to the child's long range educational or habilitation goals. The report may even go so far as to recommend specialized teaching strategies, specific materials, criterion levels, and reinforcement procedures. Given the close relationship between the evaluation and the child's educational program, report content should evolve as a result of continuous consultation among assessment team members, as well as the parents. Only in this manner can the data be transformed into a suitable program for the child.

As part of the placement procedures, information from the reports of all team members are analyzed to determine necessary services in the least restrictive environment. Team meetings are usually necessary to collate impressions and reach consensus. Parents should be involved in all meetings, especially those concerned with formal placement and subsequent IEP development. The point at which the educational program is implemented represents a transition from evaluation to intervention. At this time the psychologist may assume different and equally important roles. Behavioral programming may be necessary in both the home and classroom and the psychologist might serve as either a consultant or an active participant in planning and executing the program. Coordination of services and follow-up will be necessary under such circumstances and new problems may sometimes arise and require additional consultation. Many families are often unaware of the specialized legal, medical, and financial services available to them. Thus, the psychologist specializing in low incidence children acts as a resource and referral agent for many types of problems. Nowhere is the process of parental involvement more important than during the intervention or outcomes phase. In addition, the parents' role becomes increasingly more crucial as the severity of the child's handicap increases. As previously indicated, parental cooperation at the end of the evaluation process may depend on inclusion of the family in the problem solving process from the start. Ideally, a successful evaluation will create an atmosphere of trust and understanding in which the child's needs can be realistically considered and accommodated within family and community resources. If this objective is achieved, the child should move closer to the ultimate goal of special education—the achievement of the highest possible degree of social and vocational integration into the mainstream of society.

Summary

Until recently, specific information that would direct school psychologists in the formulation of approaches to low incidence assessment has been limited. This chapter has provided a procedural model and has also introduced a number of conceptual and practical issues. Procedures have been broadly explained and the reader is strongly urged to peruse the suggested references to extend awareness of problems and familiarity with materials. Due to the substantial differences associated with each low incidence group, specialization has been advocated as the best method of service provision for both the psychologist and the child.

One important aspect of low incidence evaluation that may not be clear from the above discussion involves the time required to complete the task. The suggested procedures demand much more time than is typically involved in traditional evaluations which yield the "untestable" label or other classification outcomes. Extra time is required because low incidence evaluation is very complex. School psychologists should be prepared to invest the additional effort if this previously unserved population is to receive appropriate services within the public schools.

APPENDICES

Assessment Devices

The following is a list of instruments for assessment of low incidence children. Developmental status, cognitive skills, and adaptive behavior are emphasized in these instruments. Selection of tools for specific problems requires review of specialized literature in the area of the particular exceptionality.

Behavior Checklists/Observational/ Adaptive Behavior Measures

	Publisher Key
AAMD Adaptive Behavior Scale	1
Balthazar Scales of Adaptive Behavior	7
Behavior Characteristics Progression Chart	16
Cain-Levine Social Competency Scales	15
Callier-Azusa Scale	6
Cambridge Assessment Developmental Rating and Evaluation (CADRE)	19
Camelot Behavioral Checklist	17
Denver Developmental Screening Test	11
Developmental Profile	13
Gesell Developmental Schedules	8
Learning Accomplishment Profile (and Early LAP)	20
Maxfield-Buckholz Social Maturity Scale for Blind Preschool Children	2
Pennsylvania Training Model: Individual Assessment Guide	21
Prescriptive Behavioral Checklist for the Severely and Profoundly Retarded	22
Social and Prevocational Information Battery	5
TARC Assessment Guide	18
Vineland Social Maturity Scale	12

Direct Tests and Standardized Measures

	Publisher Key
Arthur Adaptation, Leiter International Performance Scale	12
Bayley Scales of Infant Development	12
Blind Learning Aptitude Test	23
Cattell Infant Intelligence Scale	12
Columbia Mental Maturity Scale	12

183

Haptic Intelligence Scale for Adult Blind	13
Hiskey-Nebraska Test of Learning Aptitude	9
Perkins-Binet	10
Leiter International Performance Scale	14
Merrill Palmer Scale of Infant Development	14
Merrill Palmer Preschool Performance Tests	14
Peabody Picture Vocabulary Test	3
Stanford-Ohwaki-Kohs Block Design Intelligence Test for the Blind	4

Publisher Key

1. American Association on Mental Deficiency, 5101 Wisconsin Ave. N.W., Washington, D.C. 20016
2. American Foundation for the Blind, 15 W. 16th St., New York, NY 10011
3. American Guidance Service, Publishers Building, Circle Pines, MN 55014
4. Nathan P. Bauman, 400 Orchard Lane, Fort Washington, PA 19034
5. CTB/McGraw-Hill, Del Monte Research Park, Monterey, CA 93940
6. Callier Center for Communications Disorders, University of Texas-Dallas 1966 Inwood Road, Dallas, TX 75235
7. Consulting Psychologists Press, 577 College Ave., Palo Alto, CA 94306
8. Nigel Cox, 69 Fawn Drive, Cheshire, CT 06410
9. Marshall S. Hiskey, 5640 Baldwin, Lincoln, NB 68508
10. Howe Press of Perkins School for the Blind, Watertown, MA 02172
11. Ladoca Project & Publications, Ltd., E. 51st Ave. & Lincoln St., Denver, CO 80216
12. Psychological Corporation, 757 Third Ave., New York, NY 10017
13. Psychological Development Publishers, P.O. Box 3198, Aspen, CO 81611
14. Stoelting Company, 1350 S. Kostner Ave., Chicago, IL 60623
15. Western Psychological Services, 12031 Wilshire Blvd., Los Angeles, CA 90025
16. Vort Corporation, P.O. Box 11132, Palo Alto, CA 94306
17. Edmark Associates, 1329 Northup Way, Bellevue, WA 98005
18. H & H Enterprises, P.O. Box 1070-123, Lawrence, KS 66044
19. Cambridge Area Developmental Rehabilitation and Education Center, Cambridge, MN 55008
20. Kapplan School Supply Corporation, 600 Jamestown Rd., Winston-Salem, NC 27103
21. Project CONNECT, 236 Union Deposit Mall, Harrisburg, PA 17111, Attention: PTM Materials
22. University Park Press, Chamber of Commerce Building, Baltimore, MD 21202
23. University of Illinois Press, 702 Race St., Urbana, IL 61801

References

Abel, T. M. *Psychological testing in cultural contexts.* New Haven, CT: College & University Press, 1973.

Abeson, A., Burgdorf, R. L. Jr., Casey, P. T., Kunz, J. W., & McNeil, W. Access to opportunity. In N. Hobbs (Ed.), *Issues in the classification of children* (Vol. II). San Francisco: Jossey-Bass, 1975.

Abeson, A., & Zettel, J. The end of the quiet revolution: The Education for all Handicapped Children Act of 1975. *Exceptional Children,* 1977, *44,* 114-128.

Allen, R. M., & Jefferson, T. W. *Psychological evaluation of the cerebral palsied person.* Springfield, IL: Thomas, 1962.

Alpern, G. D., & Boll, T. J. *Developmental Profile.* Aspen, CO: Psychological Development Publications, 1972.

Alpern, G. D., Boll, T. J., & Shearer, M. S. *Developmental profile II.* Aspen, CO: Psychological Development Publications, 1980.

Altman, I., & Wohlwill, J. F. *Children and the environment.* New York: Plenum Press, 1978.

Anastasi, A. *Psychological testing* (4th ed.). New York: Macmillan, 1976.

Anastasiow, N. J., & Hanes, M. L. *Language patterns of poverty children.* Springfield, IL: Thomas, 1976.

Anderson, G., Bass, B. A., Munford, P. R., & Wyatt, G. E. A seminar on the assessment and treatment of black patients. *Professional Psychology,* 1977, *8,* 340-348.

Arnold, M. B. *Story sequence analysis.* New York: Columbia University Press, 1962.

Atkeson, B. M., & Forehand, R. Home-based reinforcement programs designed to modify classroom behavior: A review and methodological evaluation. *Psychological Bulletin,* 1979, *86,* 1298-1308.

Backer, T. E. *Methods of assessing the disadvantaged in manpower programs: A review and analysis.* Washington, D.C.: U.S. Department of Labor, 1973.

Bailey, B. E., & Green, J. Black thematic apperception test stimulus material. *Journal of Personality Assessment,* 1977, *41,* 25-30.

Baker, B. L. Parent involvement in programming for developmentally disabled children. In L. L. Lloyd (Ed.), *Communication assessment and intervention strategies.* Baltimore: University Park Press, 1976.

Baker, E. H., & Tyne, T. F. The use of observational procedures in school psychological services. *School Psychology Monograph,* 1980, *4,* 25-44.

Baker, H. J., & Leland, B. *The Detroit tests of learning aptitude.* Indianapolis, IN: Bobbs-Merrill, 1967.

Ballard, J., & Zettel, J. Public Law 94-142 and Section 504: What they say about rights and protections. *Exceptional Children,* 1977, *44,* 177-185.

Bamgbose, O., Edwards, D., & Johnson, S. The effects of race and social class on clinical judgment. *Journal of Clinical Psychology,* 1980, *36,* 605-609.

Bandura, A. *Principles of behavior modification.* New York: Holt, Rinehart & Winston, 1969.

Bandura, A. *Social learning theory.* Englewood Cliffs, NJ: Prentice-Hall, 1977. (a)

Bandura, A. Self-efficacy: Toward a unifying theory of behavior change. *Psychological Review,* 1977, *84,* 191-215. (b)

Bandura, A. The self system in reciprocal determinism. *American Psychologist,* 1978, *33,* 344-358.

Barnett, D. W., & Zucker, K. B. Assessment of the others-concept. In R. H. Woody (Ed.), *Encyclopedia of clinical assessment* (Vol. 1). San Francisco: Jossey-Bass, 1980. (a)

Barnett, D. W., & Zucker, K. B. The others-concept: Explorations into the quality of children's interpersonal relationships. In H. C. Foot, A. J. Chapman, & J. R. Smith, (Eds.), *Friendship and social relationships in children.* London: Wiley, 1980. (b)

Bartel, N. R., & Bryen, D. N. Problems in language development. In D. D. Hammill & N. R. Bartel (Eds.), *Teaching children with learning and behavior problems* (2nd ed.). Boston: Allyn & Bacon, 1978.

Bartel, N. R., Grill, J. J., & Bryen, D. N. Language characteristics of black children: Implications for assessment. *Journal of School Psychology,* 1973, *41,* 351-364.

Basic educational skills inventory. Torrance, CA: Winch & Associates, 1971.

Bates, E. Pragmatics and sociolinguistics in child language. In D. M. Morehead & A. E. Morehead (Eds.), *Normal and deficient child language.* Baltimore: University Park Press, 1976.

Bauman, M. K. Psychological and educational assessment. In B. Lowenfeld (Ed.), *The visually handicapped child in school.* New York: Day, 1973.

Bauman, M. K., & Kropf, C. A. Psychological tests used with blind and visually handicapped persons. *School Psychology Digest,* 1979, *8,* 257-270.

Becker, H. S. *Outsiders: Studies in the sociology of deviance.* New York: Free Press, 1963.

Becker, R. L. *Reading free vocational interest inventory.* Washington, D.C.: American Association on Mental Deficiency, 1975.

Beery, K. E. *Developmental test of visual-motor integration.* Chicago: Follett, 1967.

Bellack, A. S., & Schwartz, J. S. Assessment for self-control programs. In M. Hersen & A. S. Bellack (Eds.), *Behavioral assessment: A practical handbook.* New York: Pergamon, 1976.

Bellak, L., & Bellak, S. S. *Children's apperception test (human figures).* Los Angeles: Western Psychological Services, 1965.

Bem, D. J., & Allen, A. On predicting some of the people some of the time: The search for cross-situational consistencies in behavior. *Psychological Review,* 1974, *81,* 506-520.

Bender, M. L. *The Bender-Purdue reflex test and training manual.* San Rafael, CA: Academic Therapy Publications, 1976.

Bennett, F., Hughes, A., & Hughes, H. Assessment techniques for deaf-blind and visually handicapped persons. *School Psychology Digest,* 1979, *45,* 287-289.

Bennett, H., Seashore, G., & Wesman, A. G. *Differential aptitude tests.* New York: Psychological Corporation, 1969.

Bergan, J. R. *Behavioral consultation.* Columbus, OH: Merrill, 1977.

Bersoff, D. N. "Current functioning" myth: An overlooked fallacy in psychological assessment. *Journal of Consulting and Clinical Psychology,* 1971, *37,* 391-393.

Bersoff, D. N. Silk purses into sow's ears: The decline of psychological testing and a suggestion for its redemption. *American Psychologist,* 1973, *28,* 892-899. (a)

Bersoff, D. N. The ethical practice of school psychology: A rebuttal and suggested model. *Professional Psychology,* 1973, *4,* 305-312. (b)

Bersoff, D. N. *Legal and psychometric critique of school testing litigation.* Paper presented at the meeting of the American Psychological Association, New York, September 1979.

Bersoff, D. N., & Greiger, R. M. An interview model for the psychosituational assessment of children's behavior. *American Journal of Orthopsychiatry*, 1971, *41*, 483-493.

Binet, A., & Simon, T. The development of intelligence in children. In T. Shipley (Ed.), *Classics in psychology*. New York: Philosophical Library, 1961. (Originally published, 1905.)

Birch, J. W. *Mainstreaming: Educable mentally retarded children in regular classes*. Reston, VA: The Council for Exceptional Children, 1974.

Bitter, J. A. *Introduction to rehabilitation*. St. Louis: Mosby, 1979.

Bloom, L., & Lahey, M. *Language development and language disorders*. New York: Wiley, 1978.

Boehm, A. E. *Boehm test of basic concepts manual*. New York: Psychological Corporation, 1971.

Boehm, A. E. *Boehm resource guide for basic concept teaching*. New York: Psychological Corporation, 1976.

Boll, T. J. A rationale for neuropsychological evaluation. *Professional Psychology*, 1977, *8*, 64-71.

Bosma, B. The NEA testing moratorium. *Journal of School Psychology*, 1973, *11*, 304-306.

Boyd, J. E., & Bartel, N. R. Teaching children with reading problems. In D. D. Hammill & N. R. Bartel (Eds.), *Teaching children with learning and behavior problems* (2nd ed.). Boston: Allyn & Bacon, 1978.

Braud, L. W. The effects of frontal EMG biofeedback and progressive relaxation upon hyperactivity and its behavioral concomitants. *Biofeedback and Self-Regulation*, 1978, *3*, 69-89.

Brigance, A. H. *Diagnostic inventory of basic skills* (2nd ed.). Woburn, MA: Curriculum Associates, 1977.

Brigham, C. C. *A study of American intelligence*. Princeton, NJ: Princeton University Press, 1923.

Brim, O. G. American attitudes toward testing. *American Psychologist*, 1965, *20*, 125-130.

Brody, E. B., & Brody, N. *Intelligence: Nature, determinants, and consequences*. New York: Academic Press, 1976.

Brolin, D. E., & D'Alonzo, B. J. Critical issues in career education for handicapped students. *Exceptional Children*, 1979, *45*, 246-253.

Brolin, D. E., & Gysber, N. C. Career education for persons with handicaps. *Personnel and Guidance Journal*, 1979, *58*, 258-262.

Brolin, D. E., & Kokaska, C. *Career education for handicapped children and youth*. Columbus, OH: Merrill, 1979.

Brolin, D. E., & Kolstoe, O. *Career and vocational development of handicapped learners*. Columbus, OH: National Center for Research in Vocational Education, Ohio State University, 1978.

Brooks, R. Psychoeducational assessment: A broader perspective. *Professional Psychology*, 1979, *10*, 708-722.

Brown, A. L., & French, L. A. The zone of potential development: Implications for intelligence testing in the year 2000. In R. J. Sternberg & D. K. Detterman (Eds.), *Human intelligence: Perspectives on its theory and measurement*. Norwood, NJ: Ablex, 1979.

Brown, D. R. *Neurosciences for allied health therapies*. St. Louis: Mosby, 1980.

Brown, L., Nietupski, J., & Hamre-Nietupski, S. The criterion of ultimate functioning and public school services for severely handicapped students. In

M. A. Thomas (Ed.), *Hey, don't forget about me: New directions for serving the severely handicapped.* Reston, VA: The Council for Exceptional Children, 1976.

Brown, L., Branston, M. B., Hamre-Nietupski, S., Pumpian, I., Certo, N., & Gruenwald, L. A strategy for developing chronological age appropriate and functional curricular content for severely handicapped adolescents and young adults. *Journal of Special Education*, 1979, *13*, 81-90.

Brown, L. L., Teacher strategies for managing classroom behaviors. In D. D. Hammill & N. R. Bartel (Eds.), *Teaching children with learning and behavior problems* (2nd ed.). Boston: Allyn & Bacon, 1978.

Brown, L. L., & Hammill, D. D. *Behavior rating profile: An ecological approach to behavioral assessment.* Austin, TX: Pro Ed, 1978.

Brown, V. L., Hammill, D. D., & Wiederholt, J. L. *Test of reading comprehension.* Austin, TX: Pro Ed, 1978.

Brubakken, D. M., Derouin, J. A., & Morrison, H. L. *Treatment of psychotic and neurologically impaired children: A systems approach.* New York: Van Nostrand Reinhold, 1980.

Buckley, K. J., & Oakland, T. D. *Contrasting localized norms for Mexican-American children on the ABIC.* Paper presented at the meeting of the American Psychological Association, San Francisco, August, 1977.

Budoff, M., & Friedman, M. "Learning potential" as an assessment approach to the adolescent mentally retarded. *Journal of Consulting Psychology*, 1964, *28*, 433-439.

Budoff, M., & Hamilton, J. L. Optimizing test performance of moderately and severely mentally retarded adolescents and adults. *American Journal of Mental Deficiency*, 1976, *81*, 49-57.

Burks, H. F. *Burks' behavior rating scales: Preschool and kindergarten edition.* Los Angeles, CA: Western Psychological Services, 1977.

Burns, R. C., & Kaufman, S. H. *Actions, styles and symbols in kinetic family drawings (K-F-D).* New York: Brunner/Mazel, 1972.

Buros, O. K. (Ed.). *Personality tests and reviews.* Highland Park, NJ: Gryphon Press, 1970.

Buros, O. K. (Ed.). *Seventh mental measurements yearbook.* Highland Park, NJ: Gryphon Press, 1972.

Buros, O.K. (Ed.). *Eighth mental measurements yearbook.* Highland Park, NJ: Gryphon Press, 1978.

Buscaglia, L. F. *The disabled and their parents: A counseling challenge.* Thorofare, NJ: Charles B. Slack, 1975.

Butterfield, E. C. On studying cognitive development. In G. P. Sackett (Ed.), *Observing behavior: Volume 1: Theory and application in mental retardation.* Baltimore: University Park Press, 1978.

Campbell, D. P. *Strong-Campbell interest inventory.* Stanford, CA: Stanford University Press, 1974.

Campbell, J. P. Psychometric theory. In M. D. Dunnette (Ed.), *Handbook of industrial and organizational psychology.* Chicago: Rand McNally, 1976.

Carroll, J. B. The nature of the reading process. In H. Singer & R. B. Ruddell (Eds.), *Theoretical models and processes of reading* (2nd ed.). Newark, DE: International Reading Association, 1976.

Carter, C. Prospectus on black communication. *The School Psychology Digest*, 1977, *6*, 23-30.

Chapman, L. J., & Chapman, J. P. Illusory correlation as an obstacle to the use of valid psychodiagnostic signs. *Journal of Abnormal Psychology*, 1969, *74*, 271-280.

Chinn, P. C. The exceptional minority child: Issues and some answers. *Exceptional Children*, 1979, *45*, 532-536.

Cicciarelli, A., Broen, P.A., & Siegel, G. M. Language assessment procedures (Appendix A). In L. L. Lloyd (Ed.), *Communication assessment and intervention strategies*. Baltimore: University Park Press, 1976.

Clarizio, H. F. In defense of the IQ test. *School Psychology Digest*, 1979, *8*, 79-88.

Clark, G. M. Career education for the mildly handicapped. In E. L. Meyen, G. A. Vergason, & R. J. Whelan (Eds.), *Essays from focus on exceptional children*. Denver: Love Publishing, 1975.

Clark, H. H., & Clark, E. V. *Psychology and language: An introduction to psycholinguistics*. New York: Harcourt, Brace, Jovanovich, 1977.

Clark, K. E., & Campbell, D. P. *Manual for the Minnesota vocational interest inventory*. New York: Psychological Corporation, 1965.

Cleary, T. A., Humphreys, L. G., Kendrick, S. A., & Wesman, A. Educational use of tests with disadvantaged students. *American Psychologist*, 1975, *30*, 15-41.

Cleveland, S. E. Reflections of the rise and fall of psychodiagnosis. *Professional Psychology*, 1976, *7*, 309-318.

Cohen, D. H., & Stern, V. *Observing and recording the behavior of young children* (2nd ed.). New York: Teachers College Press, 1978.

Cohen, M. A., & Gross, P. J. *The developmental resource: Behavioral sequences for assessment and program planning*. New York: Grune & Stratton, 1979.

Cohen, M. A., Gross, P. J., & Haring, N. G. Developmental pinpoints. In N. G. Haring & L. J. Brown (Eds.), *Teaching the severely handicapped* (Vol. 1). New York: Grune & Stratton, 1976.

Cohen, S., Semmes, M., & Guralnick, M. J. Public Law 94-142 and the education of preschool handicapped children. *Exceptional Children*, 1979, *45*, 279-285.

Coleman, J. C., Butcher, J. N., & Carson, R. C. *Abnormal psychology and modern life* (6th ed.). Glenview, IL: Scott & Foresman, 1980.

Coles, G. S. The learning disabilities test battery: Empirical and social issues. *Harvard Educational Review*, 1978, *48*, 313-340.

Cone, J. D. The relevance of reliability and validity for behavioral assessment. *Behavior Therapy*, 1977, *8*, 411-426.

Coveny, T. E. Standardized tests for visually handicapped children: A review of research. *New Outlook for the Blind*, 1976, *70*, 232-236.

Cratty, B. J. *Developmental sequences of perceptual-motor tasks*. Freeport, NY: Educational Activities, 1967.

Crites, J. O. *Vocational psychology*. New York: McGraw-Hill, 1969.

Cronbach, L. J. *Essentials of psychological testing* (3rd ed.). New York: Harper & Row, 1970.

Cronbach, L. J. Five decades of public controversy over mental testing. *American Psychologist*, 1975, *30*, 1-14.

Cronbach, L. J., Gleser, G. C., Nanda, H., & Rajaratnam, N. *The dependability of behavioral measurements: Theory of generalizability for scores and profiles*. New York: Wiley, 1972.

Cronbach, L. J., & Meehl, P. E. Construct validity in psychological tests. *Psychological Bulletin*, 1955, *52*, 281-302.

Cronbach, L. J., & Snow, R. E. *Aptitudes and instructional methods*. New York: Irving Publishers, 1977.

Curtis, M.J., & Zins, J. *The theory and practice of school consultation*. Springfield, IL: Thomas, 1981.

Cutrona, M. P. *A psychoeducational interpretation of test scatter on the Wechsler intelligence scale for children-revised.* Belleville, NJ: Cutronics Educational Publications, 1976.

Dale, P. S. What does observing language mean? In G. P. Sackett (Ed.), *Observing behavior: Volume 1: Theory and application in mental retardation.* Baltimore: University Park Press, 1978.

Das, J. P., Kirby, J. R., & Jarman, R. F. *Simultaneous and successive cognitive processes.* New York: Academic Press, 1979.

Davison, G. C. & Neale, J. M. *Abnormal Psychology.* New York: Wiley, 1978.

Dean, R. S. Factor structure of the WISC-R with Anglos and Mexican-Americans. *Journal of School Psychology,* 1980, *18,* 234-239.

De Avila, E. A., & Havassy, B. E. Piagetian alternatives to IQ: Mexican-American study. In N. Hobbs (Ed.), *Issues in the classification of children* (Vol. 2). San Francisco: Jossey-Bass, 1975.

Deno, E. N. Special education as developmental capital. *Exceptional Children,* 1970, *37,* 229-237.

Diebold, M. H., Curtis, W. S., & DuBose, R. F. Relationships between psychometric and observational measures of performance in low-functioning children. *American Association for the Education of the Severely and Profoundly Handicapped Review,* 1978, *2,* 123-128.

Diener, C. I., & Dweck, C. S. An analysis of learned helplessness: Continuous changes in performance, strategy, and achievement cognitions following failure. *Journal of Personality and Social Psychology,* 1978, *36,* 451-462.

Doll, E. E. *The measurement of social competence.* Minneapolis: Educational Test Bureau, 1953.

Drotar, D., Baskiewicz, N., Irving, N., Dennell, J., & Klaus, M. The adaptation of parents to the birth of an infant with a congenital malformation: A hypothetical model. *Pediatrics,* 1975, *56,* 710-717.

DuBois, P. H. *A history of psychological testing.* Boston: Allyn & Bacon, 1970.

DuBose, R. F., Langley, M. B., & Stagg, V. Assessing severely handicapped children. *Focus on Exceptional Children,* 1977, *9,* 1-13.

Dunn, L. M. *Peabody picture vocabulary test.* Circle Pines, MN: American Guidance Service, 1965.

Dunn, L. M. Special education for the mildly retarded—is much of it justifiable? *Exceptional Children,* 1968, *35,* 5-22.

Dunn, L. M., & Dunn, L. M. *Peabody picture vocabulary test-revised.* Circle Pines, MN: American Guidance Service, 1981.

Dunn, L. M., & Markwardt, F. C. *Peabody individual achievement test.* Circle Pines, MN: American Guidance Service, 1970.

Dunnette, M. D. (Ed.). *Handbook of industrial and organizational psychology.* Chicago: Rand McNally, 1976.

Durrell, D. D. *Durrell analysis of reading difficulty.* New York: Harcourt, Brace, Jovanovich, 1955.

Dweck, C. S., & Reppucci, N. D. Learned helplessness and reinforcement responsibility in children. *Journal of Personality and Social Psychology,* 1973, *25,* 109-116.

D'Zurilla, T. J., & Goldfried, M. R. Problem solving and behavior modification. *Journal of Abnormal Psychology,* 1971, *78,* 107-126.

Early, G. H. *Perceptual training in the curriculum.* Columbus, OH: Merrill, 1969.

Ekwall, E. E. *Locating and correcting reading difficulties* (2nd ed.). Columbus, OH: Merrill, 1977. (a)

Ekwall, E. E. *Teacher's handbook on diagnosis & remediation in reading.* Boston: Allyn & Bacon, 1977. (b)

Ekwall, E. E. *Ekwall reading inventory.* Boston: Allyn & Bacon, 1979.

Ellett, C. D., & Bersoff, D. N. An integrated approach to the psychosituational assessment of behavior. *Professional Psychology,* 1976, *7,* 485-494.

Epstein, L. H. Psychophysiological measurement in assessment. In M. Hersen & A. S. Bellack (Eds.), *Behavioral assessment: A practical handbook.* New York: Pergamon Press, 1976.

Evans, P. L., & Richmond, B. O. A practitioner's comparison: The 1972 Stanford-Binet and the WISC-R. *Psychology in the Schools,* 1976, *13,* 9-14.

Faas, L. A. *Children with learning problems: A handbook for teachers.* Boston: Houghton Mifflin, 1980.

Fagan, S. A., Long, N. J., & Stevens, D. J. *Teaching children self-control: Preventing emotional and learning problems in the elementary school.* Columbus, OH: Merrill, 1975.

Faris, J. A., Anderson, R. M., & Greer, J. G. Psychological assessment of the severely and profoundly retarded. In R. M. Anderson & J. G. Greer (Eds.), *Educating the severely and profoundly retarded.* Baltimore, MD: University Park Press, 1976.

Federal programs for career education of handicapped individuals. *Programs for the Handicapped.* Washington, D.C.: Office of Handicapped Individuals, Nov./Dec. 1979.

Feffer, M., & Jahelka, M. Implications of the decentering concept for the structuring of projective content. *Journal of Consulting and Clinical Psychology,* 1968, *32,* 434-441.

Feuerstein, M., Ward, M. M., & LeBaron, S. W. M. Neuropsychological and neurophysiological assessment of children with learning and behavior problems: A critical appraisal. In B. B. Lahey & A. E. Kazdin (Eds.), *Advances in clinical child psychology* (Vol. 1). New York: Plenum Press, 1977.

Feuerstein, R. A dynamic approach to the causation, prevention, and alleviation of retarded performance. In H. C. Haywood (Ed.), *Social-cultural aspects of mental retardation.* New York: Appleton-Century-Crofts, 1970.

Feuerstein, R. *The dynamic assessment of retarded performers: The learning potential assessment device, theory, instruments, and techniques.* Baltimore: Univerity Park Press, 1979.

Feuerstein, R. *Instrumental enrichment: An intervention program for cognitive modifiability.* Baltimore: University Park Press, 1980.

Filskov, S. B., & Boll, T. J. (Eds.), *Handbook of clinical neuropsychology.* New York: Wiley, 1981.

Fischer, C. T. The testee as co-evaluator. *Journal of Counseling Psychology,* 1970, *17,* 70-76.

Fisher, A. T. *Four approaches to classification of mental retardation.* Revised version of paper presented at the meeting of the American Psychological Association, Toronto, August 1978.

Fishman, J. A., Deutsch, M., Kogan, L., North, R., & Whiteman, M. Guidelines for testing minority group children. *Journal of Social Issues,* 1964, *20,* 127-145.

Flaugher, R. L. The many definitions of test bias. *American Psychologist,* 1978, *33,* 671-679.

Fleishman, E. A. (Ed.), *Studies in personnel and industrial psychology* (Rev. ed.). Homewood, IL: Dorsey, 1967.

Forcade, M. C., Matey, C. M., & Barnett, D. W. Procedural guidelines for low incidence assessment. *School Psychology Digest,* 1979, *8,* 248-256.

Freeman, R., Malkin, S. F., & Hastings, J. D. Parental reaction to loss. *American Annals of the Deaf,* 1975, *120,* 391-405.

Frostig, M., & Maslow, P. *Move, grow, learn.* Chicago: Follett, 1969.

Frostig, M., & Maslow, P. *Learning problems in the classroom: Prevention and remediation.* New York: Grune & Stratton, 1973.

Fulkerson, S. C. Some implications of the new cognitive theory for projective tests. *Journal of Consulting Psychology,* 1965, *29,* 191-197.

Fulton, R. T., & Lloyd, L. L. (Eds.). *Auditory assessment of the difficult to test.* Baltimore: Williams & Wilkins, 1975.

Garber, H. L. Bridging the gap from preschool to school for the disadvantaged child. *School Psychology Digest,* 1979, *8,* 303-310.

Garfield, S. L. Some discrepancies in research reports on activities of clinical psychologists. *American Psychologist,* 1978, *33,* 847-848.

Garfield, S. L., & Kurtz, R. Clinical psychologists in the 1970s. *American Psychologist,* 1976, *31,* 1-9.

Gates, A. I., & McKillop, A. S. *Gates-McKillop reading diagnostic tests.* New York: Teachers College Press, Columbia University, 1962.

Gay, G., & Abrahams, R. D. Does the pot melt, boil, or brew? Black children and white assessment procedures. *Journal of School Psychology,* 1973, *11,* 330-340.

Gearheart, B. R., & Weishahn, N. W. *The handicapped child in the regular classroom.* St. Louis: Mosby, 1976.

Gelman, S. R. Sociological issues. In J. T. Neisworth & R. M. Smith. *Retardation: Issues, assessment and intervention.* New York: McGraw-Hill, 1978.

Gemunder, C. *The relationship of generalized expectancies to school adjustment.* Unpublished doctoral dissertation, University of Cincinnati, 1979.

Gerken, K. C. Performance of Mexican American children on intelligence tests. *Exceptional Children,* 1978, *44,* 438-443.

Gerken, K. C. Assessment of high-risk preschoolers and children and adolescents with low-incident handicapping conditions. In G. D. Phye & D. J. Reschly (Eds.), *School psychology: Perspectives and issues.* New York: Academic Press, 1979.

Ghiselli, E. E. *The validity of occupational aptitude tests.* New York: Wiley, 1966.

Ghiselli, E. E. The validity of aptitude tests in personnel selection. *Personnel Psychology,* 1973, *26,* 461-477.

Gillespie-Silver, P. *Teaching reading to children with special needs.* Columbus, OH: Merrill, 1979.

Ginsburg, H., & Opper, S. *Piaget's theory of intellectual development: An introduction.* Englewood Cliffs, NJ: Prentice-Hall, 1969.

Goetz, T.E. & Dweck, C.S. Learned helplessness in social situations. *Journal of Personality and Social Psychology,* 1980, *39,* 246-255.

Gold, M. W. Research on the vocational habilitation of the retarded: The present, the future. In N. R. Ellis (Ed.), *International review of research in mental retardation* (Vol. 6). New York: Academic Press, 1973.

Gold, M.W. Vocational training. In J. Wortis (Ed.), *Mental retardation and developmental disabilities* (Vol. 7). New York: Brunner/Mazel, 1975.

Gold, M. W. Task analysis of a complex assembly task by the retarded blind. *Exceptional Children,* 1976, *43,* 78-84.

Gold, M. W. *Try another way training manual.* Champaign, IL: Research Press, 1980.

Gold, M. W., & Pomerantz, D. J. Issues in prevocational training. In M. E. Snell (Ed.), *Systematic instruction of the moderately and severely handicapped.* Columbus, OH: Merrill, 1978.

Goldfried, M. R., & Kent, R. N. Traditional versus behavioral personality assessment: A comparison of methodological and theoretical assumptions. In

REFERENCES   193

E. J. Mash & L. G. Terdal (Eds.), *Behavior therapy assessment: Diagnosis, design, and evaluation.* New York: Springer, 1976.

Goldman, R., Fristoe, M., & Woodcock, R. W. *Goldman-Fristoe-Woodcock auditory skills test battery.* Circle Pines, MN: American Guidance Service, 1976.

Goldstein, K. M., & Blackman, S. Assessment of cognitive style. In P. McReynolds (Ed.), *Advances in psychological assessment* (Vol. 4). San Francisco: Jossey-Bass, 1977.

Goldstein, S., Strickland, B., Turnbull, A. P., & Curry, L. An observational analysis of the IEP conference. *Exceptional Children,* 1980, *46,* 278-286.

Goodman, J. F. The diagnostic fallacy: A critique of Jane Mercer's concept of mental retardation. *Journal of School Psychology,* 1977, *15,* 197-206.

Goodman, J. F. Is tissue the issue? A critique of SOMPA's models and tests. *School Psychology Digest,* 1979, *8,* 47-62.

Goodman, K. S., & Goodman Y. M. Learning about psycholinguistic processes by analyzing oral reading. *Harvard Educational Review,* 1977, *47,* 317-333.

Goodman, Y. M., & Burke, C. I. *Reading miscue inventory.* New York: Macmillan, 1972.

Gough, H. G. *Manual for the California psychological inventory.* Palo Alto, CA: Consulting Psychologists Press, 1975.

Gridley, G. C., & Mastenbrook, J. *Research on the need for local norms for the adaptive behavior inventory for children.* Paper presented at the meeting of the American Psychological Association, San Francisco, August 1977.

Grieger, R. M., & Abidin, R. R. Psychosocial assessment: A model for the school community psychologist. *Psychology in the Schools,* 1972, *9,* 112-119.

Gronlund, N. E. *Measurement and evaluation in teaching.* New York: Macmillan, 1976.

Grossman, H. J. (Ed.), *Manual on the terminology and classification in mental retardation.* Washington, D. C.: American Association on Mental Deficiency, 1973.

Guess, D., Horner, R. D., Utley, B., Holvoet, J., Maxon, D., Tucker, D., & Warren, S. A functional curriculum sequencing model for teaching the severely handicapped. *American Association for the Education of the Severely and Profoundly Handicapped Review,* 1978, *3,* 202-215.

Gump, P. V. School environments. In I. Altman & J. F. Wohlwill (Eds.), *Children and the environment.* New York: Plenum Press, 1978.

Gutkin, T. B. WISC-R scatter indices: Useful information for differential diagnosis? *Journal of School Psychology,* 1979, *17,* 368-371.

Gutkin, T. B., & Reynolds, C. R. Factorial similarity of the WISC-R for Anglos and Chicanos referred for psychological services. *Journal of School Psychology,* 1980, *18,* 34-39.

Haber, R. N. Visual perception. In M. R. Rosenzweig & L. W. Porter (Eds.), *Annual review of psychology* (Vol. 29). Palo Alto, CA: Annual Reviews, 1978.

Hackett, M. G. *Criterion reading: Individualized learning management system.* Westminster, MD: Random House, 1971.

Halpern, A. S., Irvin, L. K., & Landman, J. T. Alternative approaches to the measurement of adaptive behavior. *American Journal of Mental Deficiency,* 1979, *84,* 304-310.

Halpern, A. S., Raffeld, P., Irvin, L. K., & Link, R. *Social and prevocational information battery.* Monterey, CA: CTB/McGraw-Hill, 1975.

Hammill, D. D. Assessing and training perceptual-motor skills. In D. D. Hammill & N. R. Bartel (Eds.), *Teaching children with learning and behavior problems* (2nd ed.). Boston: Allyn & Bacon, 1978.

Hammill, D. D., & Bartel, N. R. *Teaching children with learning and behavior problems* (2nd ed.). Boston: Allyn & Bacon, 1978.

Hammill, D. D., Brown, V. L., Larsen, S. C., & Wiederholt, J. L. *Test of adolescent language: A multidimensional approach to assessment* (TOAL). Austin, TX: Pro Ed, 1980.

Hammill, D. D., & Larsen, S. C. The effectiveness of psycholinguistic training. *Exceptional Children,* 1974, *41,* 5-14.

Hammill, D. D., & Larsen, S. C. *Test of written language.* Austin, TX: Pro Ed, 1978.

Hammill, D. D., & Newcomer, P. L. *Construction and statistical characteristics of the test of language development.* Austin, TX: Pro Ed, 1977.

Hardy, J. B., Welcher, D. W., Mellits, E. D., & Kagan, J. Pitfalls in the measurement of intelligence: Are standard intelligence tests valid instruments for measuring the intellectual potential of urban children? *The Journal of Psychology,* 1976, *94,* 43-51.

Haring, N. G. Measurement and evaluation procedures for programming with the severely and profoundly handicapped. In E. Sontag, J. Smith & N. Certo (Eds.), *Educational programming for the severely and profoundly handicapped.* Reston, VA: The Council for Exceptional Children, 1977.

Haring, N. G., & Bricker, D. Overview of comprehensive services for the severely/profoundly handicapped. In N. G. Haring & L. Brown (Eds.), *Teaching the severely handicapped* (Vol. 1). New York: Grune & Stratton, 1976.

Harrington, R. G. A review of Sattler's modifications of standard intelligence tests for use with handicapped children. *School Psychology Digest,* 1979, *8,* 296-302.

Harrison, R. Thematic apperceptive methods. In B. B. Wolman (Ed.), *Handbook of clinical psychology,* New York: McGraw-Hill, 1965.

Hartman, A. Diagrammatic Assessment of family relationships. *Social Casework,* October, 1978, 465-476. (a)

Hartman, A. The Ecomap: An ecological framework for assessment and intervention. In J. R. Newbrough (Chair), *Ecological assessment.* Paper presented at the meeting of the National Association of School Psychologists, New York, 1978.

Hartmann, D. P., Roper, B. L., & Bradford, D. C. Some relationships between behavioral and traditional assessment. *Journal of Behavioral Assessment,* 1979, *1,* 3-21.

Haywood, H. C., Filler, J. W., Jr., Shifman, M. A., & Chatelant, G. Behavioral assessment in mental retardation. In P. McReynolds (Ed.), *Advances in psychological assessment* (Vol. 3). San Francisco: Jossey-Bass, 1975.

Heber, F. R. Sociocultural mental retardation: A longitudinal study. In D. G. Forgays (Ed.), *Primary prevention of psychopathology* (Vol. 2). Hanover, NH: University Press of New England, 1978.

Heber, R., Garber, H., Harrington S., Hoffman, C., & Falender, C. *Rehabilitation of families at risk for mental retardation.* December 1972. (Progress report)

Hersen, M., & Barlow, D. H. *Single case experimental designs: Strategies for studying behavior change.* New York: Pergamon Press, 1976.

Hersen, M., & Bellack, A. S. *Behavioral assessment: A practical handbook.* New York: Pergamon Press, 1976.

Hewitt, P., & Massey, J. O. *Clinical cues from the Wechsler intelligence scale for children with special sections on testing black and Spanish speaking children.* Palo Alto, CA: Consulting Psychologists Press, 1969.

Hively, W. (Ed.). *Domain-referenced testing.* Englewood Cliffs, NJ: Educational Technology Publications, 1974.

Hobbs, N. Helping disturbed children: Psychological and ecological strategies. *American Psychologist,* 1966, *21,* 1105-1115.

Hobbs, N. *Helping disturbed children: Psychological and ecological strategies, II; Project Re-ed, twenty years later.* Nashville, TN: Center for the Study of Families and Children, Vanderbilt Institute for Public Policy Studies, Vanderbilt University, 1979.

Hoff, M. K., Fenton, K. S., Yoshida, R. K., & Kaufman, M. J. Notice and consent: The school's responsibility to inform parents. *Journal of School Psychology,* 1978, *16,* 265-273.

Hogan, R., DeSoto, C. B., & Solano, C. Traits, tests, and personality research. *American Psychologist,* 1977, *32,* 255-264.

Hohenshil, T. H. Call for redirection: A vocational educator views school psychological services. *Journal of School Psychology,* 1975, *13,* 58-62.

Hohenshil, T. H. *Vocational school psychology/vocational education for the handicapped* (Selected references). Virginia Polytechnic Institute and State University, mimeographed, 1980.

Hohenshil, T. H., & Warden, P. The emerging vocational school psychologist: Implications for special needs students. *The School Psychology Digest,* 1977, *7,* 5-17.

Holland, C. J. An interview guide for behavioral counseling with parents. In E. J. Mash & L. G. Terdal (Eds.), *Behavior therapy assessment: Diagnosis, design, and evaluation.* New York: Springer, 1976.

Hollenbeck, A. R. Problems of reliability in observational research. In G. P. Sackett (Ed.), *Observing behavior: Volume II: Data collection and analysis methods.* Baltimore: University Park Press, 1978.

Holmen, M. G., & Docter, R. *Educational and psychological testing: A study of the testing industry and its practices.* New York: Russell Sage Foundation, 1972.

Honzik, M. P., Macfarlane, J. W., & Allen, L. The stability of mental test performance between two years and eighteen years. *Journal of Experimental Education,* 1948, *17,* 309-324.

Hopper, R., & Naremore, R. C. *Children's speech: A practical introduction to communication development.* New York: Harper & Row, 1973.

Horne, M. D. Attitudes and mainstreaming: A literature review for school psychologists. *Psychology in the Schools,* 1979, *16,* 61-67.

Horst, P. The logic of personnel selection and classification. In R. M. Gagné (Ed.), *Psychological principles in system development.* New York: Holt, Rinehart & Winston, 1962.

Horstmeier, D. S., & MacDonald, J. D. *Environmental prelanguage battery.* Columbus, OH: Nisonger Center Technical Report, 1975.

Hunter, J. E., & Schmidt, F. L. Critical analysis of the statistical and ethical implications of various definitions of test bias. *Psychological Bulletin,* 1976, *83,* 1053-1071.

Hynd, G. W., & Garcia, W. I. Intellectual assessment of the Native American student. *School Psychology Digest,* 1979, *8,* 446-454.

Insel, P. M., & Moos, R. H. Psychological environments: Expanding the scope of human ecology. *American Psychologist,* 1974, *29,* 179-187.

Irvin, L. K., Halpern, A., & Reynolds, W. M. *Social and prevocational information battery, Form T.* Monterey, CA: CTB/McGraw-Hill, 1979.

Irwin, J. V., Moore, J. M., & Rampp, D. L. Nonmedical diagnosis and evaluation. In J. V. Irwin & M. Marge (Eds.), *Principles of childhood language disorders.* New York: Appleton-Century-Crofts, 1972.

Itkin, W. Needed: New approaches to evaluation and training of the retarded. *Mental Retardation,* 1972, *10,* 35-41.

Jackson G. D. On the report of the ad hoc committee on educational use of tests with disadvantaged students: Another psychological view from the association of black psychologists. *American Psychologist,* 1975, *30,* 88-93.

Jacobson, S., & Kovalinsky, T. *Educational interpretation of the Wechsler intelligence scale for children-revised.* Linden, NJ: Remediation Associates, 1976.

Jaffe, B. F. (Ed.). *Hearing loss in children: A comprehensive text.* Baltimore: University Park Press, 1977.

Jastak, J. F., Bijou, S. W., & Jastak, S. R. *Wide range achievement test.* Wilmington, DE: Jastak Associates, 1978.

Jensen, A. R. How much can we boost IQ and scholastic achievement? *Harvard Educational Review,* 1969, *39,* 1-123.

Jensen, A. R. *Bias in mental testing.* New York: The Free Press, 1980.

John, E. R. *Neurometrics: Clinical applications of quantitative electrophysiology.* Hillsdale, NJ: Earlbaum, 1977.

Johnson, J. L. Mainstreaming black children. In R. L. Jones (Ed.), *Black psychology* (2nd ed.). New York: Harper & Row, 1980.

Jones, E. E. Black-white personality differences: Another look. *Journal of Personality Assessment,* 1978, *42,* 244-252.

Jones, G. B., & Gelatt, H. B. Illustrations of program interventions. In A. M. Mitchell, G. B. Jones, & J. D. Krumboltz (Eds.), *Social learning and career decision making.* Cranston, RI: Carroll Press, 1979.

Jones, R. L. (Ed.). *Black psychology* (2nd ed.). New York: Harper & Row, 1980.

Jones, R. R., Reid, J. B., & Patterson, G. R. Naturalistic observation in clinical assessment. In P. McReynolds (Ed.), *Advances in psychological assessment* (Vol. 3). San Francisco: Jossey-Bass, 1975.

Kabler, M. L. Public Law 94-142 and school psychology: Challenges and opportunities. *The School Psychology Digest,* 1977, *6,* 19-30.

Kamin, L. J. *The science and politics of IQ.* Potomac, MD: Earlbaum, 1974.

Kamin, L. J. Social and legal consequences of IQ tests as classification instruments: Some warning from our past. *Journal of School Psychology,* 1975, *13,* 317-323.

Kamin, L. J. Jensen's last stand. *Psychology Today,* 1980, *13,* pp.117;123.

Kanfer, F. H., & Goldstein, A. P. (Eds.). *Helping people change.* New York: Pergamon Press, 1975.

Kanfer, F. H., & Saslow, G. An outline for behavioral diagnosis. In E. J. Mash & L. G. Terdal (Eds.), *Behavior therapy assessment: Diagnosis, design, and evaluation.* New York: Springer, 1976.

Kansas State Department of Education. *Assessment tools for use with the severely multiply handicapped.* Topeka, KS: Special Education Administration, 1979.

Karlsen, B., Madden, R., & Gardner, E. F. *Stanford diagnostic reading tests.* New York: Psychological Corporation, 1977.

Karoly, P. Behavioral self-management in children: Concepts, methods, issues, and directions. In M. Hersen, R. M. Eisler, & P. M. Miller (Eds.), *Progress in behavior modification* (Vol. 5). New York: Academic Press, 1977.

Kaufman, A. S. Factor analysis of the WISC-R at eleven age levels between 6½ and 16½ years. *Journal of Consulting and Clinical Psychology,* 1975, *43,* 135-147.

Kaufman, A. S. *Intelligent testing with the WISC-R.* New York: Wiley, 1979.

Kaufman, A. S., & Kaufman, N. L. *Kaufman assessment battery for children (K-ABC): Examiner's manual, national standardization program.* Circle Pines, MN: American Guidance Service, 1981.

Kazdin, A. E. *Behavior modification in applied settings.* Homewood, IL: Dorsey, 1975.

Kazdin, A. E. *Behavior modification in applied settings* (Rev. ed.). Homewood, IL: Dorsey, 1980.

Kazimour, K. K., & Reschly, D. J. Investigation of the norms and concurrent validity for the Adaptive behavior inventory for children (ABIC). *American Journal of Mental Deficiency,* 1981, *85,* 512-520.

Keat, D. B. *Multimodal therapy with children.* New York: Pergamon Press, 1979.

Kent, R. N., & Foster, S. L. Direct observational procedures: Methodological issues in naturalistic settings. In A. R. Ciminero, K. S. Calhoun, & H. E. Adams, *Handbook of behavioral assessment.* New York: Wiley, 1977.

Kephart, N. C. *The slow learner in the classroom* (2nd ed.). Columbus, OH: Merrill, 1971.

Kirk, S., McCarthy, J., & Kirk, W. *The Illinois test of psycholinguistic abilities* (Rev. ed.). Urbana, IL: University of Illinois Press, 1968.

Kirk, W. D. *Aids and precautions in administering the Illinois test of psycholinguistic abilities.* Urbana, IL: University of Illinois Press, 1974.

Klein, N. K., & Safford, P. L. Applications of Piaget's theory to the study of thinking of the mentally retarded: A review of research. *The Journal of Special Education,* 1977, *11,* 201-216.

Klopfer, W. G., & Taulbee, E. S. Projective tests. In M. R. Rosenzweig & L. M. Porter (Eds.), *Annual review of psychology* (Vol. 27). Palo Alto, CA: Annual Reviews, 1976.

Knights, R. M., & Bakker, D. J. (Eds.). *The neuropsychology of learning disorders: Theoretical approaches.* Baltimore: University Park Press, 1976.

Koppitz, E. M. *The Bender Gestalt test for young children.* New York: Grune & Stratton, 1964.

Koppitz, E. M. *Psychological evaluations of children's figure drawings.* New York: Grune & Stratton, 1968.

Koppitz, E. M. *The Bender Gestalt test for young children: Volume II: Research and application, 1963-1973.* New York: Grune & Stratton, 1975.

Kratochwill, T. R. N = 1: An alternative research strategy for school psychologists. *Journal of School Psychology,* 1977, *15,* 239-249.

Kratochwill, T. R. (Ed.). *Single subject research: Strategies for evaluating change.* New York: Academic Press, 1978.

Kratochwill, T. R., & Severson, R. Process assessment: An examination of reinforcer effectiveness and predictive validity. *Journal of School Psychology,* 1977, *15,* 293-300.

Kretschmer, R. R., & Kretschmer, L. W. *Language development and intervention with the hearing impaired.* Baltimore: University Park Press, 1978.

Krumboltz, J. D. A social learning theory of career decision making. In A. M. Mitchell, G. B. Jones, & J. D. Krumboltz (Eds.), *Social learning and career decision making.* Cranston, RI: Carroll Press, 1979.

Krumboltz, J. D., Becker-Haven, J. F., & Burnett, K. F. Counseling psychology. In M. R. Rosenzweig & L. W. Porter (Eds.), *Annual review of psychology* (Vol. 30). Palo Alto, CA: Annual Reviews, 1979.

Kuder, G. F. *Kuder occupational interest survey.* Chicago: Science Research Associates, 1975.

Kuhns, J. W. *Neurological dysfunctions of children.* Monterey, CA: Publishers Test Service/ McGraw-Hill, 1978.

Labov, W. The logic of nonstandard English. In F. Williams (Ed.), *Language and poverty.* Chicago: Markham, 1970.

Lachar, D., & Gdowski, C. L. Problem-behavior factor correlates of the personality inventory for children profile scales. *Journal of Consulting and Clinical Psychology*, 1979, *47*, 39-48.

Lambert, N. M. The adaptive behavior scale-public school version: An overview. In W. A. Coulter & H. W. Morrow (Eds.), *Adaptive Behavior: Concepts and measurement*. New York: Grune & Stratton, 1978.

Lambert, N. M. Contributions of school classification, sex, and ethnic status to adaptive behavior assessment. *Journal of School Psychology*, 1979, *17*, 3-16.

Lambert, N. M., & Cole, L. Equal protection and due process considerations in the new special education legislation. *The School Psychology Digest*, 1977, *6*, 11-21.

Lambert, N. M., & Nicoll, R. C. Dimensions of adaptive behavior of retarded and non retarded public school children. *American Journal of Mental Deficiency*, 1976, *81*, 135-146.

Lambert, N. M., Windmiller, M., Cole, L., & Figueroa, R. *Manual for the AAMD adaptive behavior scale-public school version*. Washington, D. C.: American Association on Mental Deficiency, 1975.

Lanyon, R. I., & Goodstein, L. D. *Personality assessment*. New York: Wiley, 1971.

Larry P., et al. v. *Wilson Riles, et al. Opinion*. United States District Court, Robert F. Peckham, Chief Judge, Northern District of California, Case No. C-71-2270 RFP, 1979.

Lazarus, A. A. *Behavior therapy and beyond*. New York: McGraw-Hill, 1971.

Lazarus, A. A. *Multimodal behavior therapy*. New York: Springer, 1976.

Lazarus, A. A. Has behavior therapy outlived its usefulness? *American Psychologist*, 1977, *32*, 550-554.

Lee, L. L. *The northwest syntax screening test*. Evanston, IL: Northwestern University Press, 1971.

Lee, L. L. *Developmental sentence analysis*. Evanston, IL: Northwestern University Press, 1974.

Lefcourt, H. M. *Locus of control*. Hillsdale, NJ: Earlbaum, 1976.

Leland, H. W. Theoretical considerations of adaptive behavior. In W. A. Coulter & H. W. Morrow (Eds.), *Adaptive behavior: Concepts and measurement*. New York: Grune & Stratton, 1978.

Levine, E. Psychological tests and practices with the deaf: A survey of the state of the art. *Volta Review*, 1974, *76*, 298-319.

Lezak, M. D. *Neuropsychological assessment*. New York: Oxford University Press, 1976.

Lloyd, L. L. (Ed.). *Communication assessment and intervention strategies*. Baltimore: University Park Press, 1976.

Loehlin, J. C., Lindzey, G., & Spuhler, J. N. *Race differences in intelligence*. San Francisco: Freeman, 1975.

Losen, S. M., & Diament, B. *Parent conferences in the schools: Procedures for developing effective partnerships*. Boston: Allyn & Bacon, 1978.

McClelland, D. C. Testing for competence rather than for "intelligence." *American Psychologist*, 1973, *28*, 1-14.

McCormick, E. J., & Tiffin, J. *Industrial psychology* (6th ed.). Englewood Cliffs, NJ: Prentice-Hall, 1974.

McDaniel, E. L. *Inferred self-concept scale*. Los Angeles: Western Psychological Services, 1973.

MacDonald, J. D. *Parent-child communication inventory*. Columbus, OH: The Nisonger Center, 1973.

MacDonald, J. D. Environmental language intervention. In F. B. Withrow & C. J. Nygren (Eds.), *Language, materials and curriculum management for the handicapped learner.* Columbus, OH: Merrill, 1976.

MacDonald, J. D., & Nickols, M. *Environmental language inventory manual.* Columbus, OH: Ohio State University, 1974.

McNemar, Q. On so-called test bias. *American Psychologist,* 1975, *30,* 848-851.

McPhee, J. P., & Wegner, K. W. Kinetic-family-drawing styles and emotionally disturbed childhood behavior. *Journal of Personality Assessment,* 1976, *40,* 487-491.

McReynolds, P. Historical antecedents of personality assessment. In P. McReynolds, (Ed.), *Advances in psychological assessment* (Vol. 3). San Francisco: Jossey-Bass, 1975.

McReynolds, P. Introduction. In P. McReynolds (Ed.), *Advances in psychological assessment* (Vol. 4). San Francisco: Jossey-Bass, 1977.

McReynolds, W. T. DSM-III and the future of applied social science. *Professional Psychology,* 1979, *10,* 123-132.

Machover, K. *Personality projection in the drawing of the human figure: A method of personality investigation.* Springfield, IL: Thomas, 1949.

Madden, R., Gardner, E. F., Rudman, H. C., Karlsen, B., & Merwin, J. C. *Stanford achievement test.* New York: Harcourt, Brace, Jovanovich, 1973.

Magnusson, D., & Endler, N. S. (Eds.). *Personality at the crossroads: Current issues in interactional psychology.* Hillsdale, NJ: Earlbaum, 1977.

Mahoney, M. J. *Cognition and behavior modification.* Cambridge, MA: Ballinger, 1974.

Mahoney, M. J. Reflections on the cognitive-learning trend in psychotherapy. *American Psychologist,* 1977, *32,* 5-13.

Maloney, M. P., & Ward, M. P. *Psychological assessment: A conceptual approach.* New York: Oxford University Press, 1976.

Mann, L. Psychometric phrenology and the faculty psychology: The case against ability assessment and training. *Journal of Special Education,* 1971, *5,* 3-14.

Marion, R. L. Communicating with parents of culturally diverse exceptional children. *Exceptional Children,* 1980, *46,* 616-623.

Martin, F. N., (Ed.). *Pediatric audiology.* Englewood Cliffs, NJ: Prentice-Hall, 1978.

Martin, R. *Educating handicapped children: The legal mandate.* Champaign, IL: Research Press, 1979.

Martuza, V. R. *Applying norm-referenced and criterion-referenced measurement in education.* Boston: Allyn & Bacon, 1977.

Mash, E. J., Hamerlynck, L. A., & Handy, L. C. (Eds.). *Behavior modification and families.* New York: Brunner/Mazel, 1976.

Mash, E. J., & Terdal, L. G. (Eds.). *Behavior therapy assessment: Diagnosis, design and evaluation.* New York: Springer, 1976.

Mastenbrook, J. *Analysis of the concept of adaptive behavior and two assessment instruments.* Paper presented at the meeting of the American Psychological Association, San Francisco, August 1977.

Mastenbrook, J. *Future directions in adaptive behavior assessment: The Texas environmental adaptation measure.* Paper presented at the meeting of the American Psychological Association, Toronto, September 1978.

Matarazzo, J. D. *Wechsler's measurement and appraisal of adult intelligence* (5th ed.). Baltimore: Williams & Wilkins, 1972.

Matkin, N. D., Hook, P. E., & Hixson, P. K. A multidisciplinary approach to the evaluation of hearing impaired children. *Audiology: An audio journal for continuing education.* New York: Grune & Stratton, 1979.

Matluck, J. H., & Mace, B. J. Language characteristics of Mexican-American children: Implications for assessment. *Journal of School Psychology*, 1973, *11*, 365-386.

Mealor, D. J., & Richmond, B. O. Adaptive behavior: Teachers and parents disagree. *Exceptional Children*, 1980, *46*, 386-389.

Meehl, P. E. *Clinical versus statistical prediction*. Minneapolis: University of Minnesota Press, 1954.

Megargee, E. I. *The California psychological inventory handbook*. San Francisco: Jossey-Bass, 1972.

Meichenbaum, D. *Cognitive-behavior modification*. New York: Plenum Press, 1977.

Meichenbaum, D. (Ed.). *Cognitive-behavior modification newsletter*. Waterloo, Ontario: University of Waterloo, 1979, *4*.

Meisgeier, C. A. review of critical issues underlying mainstreaming. In L. Mann & D. Sabatino (Eds.), *The third review of special education*. New York: Grune & Stratton, 1976.

Menyuk, P. *Language and maturation*. Cambridge, MA: MIT Press, 1977.

Merachink, D. Assessing work potential of the handicapped in public schools. *Vocational Guidance Quarterly*, 1970, *8*, 225-229.

Mercer, J. R. *Labeling the mentally retarded*. Berkeley: University of California Press, 1973.

Mercer, J. R. *System of multicultural pluralistic assessment technical manual*. New York: Psychological Corporation, 1979.

Mercer, J. R., & Lewis, J. F. *SOMPA: System of multicultural pluralistic assessment*. New York: Psychological Corporation, 1977.

Messick, S. Test validity and the ethics of assessment. *American Psychologist*, 1980, *35*, 1012-1027.

Miller, L.K. *Principles of everyday behavior analysis* (2nd ed.). Monterey, CA: Brooks/Cole, 1980.

Millham, J., Chilcutt, J., & Atkinson, B.L. Comparability of naturalistic and controlled observation assessment of adaptive behavior. *American Journal of Mental Deficiency*, 1978, *83*, 52-59.

Mischel, W. *Personality and assessment*. New York: Wiley, 1968.

Mischel, W. Toward a cognitive social learning reconceptualization of personality. *Psychological Review*, 1973, *80*, 252-283.

Mischel, W. On the future of personality measurement. *American Psychologist*, 1977, *32*, 246-254.

Mitchell, S. K. Interobserver agreement, reliability, and generalizability of data collected in observational studies. *Psychological Bulletin*, 1979, *86*, 376-390.

Moerk, E.L. Processes of language teaching and training in the interactions of mother-child dyads. *Child Development*, 1976, *47*, 1064-1078.

Mooney, R.L., & Gordon, L.V. *The Mooney problem checklists*. New York: Psychological Corporation, 1950.

Moos, R.H., Insel, P.M. & Humphrey, B. *Family, work and group environment scales*. Palo Alto, CA: Consulting Psychologists Press, 1974.

Moos, R.H., & Trickett, E.J. *Classroom environment scale*. Palo Alto, CA: Consulting Psychologists Press, 1974.

Morehead, D.M., & Morehead, A.E. (Eds.). *Normal and deficient child language*. Baltimore: University Park Press, 1976.

Mourouzis, A., Wemple, D., Wheeler, J., Williams, L., & Zucher, S. *Body management activities: A guide to perceptual-motor training*. Dayton, OH: MWZ Associates, 1969.

Mowder, B.A. Assessing the bilingual handicapped student. *Psychology in the Schools*, 1979, *16*, 43-50.

Murdoch, G. *The relationship between family environment, children's social perception, and classroom behavior.* Unpublished doctoral dissertation, University of Cincinnati, 1979.

Murray, H.A. *Explorations in personality.* New York: Oxford University Press, 1938.

Murray, H.A. *Thematic apperception test manual.* Cambridge, MA: Harvard University Press, 1943.

Mussen, P.H., Conger, J.J., & Kagan, J. *Child development and personality* (4th ed.). New York: Harper & Row, 1974.

Mussen, P.H., & Eisenberg-Berg, N. *Roots of caring, sharing, and helping.* San Francisco: Freeman, 1977.

Mutti, M., Sterling, H.M., & Spalding, N.V. *QNST: Quick neurological screening test.* (Rev. ed.). Novato, CA: Academic Therapy, 1978.

Myklebust, H.R. *Development and disorders of written language.* New York: Grune & Stratton, 1965.

Naremore, R.C. Language variation in a multicultural society. In T.J. Hixon, L.D. Shriberg, & J.H. Saxman (Eds.), *Introduction to communication disorders.* Englewood Cliffs, NJ: Prentice-Hall, 1980.

Nay, W.R. *Multimethod clinical assessment.* New York: Gardner Press, 1979.

Neff, W.S. *Work and human behavior* (2nd ed.). Chicago: Aldine, 1977.

Neisworth, J.T., & Smith, R.M. *Retardation: Issues, assessment, and intervention.* New York: McGraw-Hill, 1978.

Nelson, K.E. (Ed.). *Children's language* (Vol. 1). New York: Gardner Press, 1978.

Nelson, K.E. (Ed.). *Children's language* (Vol. 2). New York: Gardner Press, 1980.

Nelson, R.O., & Evans, I.M. Assessment of child behavior problems. In A.R. Ciminero, K.S. Calhoun, & H.E. Adams (Eds.), *Handbook of behavioral assessment.* New York: Wiley, 1977.

Nelson, R.O., & Hayes, S.C. The nature of behavioral assessment: A commentary. *Journal of Applied Behavior Analysis,* 1979, *12,* 491-500.

Newbrough, J.R., Walker, L.S., & Abril, S. *Ecological assessment.* Paper presented at the meeting of the National Association of School Psychologists, New York, 1978.

Newcomer, P.L., & Hammill, D.D. ITPA and academic achievement: A survey. *The Reading Teacher,* 1975, *28,* 731-741.

Newcomer, P.L., & Hammill,D.D. *Psycholinguistics in the schools.* Columbus, OH: Merrill, 1976.

Newcomer, P.L., & Hammill, D.D. *The Test of Language Development.* Austin, TX: ProEd, 1977.

Nichols, E. *A primer of social casework.* New York: Columbia University Press, 1960.

Nihira, K., Foster, R., Shellhaas, M., & Leland, H. *AAMD adaptive behavior scale, 1974 revision.* Washington, D.C.: American Association on Mental Deficiency, 1974.

Nirge, B. The normalization principle and its human management implications. In R. Kugel & W. Wolfensberger (Eds.), *Changing patterns in residential services for the mentally retarded.* Washington, D.C.: U.S. Government Printing Office, 1969.

Nunnally, J.C. *Psychometric theory* (2nd ed.). New York: McGraw-Hill, 1978.

Oakland, T. (Ed.). *Psychological and educational assessment of minority children.* New York: Brunner/Mazel, 1977.

Oakland, T. Research on the adaptive behavior inventory for children and the estimated learning potential. *School Psychology Digest,* 1979, *8,* 63-70.

Oakland, T. Nonbiased assessment of minority group children. *Exceptional Child Quarterly,* 1980, *1,* 31-46.

Oakland, T. An evaluation of the ABIC, pluralistic norms, and estimated learning potential. *Journal of School Psychology*, 1980, *18*, 3-11.

Oakland, T., & Feigenbaum, D. Multiple sources of test bias on the WISC-R and Bender-Gestalt Test. *Journal of Consulting and Clinical Psychology*, 1979, *47*, 968-974.

Oakland, T., & Feigenbaum, D. Comparisons of the psychometric characteristics of the Adaptive Behavior Inventory for Children for different subgroups of children. *Journal of School Psychology*, 1980, *18*, 307-317.

Oakland, T., & Goldwater, D.L. Assessment and interventions for mildly retarded and learning disabled children. In G.D. Phye & D.J. Reschly (Eds.), *School psychology: Perspectives and issues*. New York: Academic Press, 1979.

Oakland, T., & Matuszek, P. Using tests in nondiscriminatory assessment. In T. Oakland (Ed.), *Psychological and educational assessment of minority children*. New York: Brunner/Mazel, 1977.

O'Dell, S. Training parents in behavior modification: A review. *Psychological Bulletin*, 1974, *81*, 418-433.

O'Leary, K.D., & O'Leary, S.G. *Classroom management: The successful use of behavior modification* (2nd ed.). New York: Pergamon Press, 1977.

Paraskevopoulos, J.N., & Kirk, S.A. *The development and psychometric characteristics of the revised Illinois test of psycholinguistic abilities*. Urbana, IL: University of Illinois Press, 1969.

Park, R.D. Children's home environments: Social and cognitive effects. In I. Altman & J.F. Wohlwil (Eds.), *Children and the environment*. New York: Plenum Press, 1978.

Patterson, G.R. *Families* (Rev. ed.). Champaign, IL: Research Press, 1975.

Patterson, G.R., Reid, J.B., Jones, R.R., & Conger, R.E. *A social learning approach to family intervention* (Vol. 1). Eugene, OR: Castalia, 1975.

Paul, J.L., Turnbull, A.P., & Cruickshank, W.M. *Mainstreaming: A practical guide*. Syracuse: Syracuse University Press, 1977.

Peterson, D.R. *The clinical study of social behavior*. New York: Appleton-Century-Crofts, 1968.

Pettigrew, T.F. Negro American personality: Why isn't more known? *The Journal of Social Issues*, 1964, *20*, 4-23.

Phillips, L., Draguns, J.G. & Bartlett, D.P. Classification of behavior disorders. In N. Hobbs (Ed.), *Issues in the classification of children* (Vol. 1). San Francisco: Jossey-Bass, 1975.

Piers, E.V. *Manual for the Piers-Harris children's self concept scale*. Nashville, TN: Counselor Recordings and Tests, 1969.

Piersel, W.C., Brody, G.H., & Kratochwill, T.R. A further examination of motivational influences on disadvantaged minority group children's intelligence test performance. *Child Development*, 1977, *48*, 1142-1145.

Piotrowski, R.J., & Grubb, R.D. Significant subtest score differences on the WISC-R. *Journal of School Psychology*, 1976, *14*, 202-206.

Porter, R.B., & Cattell, R. *Children's personality questionnaire*. Champaign, IL: Institute for Personality and Ability Testing, 1975.

Prasse, D.P. Federal legislation and school psychology: Impact and implication. *Professional Psychology*, 1978, *9*, 592-601.

Progress toward a free appropriate public education: Semiannual update on the implementation of Public Law 94-142: The Education for All Handicapped Children Act. Washington, D.C.: U.S. Office of Education, August, 1979.

Prugh, D.G., Engel, M., & Morse, W.C. Emotional disturbance in children. In N. Hobbs (Ed.), *Issues in the classification of children* (Vol. 1). San Francisco: Jossey-Bass, 1975.

Pryzwansky, W.B., & Bersoff, D.N. Parental consent for psychological evaluations: Legal, ethical and practical considerations. *Journal of School Psychology*, 1978, *16*, 274-281.

Public Law 94-142, 94th Congress, § 6. *Education for all handicapped children act of 1975*, November 29, 1975.

Rabin, A. *Projective techniques in personality assessment.* New York: Springer, 1968.

Rains, P.M., Kitsuse, J.I., Duster, T., Freidson, E. The labeling approach to deviance. In N. Hobbs (Ed.), *Issues in the classification of children* (Vol. 1). San Francisco: Jossey-Bass, 1975.

Razeghi, J.A., & Davis, S. Federal mandates for the handicapped: Vocational education opportunity and employment. *Exceptional Children*, 1979, *45*, 353-359.

Reitan, R.M. Neurological and physiological bases of psychopathology. In M.R. Rosenzweig & L.W. Porter (Eds.), *Annual Review of Psychology* (Vol. 27). Palo Alto, CA: Annual Reviews, 1976.

Reitan, R.M., & Davison, L.A. (Eds.), *Clinical neuropsychology: Current status and applications.* New York: Winston/Wiley, 1974.

Remmers, H.H., & Bauerfeind, R.H. *STS youth inventory* (Grades 4-8). Bensenville, IL: Scholastic Testing Service, 1968.

Remmers, H.H., & Shimberg, B. *STS youth inventory* (Grades 7-12). Bensenville, IL: Scholastic Testing Service, 1967.

Reschly, D.J. WISC-R factor structures among Anglos, Blacks, Chicanos, and Native-American Papagos. *Journal of Consulting and Clinical Psychology*, 1978, *46*, 417-422.

Reschly, D.J. Nonbiased assessment. In G.D. Phye & D.J. Reschly (Eds.), *School psychology: Perspectives and issues.* New York: Academic Press, 1979.

Reschly, D.J., & Reschly, J.E. Validity of WISC-R factor scores in predicting achievement and attention for four sociocultural groups. *Journal of School Psychology*, 1979, *17*, 355-361.

Reschly, D.J., & Sabers, D. Analysis of test bias in four groups with the regression definition. *Journal of Educational Measurement*, 1979, *16*, 1-9.

Resnick, L.B. The future of IQ testing in education. In R.J. Sternberg & D.K. Detterman (Eds.), *Human intelligence: Perspectives in its theory and measurement.* Norwood, NJ: Ablex, 1979.

Resources for the vocational preparation of disabled youth. Washington, DC: U.S. Government Printing Office, 1980.

Reynolds, C.R. A quick-scoring guide to the interpretation of children's Kinetic Family Drawings. *Psychology in the Schools*, 1978, *15*, 489-492.

Reynolds, C.R., & Gutkin, T.B. A regression analysis of test bias on the WISC-R for Anglos and Chicanos referred for psychological services. *Journal of Abnormal Child Psychology*, in press.

Reynolds, M.C. A framework for considering some issues in special education. *Exceptional Children*, 1962, *28*, 367-370.

Reynolds, M.C., & Birch, J.W. *Teaching exceptional children in America's schools: A first course for teachers and principals.* Reston, VA: The Council for Exceptional Children, 1977.

Richmond, B.O., & Kicklighter, R.H. *Children's adaptive behavior scale.* Atlanta: Humanics, 1980.

Rie, H.E., & Rie, E.D. *Handbook of minimal brain dysfunctions: A critical review.* New York: Wiley, 1979.

Ritzer, B.A., Sharkey, K.J., & Chudy, J.F. A comprehensive projective alternative to the TAT. *Journal of Personality Assessment,* 1980, *44,* 358-362.

Roach, E.G., & Kephart, N.C. *The Purdue perceptual-motor survey.* Columbus, OH: Merrill, 1966.

Robinson, N.M. & Robinson, H.B. *The mentally retarded child: A psychological approach* (2nd ed.). New York: McGraw-Hill, 1976.

Rorschach, H. *Psychodiagnostics: A diagnostic test based on perception* (4th ed.). New York: Grune & Stratton, 1942. (Originally published, 1921).

Rosenthal, T.L., & Zimmerman, B.J. *Social learning and cognition.* New York: Academic Press, 1978.

Ross, A. A clinical psychologist "examines" retarded children. In G. Williams & S. Gordon (Eds.), *Clinical child psychology: Current practices and future perspectives.* New York: Behavioral Publications, 1974.

Rotter, J.B. *Incomplete sentences blank-high school form.* New York: Psychological Corporation, 1950.

Rotter, J.B. Generalized expectancies for internal versus external control of reinforcement. *Psychological Monographs,* 1966, *80,* (1, Whole No. 609).

Rusch, F.R., & Mithaug, D.E. *Vocational training for young adults: A behavior analytic approach.* Champaign, IL: Research Press, 1980.

Sackett, G.P. (Ed.), *Observing behavior: Volume I: Theory and application in mental retardation.* Baltimore: University Park Press, 1978.

Sailor, W., & Horner, R.D. Educational assessment strategies for the severely handicapped. In N.G. Haring & L. Brown (Eds.), *Teaching the severely handicapped* (Vol. 1). New York: Grune & Stratton, 1976.

Salvia, J., & Ysseldyke, J.E. *Assessment in special and remedial education.* Boston: Houghton Mifflin, 1978.

Samuda, R.J. *Psychological testing of American minorities: Issues and consequences.* New York: Dodd, Mead & Co., 1975.

Sanders, D.A. A model for communication. In L.L. Lloyd (Ed.), *Communication assessment and intervention strategies.* Baltimore: University Park Press, 1976.

Sandoval, J. The WISC-R and internal evidence of test bias with minority groups. *Journal of Consulting and Clinical Psychology,* 1979, *47,* 919-927.

Sandoval, J., & Miille, M.P.W. Accuracy of judgments of WISC-R item difficulty for minority groups. *Journal of Consulting and Clinical Psychology,* 1980, *48,* 249-253.

Sarason, S.B. The unfortunate fate of Alfred Binet and School Psychology. *Teachers College Record,* 1976, *77,* 579-592.

Sarason, S.B., & Doris, J. *Educational handicap, public policy, and social history: A broadened perspective on mental retardation.* New York: Macmillan, 1978.

Sattler, J.M. *Intelligence test modifications on handicapped and non-handicapped children, final report.* San Diego, CA: San Diego State University Foundation, 1972. (ERIC Document Reproduction Service Number ED 095 673)

Sattler, J.M. *Assessment of children's intelligence.* Philadelphia: Saunders, 1974.

Sattler, J.M., & Anderson, N.E. Peabody Picture Vocabulary Test, Stanford-Binet, and Stanford-Binet modified with normal and cerebral palsied preschool children. *Journal of Special Education,* 1973, *7,* 119-123.

Sattler, J.M., & Tozier, L.L. A review of intelligence test modifications used with cerebral palsied and other handicapped groups. *Journal of Special Education,* 1970, *4.* 391-398.

Savage, J.E., & Adair, A.V. Testing minorities: Developing more culturally relevant assessment systems. In R.L. Jones (Ed.), *Black psychology* (2nd ed.). New York: Harper & Row, 1980.

Scheff, T.J. *Being mentally ill.* Chicago: Aldine, 1966.

Schiefelbusch, R.L. (Ed). *Nonspeech language and communication: Analysis and intervention.* Baltimore: University Park Press, 1980.

Schiefelbusch, R.L., & Lloyd, L.L. (Eds.). *Language perspectives-acquisition, retardation, and intervention.* Baltimore: University Park Press, 1974.

Schmidt, F.L., & Hunter, J.E. Racial and ethnic bias in psychological tests: Divergent implications of two definitions of test bias. *American Psychologist,* 1974, *29,* 1-8.

Scholl, G., & Schnur, R. *Measures of psychological, vocational, & educational functioning in the blind and visually handicapped.* New York: American Foundation for the Blind, 1976.

Scott, L.S. *Texas environmental adaptation measure: Adaptive behavior in sociocultural, emotional environments.* Paper presented at the meeting of the American Psychological Association, Toronto, September 1978.

Sechrest, L. Incremental validity: A recommendation. *Educational and Psychological Measurement,* 1963, *23,* 153-158.

Seligman, M.E.P. *Helplessness: On depression, development, and death.* San Francisco: Freeman, 1975.

Semel, E.M., & Wiig, E.H. *Clinical evaluation of language functions.* Columbus, OH: Merrill, 1980.

Senna, C. (Ed.). *The fallacy of IQ.* New York: The Third Press, 1973.

Sewell, T.E. Intelligence and learning tasks as predictors of scholastic achievement in black and white first-grade children. *Journal of School Psychology,* 1979, *17,* 325-332.

Sewell, T.E., & Severson, R.A. Learning ability and intelligence as cognitive predictors of achievement in first-grade black children. *Journal of Educational Psychology,* 1974, *66,* 948-955.

Shavelson, R.J., Hubner, J.J., & Stanton, G.C. Self-concept: Validation of construct interpretations. *Review of Educational Research,* 1976, *46,* 407-441.

Shub, A.N., Carlin, J.A., Friedman, R.L., Kaplan, J.M., & Katien, J.C. *Diagnosis: An instructional aid (Reading).* Chicago: Science Research Associates, 1973.

Siegel, G.M., & Broen, P.A. Language assessment. In L.L. Lloyd (Ed.), *Communication assessment and intervention strategies.* Baltimore: University Park Press, 1976.

Silvaroli, N.J. *Classroom reading inventory.* Dubuque, IA: Brown, 1976.

Simon, A., & Boyer, E.G. (Eds.). *Mirrors for behavior III: An anthology of classroom observation instruments.* Philadelphia: Research for Better Schools, 1974.

Singer, H., & Ruddell, R.B. (Eds.). *Theoretical models and processes of reading* (2nd ed.). Newark, DE:International Reading Association, 1976.

Slingerland, B.H. *Slingerland screening tests for identifying children with specific language disabilities* (Rev. ed.). Cambridge, MA: Educators Publishing Service, 1970.

Sloves, R.E., Docherty, E.M., Jr., & Schneider, K.C. A scientific problem-solving model of psychological assessment. *Professional Psychology,* 1979, *10,* 28-35.

Smith, E.J. Profile of the black individual in vocational literature. In R.L. Jones (Ed.), *Black Psychology* (2nd ed.). New York: Harper & Row, 1980.

Smith, R.M., Forsberg, S.J., Herb, S.L., & Neisworth, J.T. Instructional intervention. In J.T. Neisworth & R.M. Smith. *Retardation: Issues, assessments and intervention.* New York: McGraw-Hill, 1978.

Snow, C.E. Mother's speech research: From input to interaction. In C.E. Snow & C.A. Furguson (Eds.), *Talking to children: Language input and acquisition.* New York: Cambridge University Press, 1977.

Solomon, I.L., & Starr, B.D. *School apperception method.* New York: Springer, 1968.

Somerton, M.E., & Meyers, D.G. Educational programming for the severely and profoundly mentally retarded. In N.G. Haring & L. Brown (Eds.), *Teaching the severely handicapped* (Vol. 1). New York: Grune & Stratton, 1976.

Sommers, R.K., Erdige, S., & Peterson, M.K. How valid are children's language tests? *The Journal of Special Education,* 1978, *12,* 393-407.

Spache, G.D. *Diagnostic reading scales* (Rev. ed.). Monterey, CA: CTB/McGraw-Hill, 1972.

Spivack, G., Haimes, P.E., & Spotts, J. *Devereux adolescent behavior rating scale manual.* Devon, PA: The Devereux Foundation, 1967.

Spivack, G., Platt, J.J., & Shure, M.B. *The Problem-solving approach to adjustment.* San Francisco: Jossey-Bass, 1976.

Spivack, G., & Shure, M. *Social adjustment of young children: A cognitive approach to solving real-life problems.* San Francisco: Jossey-Bass, 1974.

Spivack, G., & Spotts, J. *Devereux child behavior rating scale.* Devon, PA: Devereux Foundation Press, 1966.

Spivack, G., & Swift, M. *Devereux elementary school behavior rating scale.* Devon, PA: Devereux Foundation, 1967.

Standards for educational and psychological tests. Washington, DC: American Psychological Association, 1974.

Stern, A. *Diagnosis and assessment of mental retardation.* In B.R. Gearheart & F.W. Litton (Eds.), *The trainable mentally retarded.* St. Louis, MO: Mosby, 1975.

Stern, G.G., Stein, M.I., & Bloom, B.S. *Methods in personality assessment.* Glencoe, IL: The Free Press, 1956.

Stokols, D. (Ed.). *Perspectives on environment and behavior: Theory, research, and applications.* New York: Plenum Press, 1977. (a)

Stokols, D. Origins and directions of environment-behavioral research. In D. Stokols (Ed.), *Perspectives on environment and behavior: Theory, research, and applications.* New York, Plenum Press, 1977. (b)

Stokols, D. Environmental psychology. In M.R. Rosenzweig & L.W. Porter (Eds.), *Annual review of psychology* (Vol. 29). Palo Alto, CA: Annual Reviews, 1978.

Sugarman, A. Is psychodiagnostic assessment humanistic? *Journal of Personality Assessment,* 1978, *42,* 11-21.

Sullivan, P.M., & Vernon, M. Psychological assessment of hearing impaired children. *School Psychology Digest,* 1979, *8,* 271-290.

Sundberg, N.D. *Assessment of persons.* Englewood Cliffs, NJ: Prentice-Hall, 1977.

Super, D.E. A life-span, life-space approach to career development. *Journal of Vocational Behavior,* 1980, *16,* 282-298.

Super, D.E. A theory of vocational development. *American Psychologist,* 1953, *8,* 185-190.

Super, D.E., & Crites, J.O. *Appraising vocational fitness by means of psychological tests* (Rev. ed.). New York: Harper & Row, 1962.

Super, D.E., & Hall, D.T. Career development: Explorations and planning. In M.R. Rosenzweig & L.W. Porter (Eds.), *Annual review of psychology* (Vol. 29). Palo Alto, CA: Annual Reviews, 1978.

Swan, G.E., & MacDonald, M.L. Behavior therapy in practice: A national survey of behavior therapists. *Behavior Therapy,* 1978, *9,* 799-807.

Swanson, E.N., & Deblassie, R.R. Interpreter and Spanish administration effects of the WISC performance of Mexican-American children. *Journal of School Psychology,* 1979, *17,* 231-236.

Switzky, H., Rotatori, A.F., Miller, T., & Freagon, S. The developmental model and its implications for assessment and instruction for the severely/profoundly handicapped. *Mental Retardation,* 1979, *17,* 167-170.

Symonds, P.M. *Symonds picture-story test.* New York: Teachers College Press, 1948.

Tebeleff, M., & Oakland, T.D. *Relationship between the ABIC, WISC-R and achievement.* Paper presented at the meeting of the American Psychological Association, San Francisco, August 1977.

Templin, M.C., & Darley, F.L. *The Templin-Darley tests of articulation.* Iowa City: Bureau of Educational Research and Service, University of Iowa, 1960.

Terman, L.M. *The measurement of intelligence.* Boston: Houghton Mifflin, 1916.

Terman, L.M., & Merrill, M.A. *Stanford-Binet intelligence scale: 1972 norms edition.* Boston: Houghton Mifflin, 1973.

Terman, L.M., & Oden, M.H. *Genetic studies of genius: Volume V: The gifted children at mid-life.* Stanford, CA: Stanford University Press, 1959.

Theimer, R.K., & Rupiper, O.J. Special education litigation and school psychology, *Journal of School Psychology,* 1975, *13,* 324-334.

Thompson, C.E. *Thematic apperception test: Thompson modification.* Cambridge, MA: Harvard University Press, 1949.

Thompson, J.M., & Sones, R.A. *Education apperception test.* Los Angeles, Western Psychological Services, 1973.

Torres, S. (Ed.). *A primer on individualized educational programs for handicapped children.* Reston, VA: The Council for Exceptional Children, 1977.

Tortelli, J.P. Simplified psycholinguistic diagnosis. *The Reading Teacher,* 1976, *29,* 637-639.

Trahan, D., & Stricklin,A. Bender-Gestalt emotional indicators and acting-out behavior in young children. *Journal of Personality Assessment,* 1979, *43,* 365-375.

Trupin, E.W., & Townes, B.D. Neuropsychological evaluation as an adjunct to behavioral interventions with children. *Professional Psychology,* 1976, *7,* 153-160.

Tucker, J.A. Operationalizing the diagnostic-intervention process. In T. Oakland (Ed.), *Psychological and educational assessment of minority children.* New York: Brunner/Mazel, 1977.

Turnbull, A.P., & Schultz, J.B. *Mainstreaming handicapped students: A guide for the classroom teacher.* Boston: Allyn & Bacon, 1979.

Turnbull, A.P., Strickland, B.B., & Brantley, J.C. *Developing and implementing individual educational programs.* Columbus, OH: Merrill, 1978.

Turnbull, H.R., Turnbull, A.P., & Strickland, B. Procedural due process: The two-edged sword that the untrained should not unsheath. *Journal of Education,* 1979, *161,* 40-59.

U.S. Department of Labor, Manpower Administration. *Manual for the USES general aptitude test battery.* Washington, DC: U.S. Employment Service, 1970.

Uzgiris, I.C., & Hunt, J. McV. *Assessment in infancy: Ordinal scales of psychological development.* Urbana, IL: University of Illinois Press, 1975.

Vernon, M., Bair, R., & Lotz, S. Psychological evaluation and testing of children who are deaf-blind. *School Psychology Digest*, 1979, *8*, 291-295.

Voeltz, L.M. Children's attitudes towards handicapped peers. *American Journal of Mental Deficiency*, 1980, *84*, 455-464.

Vygotsky, L.S. *Mind in society: The development of higher psychological processes*, (Cole, M., John-Steiner, V., Scribner, S., & Souberman, E., Eds.). Cambridge, MA: Harvard University Press, 1978.

Waddell, D.D. The Stanford-Binet: An evaluation of the technical data available since the 1972 standardization. *Journal of School Psychology*, 1980, *18*, 203-209.

Wade, T.C., & Baker, T.B. Opinions and the use of psychological tests: A survey of clinical psychologists. *American Psychologist*, 1977, *32*, 874-882.

Wade, T.C., & Baker, T.B. Representativeness of the Wade and Baker sample: A reply to Garfield. *American Psychologist*, 1978, *33*, 848-850.

Wahler, R.G., House, A.E., & Stambaugh, E.E. *Ecological assessment of child problem behavior*. New York: Pergamon Press, 1976.

Waisbren, S.E. Parents' reactions after the birth of a developmentally disabled child. *American Journal of Mental Deficiency*, 1980, *84*, 345-351.

Wallace, G., & Larsen, S.C. *Educational assessment of learning problems: Testing for teaching*. Boston: Allyn & Bacon, 1978.

Walker, H.M. *Walker behavior identification checklist*. Los Angeles: Western Psychological Services, 1976.

Waugh, R.P. The ITPA: Ballast or bonanza for the school psychologist. *Journal of School Psychology*, 1975, *13*, 201-208.

Wechsler, D. *The measurement and appraisal of adult intelligence* (4th ed.). Baltimore: Williams & Wilkins, 1958.

Wechsler, D. *Wechsler intelligence scale for children-revised*. New York: Psychological Corporation, 1974.

Weinberg, R.A., & Wood, F.H. (Eds.). *Observation of pupils and teachers in mainstream and special education settings: Alternative strategies*. Minneapolis: Leadership Training Institute/Special Education, University of Minnesota, 1975.

Weiner, I.B. Does psychodiagnosis have a future? *Journal of Personality Assessment*, 1972, *36*, 534-546.

Weinrott, M.R. A training program in behavior modification for siblings of the retarded. *American Journal of Orthopsychiatry*, 1974, *44*, 362-375.

Wepman, J. *The auditory discrimination test*. Chicago, IL: Language Research Associates, 1958.

Wesman, A.G. Intelligent testing. *American Psychologist*, 1968, *23*, 267-274.

Whalen, C. K., & Henker, B. (Eds.). *Hyperactive children: The social ecology of identification and treatment*. New York: Academic Press, 1980.

Whitehurst, G. J., Novak, G., & Zorn, G. A. Delayed speech studied in the home. *Developmental Psychology*, 1972, *7*, 169-177.

Whitely, J. W., & Resnikoff, A. (Eds.). *Career counseling*. Monterey, CA: Brooks/Cole, 1978.

Wiggins, J. S. *Personality and prediction: Principles of personality assessment*. Reading, MA: Addison-Wesley, 1973.

Wiig, E. H., & Semel, E. M. *Language assessment and intervention for the learning disabled*. Columbus, OH: Merrill, 1980.

Willems, E. P. Steps toward an ecobehavioral technology. In A. Rogers-Warren & S. F. Warren (Eds.), *Ecological perspectives in behavioral analysis*. Baltimore: University Park Press, 1977.

Williams, R. L. Abuses and misuses in testing black children. *The Counseling Psychologist*, 1971, *2*, 62-73.

Williams, R.L. The BITCH-100: A culture specific test. *Journal of Afro-American Issues,* 1975, *3,* 103-116.

Winter, W. D., Ferreira, A. J., & Olsen, J. L. Story sequence analysis of family TATs. *Journal of Projective Techniques and Personality Assessment,* 1965, *29,* 392-397.

Wirt, R. D., Lachar, D., Klinedinst, J. K., & Seat, P. D. *Multidimensional description of child personality: A manual for the personality inventory for children.* Los Angeles: Western Psychological Services, 1977.

Wolf, T. H. *Alfred Binet.* Chicago: University of Chicago Press, 1973.

Wolfensberger, W. *The principle of normalization in human services.* Toronto: National Institute on Mental Retardation, 1972.

Woodcock, R. W. *Woodcock reading mastery tests.* Circle Pines, MN: American Guidance Services, 1973.

Woody, R. H. (Ed.). *Encyclopedia of clinical assessment* (2 vols.). San Francisco: Jossey-Bass, 1980.

Workman, E. A., & Hector, M. A. Behavioral self-control in classroom settings: A review of the literature. *Journal of School Psychology,* 1978, *16,* 227-236.

Wylie, R. *The self-concept.* Lincoln, NE: University of Nebraska Press, 1961.

Wylie, R. *The self-concept: A review of methodological considerations and measuring instruments* (Vol. 1, Rev. ed.). Lincoln, NE: University of Nebraska Press, 1974.

Yando, R., Seitz, V., & Zigler, E. *Intellectual and personality characteristics: Social class and ethnic-group differences.* Hillsdale, NJ: Earlbaum, 1979.

Yarrow, L. J. Interviewing children. In P. H. Mussen (Ed.), *Handbook of research methods in child development.* New York: Wiley, 1960.

Ysseldyke, J. E. Remediation of ability deficits: Some major questions. In L. Mann, L. Goodman, & J. L. Wiederholt (Eds.), *Teaching the learning disabled adolescent.* Boston: Houghton Mifflin, 1978.

Zipperlen, H. R. Normalization. In J. Wortis (Ed.), *Mental retardation and developmental disabilities* (Vol. 7). New York: Brunner/Mazel, 1975.

Zubin, J., Eron, L. D., & Schumer, F. *An experimental approach to projective techniques.* New York: Wiley, 1965.

Zucker, K. B., & Barnett, D. W. *The paired hands test.* Dallas: McCarron Dial Systems, 1977.

Zweig, R. L., & Associates. *Fountain Valley teacher support system in reading.* Huntington Beach, CA: Zweig Associates, 1971.

INDEX